TQM: A Step-by-Step Guide to Implementation

TQM: A Step-by-Step Guide to Implementation

by
Charles N. Weaver, Ph.D.

TQM: A Step-by-Step Guide to Implementation

Charles N. Weaver, Ph.D.

Library of Congress Cataloging-in-Publication Data

Weaver, Charles N.
    TQM: a step-by-step guide to implementation / by Charles N.
Weaver.
        p. cm.
    Includes bibliographical references and index.
    ISBN 0-87389-116-3
    1. Total quality management.   I. Title.
HD62.15.W42   1991
658.5—dc20   91-14304
                                                                  CIP

10987654321

ISBN 0-87389-116-3

Acquisitions Editor: Jeanine L. Lau
Production Editor: Mary Beth Nilles
Set in Bem by DanTon Typographers. Cover design by Wayne Dober. Printed and bound by BookCrafters.

For a free copy of the ASQC Quality Press Publications Catalog, including ASQC membership information, call 800-952-6587.

Printed in the United States of America

ASQC Quality Press
611 East Wisconsin Avenue
Milwaukee, Wisconsin 53202

Contents

Preface

This book describes a method for increasing organizational effectiveness. It should be explained that the method is not *instant pudding*. Instant pudding is Dr. W. Edwards Deming's term to describe a nonexistent, but often sought after quick fix for a company's problems so it can produce quality.[7]

To understand why the method described in this book is not instant pudding, consider the following: To bring about meaningful and permanent improvements in an organization's performance, we must carry out a comprehensive educational effort which has two objectives: first, to change the organization's culture and, second, to increase its effectiveness.

An organization's culture consists of the widely shared beliefs of its personnel about what is important and how things are to be done. For instance, how an organization treats its customers or its workers is part of its culture. How an organization deals with its suppliers or determines how well it's doing is part of its culture.

An organization's effectiveness, on the other hand, is how well it accomplishes what it's in business to do, how well it accomplishes its mission. For example, Do its products work? Are they delivered to customers on time? Are repairs infrequent and reasonably priced? Is service readily available and exemplary? Do customers brag about the products?

Through the years, there has been a parade in the United States of organizational development efforts, usually called programs. Every employee who has been on the job for a period of time can name several of these programs. Such employees can half-humorously tell how each program was introduced by management with great fanfare, speeches, and promises about how much good it was going to do for the company and its employees. With time, however, management always seems to lose interest. Consequently, the current program loses its vitality and is swept off stage. Soon another program is introduced with equal fanfare and promises.

Experience shows that in the short run organizational development efforts in the United States have had some success at increasing effectiveness, but have almost always failed miserably at changing organizational culture. It is important to understand that when an organization's culture does not change, it is virtually impossible to sustain improvements in effectiveness that may have been achieved. Through lack of culture change this kind of failure can happen to the method described in this book because it, too, is an organizational development effort. Thus, although the method described herein can dramatically improve an organization's effectiveness, until its culture changes, those improvements eventually will be lost. Unless an organization's culture changes, this method will be swept off stage and remembered as just another management program.

To avoid the problem of paralysis of organizational culture, the following approach is recommended. At least several months before introducing the method described in this book, or any other organizational development effort, an organization should begin comprehensive education aimed at its culture. This education should be based on the teachings of Dr. W. Edwards Deming,[7] Dr. Joseph M. Juran,[22] and other quality philosophers. When this cultural transformation has taken place, the resulting management style is called total quality management (TQM). TQM is a participative management style which focuses on satisfying customer expectations by continually improving the way business is conducted. This definition is self-explanatory except for the first phrase, "participative management style." This means that achieving a cultural transformation requires going beyond necessary worker involvement to include continual, direct involvement by senior management.

The method described in this book is a systematic process for implementing TQM. It can be used to tailor TQM to meet the specific needs of any organization. In addition to implementing TQM, using this process establishes a management information system (MIS) which provides a set of powerful new tools for improved leadership. This MIS is developed by employees using consensus-building techniques, and is a means of comprehensively measuring organizational performance. It is called the methodology for generating efficiency and effectiveness measures (MGEEM). Although this process has many attractive features, the main purpose of MGEEM is to implement TQM. To emphasize this purpose, in this book the process is referred to as TQM/MGEEM.

As managers begin the work of transforming the culture of their organizations, they usually attend seminars and read the books of TQM's quality philosophers. After discussing these great teachings among themselves, managers can be expected to raise questions about how they are supposed to actually implement TQM. They want guidance on exactly what to do. They want a checklist or set of operating instructions. On the other hand, managers who have achieved knowledge about organizational development understand that the enlightenment that moves an organization toward a culture of quality, in itself, has highly positive impacts on effectiveness. In other words, accepting and practicing the teachings of the quality philosophers about TQM not only changes organizational culture, but also greatly improves effectiveness.

Unfortunately, increasing effectiveness through culture change is too slow for most managers. In most cases, they are impatient and want to increase effectiveness in the short-term. Usually they are completely justified in their impatience. Many see the writing on the wall and realize that unless effectiveness is increased in the short-term, there may not be an intermediate- or long-term. They may lose their jobs, or their businesses may go broke!

The TQM/MGEEM approach described in this book provides a systematic and comprehensive method of applying the teachings of the quality philosophers. For instance, TQM/MGEEM provides a systematic, structured process in which managers may seek to employ Dr. Deming's famous 14 points, his suggested road map for creating culture change within an organization.[7] In using TQM/MGEEM, personnel also become involved in direct, hands-on opportunities to use Dr. Juran's many contributions to the culture of quality, including his highly useful definitions of quality, customer, product, and process; his discussion of the process by which quality is managed (quality planning, control, and improvement); and his unparalleled discussion of the infrastructure required to bring about quality improvements (quality councils and project improvement teams).[22] As personnel are involved in the TQM/MGEEM process, they begin to comprehend how the teachings of Dr. Deming, Dr. Juran, and other quality philosophers of TQM have real meaning in their organizations. They begin to understand how TQM doctrine can be put into actual use.

This book is not intended to provide a complete explanation of the teachings of TQM's quality philosophers. This book's purpose is to explain how to use TQM/MGEEM, a systematic and comprehensive means of implementing these great teachings.

The reader who is unfamiliar with the works of the quality philosophers of TQM is advised to begin to learn the teachings of Deming by first reading what many consider the *Reader's Digest* version of his philosophy in a clearly written book by Mary Walton, *The Deming Management Method*.[44] Next, read *The Deming Route to Quality and Productivity* by William W. Scherkenbach,[37] and *The Deming Guide to Quality and Competitive Position* by Howard S. Gitlow and Shelly J. Gitlow.[12] With that much background, the reader should be ready for Deming's book, *Out of the Crisis*, a text worthy of many readings and much close study.[7] My favorite book by Dr. Juran is *Juran on Leadership for Quality: An Executive Handbook*,[27] but he has written many excellent books and handbooks. Selected works by other quality philosophers of TQM are listed in the References.

Returning to the original question, "Why is TQM/MGEEM not instant pudding?" The answer is that TQM/MGEEM, like many other organizational development efforts, will increase effectiveness, but eventually fall apart unless a user organization changes its culture. By itself, TQM/MGEEM is not instant pudding. Coupled, however, with the culture-changing teachings of the quality philosophers, TQM/MGEEM can greatly increase the effectiveness of any organization. TQM/MGEEM is the answer to the question so often asked after attending a seminar by one of the quality philosophers, "What do we do next?"

Acknowledgments

Much of the information contained in this book resulted from my association with the research and development (R&D) program in organizational performance measurement and enhancement at the Human Resources Directorate (HRD) of the Armstrong Laboratory. This R&D appears in HRD technical reports and is, therefore, in the public domain. Nothing contained in this book is intended or should be inferred to represent the policy of the United States Air Force or Department of Defense.

Many people contributed in a variety of ways to what I learned at HRD and I gratefully acknowledge them. They include: Dr. William E. Alley, Larry T. Looper, Dr. Herbert J. Clark, William J. Phalen, Colonel Harold G. Jensen, Dr. R. Bruce Gould, and Lieutenant Colonel David E. Brown (HRD); Dr. Michael D. Matthews (Drury College); Dr. Thomas C. Tuttle (Maryland Center for Productivity and Quality of Working Life); and Robert D. Pritchard (Texas A&M University).

My thinking about organizational development has been influenced by conversations with many people. Among the most influential of these were Dr. W. Edwards Deming (New York University); Dr. Joseph M. Juran (Juran Institute); Dr. Stephen L. Dockstader and Dr. Chandler Shumate (Navy Personnel Research and Development Center); Dr. Laurie Broedling (Deputy Under Secretary of Defense for Total Quality Management); Dr. Norval D. Glenn (University of Texas at Austin); Dr. Stanley Dickinson (Office of the Secretary of the Air Force); Mr. Del Nelson (Sacramento Air Logistics Center); Major Don M. Reimensnider and Chief Master Sergeant Joseph F. Dymon (Air Force Management Engineering Agency); Luis Salinas (Corpus Christi Army Depot); John E. Hornbeak and Louis Garcia (Southwest Texas Methodist Hospital); D. Scott Bushnell (McCormick-Schilling Division of McCormick & Company, Inc.); Anthony Gallegos (Installations Assistance Office—West, Office of the Secretary of Defense); and Robert A. Stone (Deputy Assistant Secretary of Defense—Installations).

Most of what I know about organizational development, however, resulted from my experiences in implementing total quality management through the technology described in this book. I benefited in these experiences from contact with many knowledgeable people to whom I acknowledge my gratitude. Among them are Colonel John C. Handy and Colonel Donald Scooler (437th Military Airlift Wing); Colonel Robert B. Stephens (315th Military Airlift Wing); Colonel Arnold L. Weinman (92nd Bombardment Wing); Colonel Chuck Ferguson (Air Force Reserve); Colonel Chuck Churchill (Ft. Dietrick); Brigadier General Frank K. Martin and Colonel John A. McClanathan, Jr. (Air Force Office of Security Police);

Rear Admiral Jimmie W. Taylor, Captain Donald W. Scott, Captain Richard A. Catone, Captain W. P. Burtch, Jr., and Commander Donald B. Clark (Naval Air Training Command); Commander Frederick C. Orton (Anti-Submarine Warfare Wing, U.S. Pacific Fleet); John J. Boland and Larry Hermann (Naval Aviation Depot-Alameda); Rear Admiral Wayne E. Rickman (Training Command, U.S. Atlantic Fleet); Rear Admiral D. M. Lichtman (San Francisco Medical Command); Brigadier General (Dr.) Thomas E. Bowen and Colonel (Dr.) Edwin M. Healey (Fitzsimons Army Medical Center); Captain (Dr.) John R. Aguillar (Corpus Christi Navy Hospital); Captain Medhat Ashamalla (Roosevelt Roads Naval Hospital, Puerto Rico); Major General John E. Major, Colonel (Dr.) Osvaldo Bustos and Colonel Johnny L. Connor (U.S. Army Health Services Command); Major General Robert F. Swarts and Rose Mary Alais (Air Force Commissary Service); James C. Wallin (Material Management Directorate, San Antonio Air Logistics Center); Gus Damon (Pearl Harbor Naval Shipyard); Al Russell; Charles P. Skipton; Gary Thurber; Gary Zura; Anthony Buquor; Ralph M. Lentz; Sandra Edsall; Van "Butch" Robbins; and Ray Hicks.

In addition, word processing support was provided, in part, at St. Mary's University by Kathy Pope and a cadre of federally funded Work-Study students: Brian Moy, Angie Lyssy, David Thomas, Araceli Sifuentes, Jeanette Mora, and Gary Garcia. A colleague at St. Mary's University and the University of Texas Health Science Center to whom I express my thanks is Dr. Michele L. Trankina. The ultimate in high-quality customer support was provided by the staff of ASQC Quality Press. I am especially indebted to Jeanine L. Lau, ASQC Quality Press acquisitions editor.

THE QUALITY CRISIS

If you're like me, you grew up believing the United States is the greatest country in the world. You like to think the United States dominates the world in everything. Although this certainly used to be true in most areas, things have changed. For instance, in many ways the United States is not the world's greatest economic power. If you don't believe it, consider some statistics.

Suppose we made a list of the 35 largest banks in the world (ranked by assets in 1989). How many of these banks would you say are United States banks? The answer is only one! That means the United States isn't even close to dominating the world of banking. Where do the largest banks

1

come from? If you look at such a list, you'll find Japan on top with France and West Germany following. To experience firsthand the huge expansion of Japanese banking, go out to the West Coast (e.g., San Diego) and walk around downtown. As you find bank buildings try to pronounce the names on the signs.

You also may think the United States dominates the world of industry and commerce. Suppose we make another list, this time of the world's largest corporations (ranked on market value as of June 30, 1989). How many would you say are United States corporations? The answer is only three of the largest 10, only 12 of the largest 30, and only 21 of the largest 50. That's not as bad as the situation in banking, but it shows that the United States hardly dominates the world's industry and commerce. Roughly the same pattern exists for the United States among the world's largest insurers (ranked on assets in 1989). There are only four United States insurers in the largest 10, only eight in the largest 20, and only 12 in the largest 30 (*Wall Street Journal*, September 23, 1990).

Statistics also show that United States industry is slipping in a number of important markets. For instance, the United States share of the electronics market has declined from 100 percent in 1970 to less than 5 percent today. Over the same period, the United States' share in phonographs fell from 100 to 1 percent, in color televisions from 90 to 10 percent, in machine tools from 100 to 35 percent, and in VCRs from 10 to 1 percent (*Wall Street Journal*, November 14, 1988).

In *Fortune* magazine (September 24, 1990), Edmund Faltermayer cites the percentage losses from 1979 to 1989 of United States industry's share of a number of other United States markets. These losses include: computers, 28 percent; semiconductors, 23 percent; telephone equipment, 14 percent; apparel, 12 percent; industrial machinery, 12 percent; household appliances, 11 percent; tires, 9 percent; nuts, bolts, and washers, 7 percent; ball and roller bearings, 5 percent; and cement, 7 percent. Other statistics add to this gloomy picture.

Americans no longer have the highest per capita income or highest level of individual productivity in the world. Norval D. Glenn and I reported in *Public Opinion Quarterly* (1982–1983) results from nationwide public opinion surveys which show that the job satisfaction of American workers has fallen dramatically since 1955. In 1987 Japan for the first time became the world's richest nation (*Wall Street Journal*, August 22, 1989, p. A10). The evidence that the United States is slipping continues.

There is considerable debate, of course, about what is causing the United States to slip from its position as the world's number one economic power. Almost every current news magazine, newspaper, and business program on television has something to say about these causes. Pessimists comment that the United States never *was* number one. They contend that any economic glory we ever had was because we had no competition. They claim our competitors lost their economic strength in World War II. As these nations get back on their feet, it's only natural, they say, that the role of the United States will become less important. Others blame the United States government. Some of them say the government doesn't do enough for business. Others declare the government does too much. Still others say United States workers are to blame, claiming that they don't receive good educations, are overpaid, lack the proper work ethic, and, as a group, are getting too old. Still others argue that United States managers are to blame because they don't spend enough money on research and development, fail to innovate, and have out-of-date attitudes.

I take a somewhat different viewpoint about why the United States is in this mess. I agree that our loss of economic position is the result of various root causes, but I think that before we can make a serious start down the road to recovery, we must appreciate that there is an intermediate step between these root causes and our loss of economic power. The intermediate step is that we have suffered a severe decline in quality. So, various root causes have resulted in a serious decline of quality in the United States. In turn, this decline in quality has caused our loss of economic position.

Why is it important to know about this intermediate step? Because, as a country, we need to work vigorously on the root causes. There can be no question about that. For instance, we must make changes so that our government promotes rather than hinders business interests. We must introduce broad improvements in our educational system. We must spend more money on research and development in key areas.

These kinds of changes seldom take place overnight. Some of them will require years, even decades, but if we work at them we eventually will reverse the crisis. As a nation, we have always been able to meet the serious challenges that have faced us. In addition to working on the root causes, however, we must work on the intermediate step itself. We must take direct and deliberate action to turn quality around in every organization in the United States.

How this can be and is being done in many United States organizations is this text's subject. Before addressing the solution to the quality problem, however, let's clarify what is meant by declining quality.

What Is Declining Quality?

When I make a speech, I like to start it with a joke, but when I make a speech about quality in the United States, I have a tough time finding a joke to use. The awful truth is that quality in the United States is no joking matter. Quality is no joke to the person who has twice had to replace the American-made engine in an American-made truck, to the customer who takes a number and waits and waits and waits, to the manager of a repair shop whose workers sit idle on an important job waiting for spare parts ordered weeks ago, or to the restaurant customer who asks a waiter for the correct time and is told, "Sorry, this is not my table!"

The fact is that in the United States quality is in a state of crisis. I believe that lack of quality is among the most serious problems the United States has ever faced. Years from now, historians will say that the fall of the United States from the role of economic world leader was not because of war, economics, drugs, or moral decay. It was because of a decline in quality.

Declining quality in the United States means two things. First, it means many of our products don't work as well as those produced by offshore competitors. In a recent speech on quality, I pointed to the inferiority of United States products by asking anyone in the audience who owned a foreign-made automobile to stand up. Of course, in response to this question, almost everyone stood up. These people realize that when they buy foreign-made products they may cause American workers to lose jobs. As much as they dislike the idea of United States workers losing their jobs, they are simply unwilling to tolerate the inconvenience and high repair bills of many American products which don't work well. Thus, the aforementioned markets and many others once dominated by United States firms have fallen into the hands of offshore competitors.

Declining quality in the United States has a second meaning. Not only do United States products fail to work well, but customers who want to buy these products often are not treated well, either. For these customers quality is a double-whammy. First, they are buffeted by delays, errors, abuses, and insults. Then, after they finally get their hands on the product, it doesn't work. Like everyone in the United States, I am forced to tolerate delays, abuses, errors, and insults to obtain needed goods and services. I could relate numerous horror stories about the many companies with which I deal: the cable television company, airlines, my previous insurance agency, automobile dealers who repair my car, the telephone company, the savings and loan association which holds my mortgage, my bank, the local hospital, the neighborhood veterinarian, pest exterminators, restaurants, taxis, movie theaters, and even the local ice cream parlor. To demonstrate the downtrodden state of the American customer, consider a few true incidents.

Several years ago I applied for a teaching job at a university out on the West Coast. At the time of the job interview, I entered the dean's outer office where his secretary was working at her desk. After seeming to ignore my presence for several minutes, she looked up. With a strong sense of impatience, she snapped, "What do you want?" Already uneasy about the impending interview, her harsh remark almost sent me rushing out the door to safety. In a meek voice I responded that I was there for a scheduled job interview with the dean. Upon hearing this, she smiled broadly and said, "Oh, I'm so sorry. I thought you were a student!"

She mistook me for the enemy, an accursed student. When she realized I was actually a prospective university employee, an insider, not one of "them," her attitude changed.

This secretary is typical of many university faculty and staff members who believe that "The university would be a great place to work if it weren't for the students!" These students—these outsiders, these *enemies*—are really the customers. It is through service to them that universities meet a principal part of their mission: education. It is through universities' providing education that their secretaries have jobs.

Strange as it seems, this attitude is common among the employees of many other organizations throughout the United States whose main job is to provide products and services to customers. They believe that "This would be a great place to work if we didn't have to bother with the customers."

When I was at the grocery store early one morning, I got in the quick checkout lane. There were six other shoppers and their carts ahead of me, but the lanes next to this lane were closed. In full view of the waiting line of customers were three uniformed grocery employees, including a manager. Rather than opening another checkout lane, they made us wait while they chatted! The line moved slowly, and I finally reached the checker. At that point, the checkout procedure required that I lift the groceries out of my shopping cart and place them on a conveyor. The conveyor moved the groceries down to the checker where they were rung up, sacked, and purchased. Once my groceries were sacked, I was asked, "Do you need any help with these?" This question implied that I was expected to carry my groceries out to my car. Not only was I asked to wait needlessly at the checkout counter while the three poorly trained employees chatted, I was expected to do work (put my groceries on the conveyor and get them out to my car) that was once provided as a service.

Manipulating the customer into doing more of what previously was a service is a deliberate strategy of many United States merchants to increase their revenue. Profits rise as a result of lower labor costs when customers do the work that their employees once provided as service. Lower labor costs, with the same or continually increasing prices above the inflation rate means greater profitability. The merchants argue that they pass these savings on to their customers in the form of lower prices, but how can customers know if prices really are lower? Only a few conscientious shoppers continually compare prices, and all they usually find is that all prices are rising.

A short time ago I signed a contract to have carpet installed in a vacant rental house. I made it clear to the salesperson that I would pay for the carpet only after inspecting the job and that I expected to be billed through the mail. On the agreed day and hour of installation, I drove to the rental house to unlock the door for the installers. I waited an hour, but they never showed up.

In a telephone conversation the following day, a scheduler explained that installers have no control over when they arrive to install carpet. It depends on how long their previous jobs take. I was irritated by their thoughtlessness and waste of my time.

To prevent this from recurring I agreed to leave the door key in the mailbox. This could have led to the theft of the stove, refrigerator, and other appliances which I provide to renters, but I had no other choice; I had signed a contract for carpet and could not spare the time to wait for the installers. Finally, installation was completed.

About ten o'clock that evening, a company representative telephoned me at home to ask if he could come to my home to pick up a check for the balance due. I angrily told him it was too late in the day for such a call and that it had been agreed that I would not pay until after inspection of the work and, then, only when the bill was received through the mail.

My inspection of the work the next day revealed that carpet had not been laid in two closets as agreed. A call to the company got the crew back the following day, but they laid carpet in only one of the two closets. Another call resulted in the crew returning a third time to complete the job. Of course, each of these times I had to leave the door key in the mailbox exposing my appliances to theft.

Another problem detected in the final inspection was that the new carpet was thicker than the old carpet. Consequently the doors would not open and close easily. After four attempts, I finally reached the manager who said that it was not their policy to do carpentry work. He took no responsibility for his salesman's not informing me that carpets are of different thicknesses. To plane one quarter inch from the bottoms of nine doors cost me the time of locating a carpenter and an additional $90.

Customers in the United States are constantly buffeted by a never-ending series of delays, errors, abuses, and insults. When was the last time you tried to do business with an American company only to have an employee tell you to take a number and wait? How many times have you wanted to do business with a United States company on the telephone only to be placed on hold for five minutes by a "customer representative?" You wanted to buy. You were willing to spend your money, but they were too busy. How many times has your flight's takeoff been delayed 30 minutes while you and 150 other people sat in a crowded airplane?

My favorite example of the deterioration of customer service follows. Think about the comments that are exchanged between salesclerks and customers after transactions. Years ago, salesclerks said "Thank you" and customers said "You're welcome," but now it's the other way around. Customers somehow feel pressure to express appreciation for the privilege of buying the goods or services in question. Nowadays, customers say "Thank you" (seemingly for taking their money). Clerks, on the other hand, have the attitude that:

> I have done you a favor by waiting on you. I took my valuable time away from smoking a cigarette or talking to another clerk to do you a favor. But, it's ok, you said thanks. And, anyway, the next time you come in this store, you'll have to wait on yourself because the owner is instituting self-service!

If you still don't believe that customers in the United States are buffeted by delays, errors, abuses, and insults, I would say that you've become accustomed to the problems. To better appreciate the problem, do something for me. The next time you do your shopping and errands, carry a 3x5-inch index card and pencil. Briefly note on the card each delay, error, abuse, and insult you suffer. Remember, *you* have the money and the merchants want your money. As a customer, you should be treated like a king or queen. Your needs should be anticipated and met. You should be treated with respect. Shopping should be a joy. You should not experience long delays. You should not have to accept products that don't work. My experience is that one 3x5-inch index card won't be enough. Perhaps you should take a notebook instead!

Besides abuse of ultimate consumers, the ones who buy groceries and carpeting and say "Thank you," there are other customers who also are constantly mistreated in the United States. These customers are important and should also be served in a respectful, timely, and quality manner. These customers are *internal* customers — people who work in the various divisions, departments, and work centers of American companies. In other words, within the same company, departments are customers of each other. The contracting department is a customer of the engineering department, finance is a customer of computer services, sales is a customer of audiovisual, etc. The unfortunate fact is that many internal customers are seldom recognized as customers, much less well-treated.

People who work in so-called support or supplier departments, who are supposed to treat their customers well, often focus more on satisfying their boss' requirements. Oddly enough, the focus of many bosses is not on their customers. Bosses of many support organizations do not realize that the in-house departments they are chartered to support are their customers. To them, customers are *external* to the company. To make matters even worse, most bosses are preoccupied with their own promotions and are forever searching for ways to look good to their own bosses. They seldom appreciate the fact that the best way to look good is to show leadership in their department by satisfying the expectations of their customers, whether internal or external.

Unbelievably, many bosses of support departments may even *create* hostility between their department and its customers. For example, they may demand that their subordinates adhere to out-of-date rules and regulations that run counter to their customers' best interests. "You must make out your request in triplicate." (We won't make copies.) "You must wait in long lines at our service counter." (This saves our labor costs since we don't have to hire extra customer representatives.) "Your boss must sign all requisitions." (We don't trust you.) "Sometimes you must wait two weeks for delivery." (We keep our costs down by not hiring part-time employees to handle peak customer activity.) As a result, the subordinates of such bosses often see customers who request better or more timely service as interfering with their efforts to do what the boss wants, to adhere to the rules and regulations.

It is not unusual for personnel from internal customer departments to have to "know someone" or "do someone a favor" to obtain needed support. In such situations, it is difficult to imagine that these departments are within the same company! They should be working together for the common good. They should help each other. They should have a relationship based on harmony and cooperation. Too often they do not! This condition is common throughout both the private and public sectors of the United States, and eats into profits and market share. It makes Americans less competitive in the marketplace.

Failure to treat internal customers as kings and queens contributes significantly to the decline of the United States because it dramatically reduces effectiveness. It suboptimizes efforts. A good business principal is that no department can provide quality products and services to its customers unless its suppliers (support departments) reciprocate. So, the United States has a domino effect. Department A doesn't treat its customer (Department B) well with high-quality products and service. Therefore, Department B cannot treat its customers (Departments C, D, E, and F) well with high-quality products and service, etc. Thus, individual businesses as well as the entire United States business structure suffers. As a result, offshore producers who seldom make the fatal mistake of not satisfying their customers' expectations have gotten the upper hand. It is astonishing how often problems of customer service are overlooked by otherwise excellent United States managers. Somehow they have allowed their employees to assume that customers are not important! Poor customer service is virtually the rule of United States businesses, rather than the exception.

What Caused the Crisis of Quality in the United States?

It is important to address the question *Why* are so many organizations in the United States and many other Western countries failing to produce high-quality products and mistreating customers? Of course there are a variety of causes, but the answer lies in the failure of Western managers to appreciate that we are now in a new era of quality.

Many managers in the Western world remain in the statistical quality control or quality assurance eras. Using statistics to control processes, and as a basis for inspection, are important contributions made to the quality movement in the 1930s. Similarly, the contributions in the 1950s of quality assurance, including the concepts of the cost of quality, total quality control, reliability engineering, and zero defects, are also valuable contributions to the quality movement. Most Western managers, however, still operate as if these contributions are the most recent developments in quality. (For further elaboration on this point, see Garvin.[11]) For example, many managers of United States organizations regard their companies as progressive with respect to quality, yet they rely almost exclusively on statistical control charts to assure quality. In their companies virtually all line personnel, especially those in manufacturing activities, are taught to use control charts and to self-control the quality of their work. Many other United States organizations base quality control on the activities of their quality assurance departments.

I do not recommend that statistical quality control and quality assurance be discarded and forgotten. Many of the concepts involved in these approaches (e.g., controlling processes with statistics, basing inspection on statistics, considering the costs of quality, encouraging interfunctional coordination, and encouraging the application of quality concepts beyond manufacturing throughout a company) play a vital role in today's efforts to improve quality. These concepts are important, but I am convinced they form a bare minimum quality level on which to build a quality improvement program. Recent quality improvement innovations must be added.

As Garvin insightfully explains, the underlying philosophy of both statistical quality control and quality assurance is basically defensive in nature.[11] These approaches suggest that we must forever be on guard to prevent something bad from happening. We must continually inspect regular work to ensure that nothing is done that will hurt the company.

Consequently, the basic objective of quality efforts in companies that follow this philosophy is to control and contain potential mistakes, and prevent defects to keep mistakes from happening. "Let's not do something that could get us into a liability lawsuit. Let's not do something that could cause the embarrassment of a product recall."

The recommended approach is to stop being defensive about quality. Quality should be treated proactively. Western managers must realize that today quality is a competitive weapon! Some managers who realize this recommend dropping the defensive phrase *quality control* for a more proactive term such as *quality management, strategic quality management,* or *total quality management.*

In today's market, quality must be viewed as an important basis for competition. Quality must be seen as a direct link to profitability and market share. As such, senior managers must realize that quality is too important to delegate (as many now do to their quality assurance departments). Instead, managers at all levels must become directly and continually involved in the quality effort.

Another important component of the new approach to quality is explained in a recent report by John T. Hagan to the American Society for Quality Control.[15] For quality to serve as an effective basis for competition it must be defined by the customer rather than by so-called *expert* in-house personnel. It is not the design engineers, senior managers, technical directors, or staff physicians who know how to define quality. Quality can be defined only by the user — the customer.

Before managers launch into an effort to learn how customers define the quality of their products and services, they should appreciate some simple, commonsense ideas about customers. First, as everyone knows, most customers are not required to buy from one supplier. They look at alternative suppliers. They shop around to compare the product or service features offered by several or even many suppliers. Customers buy where the composite of product and service features best satisfy their expectations. Consider an example. When you go out to buy a half-gallon of milk, there are alternative suppliers who offer somewhat different features. The supermarket has lower prices, but is farther away and usually requires a longer checkout time. A neighborhood convenience store is closer and faster, but has higher prices. Important supplier features apply not only to products but, as in this example, to other characteristics of a supplier. A grocery store may have fresher milk because it sells more milk. One must weigh these various features in terms of his/her needs and make a choice. To compete, suppliers must learn how customers perceive their strengths relative to their competitors and continually improve the manner in which they conduct business to strengthen themselves. In this example, the supermarket should strive to reduce checkout time and the convenience store should strive to reduce prices.

The milk purchase example crystallizes two important commonsense ideas about customers. First, they weigh a variety of features when making a decision about where to buy something. Price is not always the most important feature. Sometimes it's convenience of location, speed of checkout, courtesy, cleanliness, reliability of the product over its lifetime, frequency and life-cycle cost of repair, etc. Customers also weigh the features offered by alternative suppliers. Managers, therefore, must study their customers to understand their current and changing product and service expectations against what the competition is offering.

There is another key about consumers. Their expectations change constantly. For instance, the average age of consumers is increasing so that over time more of the United States population will be over 65. Older people often have different expectations about products and services, e.g., they may be more concerned about their health and buy more low-fat milk.

Consider another example. Over recent years, more United States households have both spouses employed full-time and, as the divorce rate has increased, more single-parent households have emerged. Customer expectations change not only as their demographic characteristics change, but also as competitive offerings and technology change. For example, automatic tellers changed customer expectations about service in the banking industry. The invention of the quartz movement changed customer expectations about the cost and accuracy of wristwatches. The development of the jet engine changed customer expectations about travel, vacations, and delivery service. These types of changes influence customers' expectations about products and services. Companies that expect to be around next year must respond to these changes.

The new era of quality has changed business rules. Literally faced with extinction, Western managers at all levels need to adapt to these new rules. Almost daily evidence in the newspapers about increasing losses of United States market shares to offshore producers, liability lawsuits, business failures, increasing activities of consumer-related government agencies (e.g., the National Highway Safety Administration, Environmental Protection Agency, and the Consumer Product Safety Commission), and product recalls demonstrate the urgent need to adopt the new quality rules of business.

It is unfortunate that many Western managers possess attitudes which cause them to view this new era of quality as a threat rather than as an opportunity. Increasing numbers of observers believe that many Western managers are present-day dinosaurs destined for extinction, or for employment and retraining by the Japanese. Among these *blinding* attitudes is the notion that there is one best way to do things. "If it ain't broke, don't fix it." This attitude keeps managers from changing the features of their product and service offerings to satisfy the changing expectations of their customers.

Another blinding attitude is that if everyone pursues his/her selfish interests an invisible hand will maximize everyone's well-being. This leads to dog-eat-dog competition — even among co-workers and departments in the same company. People must learn to cooperate in a spirit of harmony and goodwill.

Another blinding attitude is the emphasis on short-term results. Western managers believe a venture must show solid quarterly returns. They make a budget which often blinds them to what *is* important — continual improvement. For instance, a manager may want to commit funds to a project that promises to lead to quality improvement. If the funds are not in the budget, however, chances are the project will not be funded. When managers want to see immediate payoff, commitment to the long haul is more difficult to practice. This kind of thinking limits interest in R&D which opens the door to innovation and opportunities to even greater customer satisfaction in the future. Short-term thinking also creates an unfortunate focus among managers on results rather than on continuous improvement of processes which produce the results. These blinding attitudes and their unfortunate consequences will be explained later in greater detail.

The approach explained in this text provides a framework by which managers can move deliberately, but at their own pace, toward the new era of quality. In addition, this framework provides unending opportunities for managers to learn to shake off their blinding attitudes and begin to create an organizational culture within which continuous improvement can occur.

CHAPTER 2

WHAT CAN BE DONE
TO SET THINGS RIGHT?

Let's suppose you're convinced that quality in the United States is in a state of crisis, that many of our products are not as good as those produced offshore, and that our internal and external customers are seldom treated like kings or queens. Naturally, no American feels comfortable with these thoughts. Americans like to win. We like to be Number One. The questions are, What can be done to set things right? and What can be done to restore quality in America?

Sufficient knowledge already exists to solve our quality problems.

There are literally thousands of books and magazine articles on how to improve quality. There is information on every conceivable topic related to achieving profitability and excellence. There are quality philosophers, such as Dr. W. Edwards Deming, Dr. Joseph M. Juran, Tom Peters, and Philip B. Crosby, who provide seminars, training, videos, and reading materials on how to improve quality. We have access to the philosophies and techniques used by the Japanese in their successful achievements in increasing quality, many of which originated in the United States.[18, 23, 25, 28, 29, 38]

To ensure that their personnel are exposed to knowledge about quality, many companies not only send their people to training in this area, but also maintain their own training departments, which routinely offer courses, workshops, seminars, and video presentations on quality improvement. If knowledge about quality does, in fact, exist (and there can be little doubt that it does), why don't United States businesses use it to produce higher quality?

Most American managers are only too aware that the quality of their products and services is inadequate. Many feel a deep sense of helplessness about how to turn around this bad situation. Reading books and attending seminars on improving quality is stimulating and provides many good ideas, yet managers worry about how to effectively *apply* what they have learned. Many new ideas about improving quality make sense, and most managers have tried one or two, but usually with little permanent impact. Privately they confess that neither they nor their staffs really understand how to implement a complete organization-wide program of quality improvement.

The Solution

After years of consulting with hundreds of organizations, I am convinced that the main barrier to improving quality and increasing organizational effectiveness is the absence of a simple, step-by-step procedure which permits the systematic implementation of existing knowledge on this subject. What is needed is a fabric that holds together the excellent existing methods to improve organizational effectiveness and gives those methods direction and meaning.

Experience shows that to be successful, a procedure to bring about companywide improvement must address a number of key concerns:

1. The procedure must provide managers with frequent and reliable information about the state of quality and effectiveness. Without such measures, managers have no way of knowing the effects, good

or bad, of their improvement initiatives, e.g., an initiative in one department could help that section, but might have negative repercussions elsewhere.

2. It is important that information about the state of quality and effectiveness go beyond the measures available from accounting and engineering. This is because the many important measures of quality and effectiveness, such as customer satisfaction and timeliness, cannot be directly assessed with dollars and man-hours.

3. Managers are the first to recognize that organizations differ in an infinite number of ways. Some are manufacturers; some provide service. Some are in the private sector; some are public. Some are highly centralized; others are not. Some are huge multinationals while others are small partnerships or proprietorships. Managers know it is senseless to suggest that there is one best way to initiate improvement in organizations. They understand that the specific techniques needed to improve organizations are not rigidly predetermined. It is almost always incorrect, therefore, to try to duplicate the approaches to improvement used by currently successful companies, American, Japanese, or otherwise. To be successful, an implementation approach should be adaptive enough to reflect the unique features of the organization using it.

4. A procedure for companywide improvement should also be capable of promoting the application of any specific quality improvement approach or, more likely, any combination of approaches. For instance, if an organization's personnel are as impressed as I am by Deming's prophetic 14 points,[7] the implementation procedure should make accomplishment of the 14 points easier and more straightforward. Another organization, however, may prefer to begin their improvement effort with the excellent, more applied approach to J.M. Juran,[22] portions of the approach of Phil Crosby,[4] parts of the elements of Tom Peters' revolution,[30] or the diagnostic techniques of the late Kaoru Ishikawa.[19,20]

Most people who are serious about improvement eventually come to realize that what is best is a combination of some sort, such as Deming's philosophy combined with Juran's improvement teams using Ishikawa's seven tools. It makes no difference. A successful implementation procedure should round off the sharp edges and make any technique or combination of techniques operate more easily.

5. Managers know that it is important to be able to prioritize the significance of the problems which face them. They realize it is wrong to merely guess at what is preventing an organization from producing higher quality, or from treating customers better. Managers know it is imperative to have reliable information about which problems are the most critical. They know it is best to solve the high-priority problems first; it is not optimum to solve less important problems while serious problems are creating great damage. Furthermore, managers realize that identifying problems and assessing their importance should not be identified through judgment, nominations, or by walking around, but should be approached systematically.

6. This requirement results from the dilemma that experts in improvement caution that obtaining meaningful results takes a long time (five years or more), yet most of today's managers are driven by the need to produce short-term results. They are painfully aware that pressures to produce short-term results have harmful effects, such as limiting progress in long-range planning and commitment to long-term research. Pressures for short-term results are real, however, and most managers must produce something on their watch. They can't wait five years. Unless they produce short-term results, they won't have a job in five years. Consequently, to be valuable in a practical sense, an implementation procedure must produce immediate, short-term improvements.

This does not infer that short-term results are all that should be expected. In fact, pressures for short-term gains should be eliminated whenever possible. The real focus should be on commitment to continual, long-term improvement everywhere in an organization, but the hard realities of today's world require improvement efforts to demonstrate almost immediate benefits.

7. Managers worry that efforts to improve quality and increase effectiveness are too dependent on the assistance of outside experts. Thousands of dollars a day in consulting fees simply are not feasible for most small and many medium-sized companies. Instead of such a dependency on consultants, managers want an improvement effort that can be implemented in large part or entirely by in-house personnel.

8. Managers are concerned that many quality improvement initiatives hold individuals responsible for identifying and correcting problems.

Experience shows that most successful improvement efforts focus on teams, not individuals. There are several reasons for this:

- Most work in organizations is accomplished by people cooperating to accomplish tasks rather than by individuals working alone. Thus, it is more important to focus on improving the performance of teams than individuals.

- Workers are less likely to accept any initiative for improvement if they think it will place individuals, such as themselves, under the microscope. Additionally, when implemented, initiatives which focus on individuals are much more likely to be undermined or *gamed.*

- Unions are almost certain to object to individual-based quality improvement initiatives. If a union opposes any kind of organizational development effort, it may file a grievance to legally bring the effort to a complete stop, at least until the grievance is settled.

A much more fundamental issue underlies the question of involving individuals or teams in improvement efforts. It is a serious error to believe that individual workers or teams of workers caused or are responsible for correcting a company's problems. Managers who believe this like to think, "We wouldn't have these problems if the workers would just put their shoulders to the wheel and do what they are told."

Everyone who has ever worked at any level in any organization knows that almost all of the problems which keep workers from doing a better job are beyond their control. Everyone knows that workers don't have the authority to make changes to fix these problems. Improvement requires the authority of the bosses.

Therefore, improvement is almost always the bosses' responsibility. Workers should be involved in teams in *identifying* the problems, barriers, and constraints to improved quality and increased effectiveness, but only managers can make the necessary changes to *remove* them. This is one of this book's most important messages, and later chapters will discuss exactly how to create conditions in which this process can occur.

9. Managers' continual thirst for better ways to manage must be satisfied. Managers seek new tools that will give them a greater sense of control over what's going on in the organization. They want

solid information about performance so they can improve it. In particular, managers want early warning signals to alert them when problems are developing and other signals which notify them that problems are fixed. They also want guidance in resource allocation decisions, e.g., "Will quality benefit more from applying effort or resources to Problem A or Problem B?" "If I have to draw down resources in the organization, where will the reduction have the least harmful effects?"

10. Managers want better measurement, as suggested in concern number 1. Beyond better measurement, however, some want a measurement system that can be aggregated or rolled up. This would permit them to combine measures of different aspects of quality and effectiveness into one number. For example, they could add measures of customer satisfaction and timeliness to traditional accounting and engineering measures. They could roll up measures from several, even unlike, organizational subunits into one number that would be an index of the quality or effectiveness of the larger organization of which the subunits are components.

11. The final requirement of a procedure to improve quality and increase effectiveness is that everyone in the company must be involved in the undertaking. It is common to see senior management fully committed to improvement and people at the worker level highly enthusiastic about the promised benefits. Yet, many organizations fail to involve the critical layer of middle managers in their improvement effort. Without the full support of middle managers little progress in improvement usually takes place.

Each of these requirements is fully satisfied by the technique outlined in this book. Before previewing this technique, however, it is important to explain why it is so difficult, often impossible, for many United States companies to turn themselves around on quality and effectiveness.

Most United States companies have enormous difficulty reorienting themselves toward quality and effectiveness because through the years they have developed organizational characteristics which, strange as it seems, have resulted directly from the decisions and behavior of their managers. These undesirable characteristics severely limit the full utilization of human and organizational potential.

Therefore, despite the fact that the tools and knowledge for organizational improvement are available through this book and others, my experience suggests that United States companies with these characteristics have extreme difficulty changing. Despite their best efforts to bring about organizational change, there is every reason to believe that favorable results often are impossible to achieve. This is not because the techniques for bringing about improvement are unsound, but because most United States organizations have huge mountains, built by their own managers, which stand in the way!

Mountains to Climb

Two mountains stand in the path of improvement in most United States organizations. The first mountain concerns the treatment of personnel. In virtually all of the hundreds of organizations with which I have worked over the past 25 years, there is a history of horrendous abuses of personnel, both at the managerial and worker levels. To better explain what I mean by abuses of personnel, consider several examples from my files.

A deputy director of personnel with 15 years of outstanding performance ratings was dismissed in the following way. To create a position for a friend of the president, a letter was left on the deputy director's desk to be read when she arrived at work on a Monday morning. The letter read, "Your services at XYZ company are no longer required. Please gather your personal belongings and be off company property before noon. If you are not, the security office will be asked to assist in your departure."

How do you suppose she and other people in the company felt about this tragedy? How did it affect their morale and sense of job security? What do you suppose they say to their friends about this company?

In a second company, a midlevel manager with a long, successful service record was sent a similar "Dear John" letter via special delivery mail while he was away on vacation. The letter informed him of his dismissal and said, "When you return from your vacation, don't bother to come into the office. We will gather your belongings and have them delivered to your home with your last paycheck."

How do you suppose this manager and his friends in the company felt about this? Did it make them feel more secure in their jobs? How did they feel about the senior managers who let this happen?

In a third company, an employee with 10 years of satisfactory service was terminated, and the company's contributions to his retirement fund were withdrawn as well as the interest on the money he had contributed. (This took place before the federal law requiring vesting of retirement contributions was passed.) How secure did other employees feel about their retirement when they heard about this? Did they have more trust in the company?

In a fourth company, a committee of peers formed for the specific purpose of evaluating applications for promotion was severely, publicly reproached by the company president for not agreeing with his opinion that an employee who was his personal friend should be promoted. The committee had unanimously concluded that the applicant lacked the qualifications for promotion. How motivated were these committee members when they had another application to review? How did they feel about the president?

In another instance, a company executive created a new position for her husband who had recently retired from the Army, not allowing others in line for the job to apply for it. The new job was director of quality! How do you suppose the people who were up for the job felt about the company's promotion policies after this tragic event? Did their loyalty to the company increase? Did their support for the company's goals increase?

In another organization, a powerful midlevel executive had two young executives who were his favorites. As he was promoted through the ranks into upper management, he saw to it that his two "boys" got promotions to move up behind him. How do you suppose other young executives felt when they saw this executive and his boys together at lunch? How did they feel when they later had to work for one of the boys whom they knew got promoted largely out of favoritism rather than merit? What respect could they have had for the company or the executive? How happy were they in their work?

Employees in virtually every organization can recount many such stories. You can probably tell stories of similar abuses yourself.

Not only is it patently unethical and unprincipled, it is impossible to keep knowledge of personnel abuses a secret. Word gets out. A secretary who types a "Dear John" letter will confide its contents to one trusted friend, and the friend will confide in one trusted friend, etc.

Are employees justified in taking knowledge of such abuses seriously? Will they ever forget them? When they see a friend or co-worker mistreated, do they realize that if it can happen to others it can happen to them?

Here's another important point: When the president stands up before employees to talk about a new program to improve this or that, do employees remember the abuses the manager instigated or choose to ignore them? With memories like these, can employees be proud of the company and its management? Can they feel secure in their jobs? Can they take joy in their work? Importantly, can they trust the manager's comments about improving quality when they remember how the manager got promoted into that job through favoritism, or some other gross abuse? They cannot!

Managers who look to this book for guidance about how to improve their company may have *the abuse of personnel* mountain to climb. These managers must ask themselves whether their leadership and that of others in the company has always been principled. They must ask themselves whether their leadership has created an organizational climate which, *itself,* is an obstacle to the improvement of quality and effectiveness? They must ask themselves whether all the company systems which touch personnel are characterized by trustworthiness and integrity. They must realize that problems in this area will doom any improvement effort to failure.

A company history of personnel abuses and the continuing existence of conditions which produce them severely limit the development of high-quality interpersonal relations, a prime requisite of improvement. Where there is fear and suspicion, instead of trust and integrity, there can be no cohesiveness and teamwork. Thus, there can be no permanent improvement.

A second mountain stands in the path to improved quality and effectiveness in most United States organizations. Every boulder and ton of earth in this mountain were put there by a well-intentioned person playing the role of manager who may never have been trained properly for the job. This person is the biology, philosophy, or political science professor who becomes a university dean or president; the ace fighter pilot who becomes the commander of a military science center; the crackerjack vacuum cleaner salesperson who becomes president of a fast-food chain; the CPA, psychologist, statistician, or engineer who becomes a corporate manager. These types of promotions occur because of the often erroneous belief that if someone is skilled at a given craft, such as biology, sales, or accounting, he/she will make a good manager. Making this assumption usually has harmful consequences. The truth is that most of the skills required to make a good craftsperson are different from the skills required for management. The two sets of skills may overlap, but not always.

To compound this problem, those who are aware of this fallacy usually are satisfied to accept a craftsperson as a manager if the applicant will take a couple of supervisory training courses or, even worse, earns a degree in management at a college or university. These forms of training teach the same management principles that were followed to build many of the mountains of organizational problems discussed herein.

In other words, this second mountain which stands in the path to improved quality and effectiveness stems from the fact that many managers are not properly trained for leadership. As virtually any business book on the subject states, management involves the processes of planning, organizing, directing, and controlling. The problem with this basically sound approach is that poorly trained managers often become obsessed with the controlling process, resulting in too much emphasis being placed on evaluation and compliance. Eventually this obsession results in the creation of a multitude of constraints and barriers to organizational effectiveness. From the viewpoint of line personnel who are trying to accomplish the critical aspects of the organization's mission, these constraints and barriers are a massive bureaucracy which impedes, stifles, and harasses their efforts. These constraints and barriers include excessive paperwork, overemphasis on procedure, repressive regulations, inflexibility, dilution of single point authority with staff redundancy, and an increasingly unfavorable ratio of management and staff to line personnel which generates dysfunctional bureaucratic requirements.

Consider my favorite example of how management overconcern with evaluation and compliance can impede line efforts. This is a military tale from the Battle of Isandhlwana in the 1879 Zulu War in South Africa. This battle was the worst defeat ever inflicted on a modern army by native troops.

As the battle began, imagine the British private on the firing line who looked out to see 30,000 Zulu warriors coming over a distant hill into firing range of the 1,800 troops in the camp. He was willing to do his job, to fire his single-shot Martini-Henry carbine rapidly and accurately to help win the battle.

Now, consider the bureaucratic constraints which the British military authorities had created, supposedly to ensure an effective fighting unit. When the private needed more ammunition, he was required to indicate his need to his color sergeant for verbal permission to leave the firing line.

Privates were not trusted. Despite the fact that there were countless examples of a strong sense of comradeship and loyalty among privates in the British army, the officers believed that privates would abandon their mates to flee in the face of the enemy. (Another reason for monitoring privates' use of ammunition was the officers' belief that they might take too many cartridges and later sell them on the black market.)

In any case, after receiving permission from his color sergeant, the private had to work his way through the battle's incessant din and confusion to locate the ammunition wagon assigned to his company. Even though another ammunition wagon might be closer, he could only draw ammunition at the assigned wagon. If he tried to do otherwise, he would be told by another wagon's quartermaster, "We'll not issue ammunition from this wagon to any but authorized companies!" (This was because the officers wanted to compare companies on ammunition usage rates.)

At last the private located the correct wagon and implored a private assisting the wagon's quartermaster for ammunition. He was told, "Wait your bloody turn and get in line!"

He got in line, and when his turn came, the quartermaster checked the company insignia on his uniform to ensure that he was qualified to receive ammunition from this wagon.

Now the sea of Zulu warriors with shields held high and spears flashing in the sunlight was getting dangerously close, 300 yards and closing rapidly on the firing line. By this time, the private was desperate to grab a handful of ammunition and rejoin his mates back at the line. There was, however, another regulation. Until there was an immediate requirement for its use, "All ammunition must remain in their proper boxes banded with their lids screwed down, as his lordship ordered." The quartermaster wanted to do his job properly. He would never unscrew several boxes at once and empty the cartridges out in a large pile on a blanket so they could be scooped up by desperately needy privates. Rather, each man had to be given ammunition from a single open box. For the private in question the last cartridge from the only open box was given to the previous man, so he had to wait while another box was opened.

There were two other regulations. First, privates could only be given 20 rounds of ammunition at any one time. This was because the cartridge case on their belts would not hold more. Second, spent brass cartridge cases had to be returned to and accounted for by a quartermaster. Because of the emergency, however, the last regulation was waived, and the private was finally given 20 rounds of ammunition.

By this time his company had been overrun at its former position and he had to fire at the approaching Zulus, now only 50 yards away, from where he stood beside the ammunition wagon.

After he fired one round, the quartermaster shouted at him that it was unsafe to discharge a weapon within 10 yards of the ammunition wagon and wanted to make a record of the private's name and serial number for a subsequent disciplinary action. As the reluctant private was providing this information, the Zulus closed on the ammunition wagon and killed everyone around it including the private, who only wanted to fire his rifle at the enemy, and the quartermaster, who only wanted to follow his lordship's orders.

In a subsequent review of the battle and the causes of the defeat, a colonel reported to a general that the fault lay, in part, with privates who were insufficiently disciplined for battle and were seen leaving the firing line. In response, the general directed that his staff conduct a study to determine how a regulation could be written to prevent this problem in the future!

Similar to these British officers, United States managers at every level believe they make important contributions to winning the battle of competition. Indeed, most do a reasonably good job of the first three management functions — planning, organizing, and directing. Through the years, however, the many people who cycle through as managers overemphasize the control function until control becomes excessive and produces a mountain of constraints and barriers to organizational effectiveness. It is possible, as previously noted, that each successive manager may have no direct experience with the organization, e.g., the fighter pilot who manages a science center. The bosses who promoted this individual mistakenly believe that a good craftsman is a good manager. "If you can fly an aircraft, you can manage a science center!"

The result is that persons managing organizations often don't fully understand the work they are managing. How do they get a good feeling about whether things they manage are going well? How do they maintain a sense of control? How do they demonstrate to the central boss that they are doing a good job and deserve a raise and promotion?

In the backs of their minds, they know that soon they will rotate by reassignment or through job-hopping to other positions to manage other organizations. They realize and usually lament that there isn't enough time to thoroughly understand the work they now manage, although sincere effort may be made in that direction. Instead, they rely on the accounting and financial tools learned in a weekend MBA program as measures of how well things are going.

A reasonable use of accounting and finance is appropriate and, of course, required for many purposes by stockholders, regulatory bodies, and the Internal Revenue Service. Unfortunately, too many managers are unable to keep the use of these tools at a reasonable level. Whenever a difficult problem or crisis develops which puts the manager on the hot seat, a new accounting or financial procedure is enacted to ensure that this won't recur. Often when a senior manager makes a simple inquiry, a new reporting system is developed.

Such reactions among subordinates occur repeatedly across the tenure of each successive senior manager until a staggering amount of bureaucracy is built up. As an organization's environment changes, controls and reporting systems of all kinds continue to exist for contingencies that may have no potential for recurrence. Increasing staff and resources are required to support this growing bureaucracy. Eventually what once was a flexible organization able to keep pace with changing and rising customer expectations becomes unwieldy, stress-filled, and increasingly stagnant.

To consultants who are trying to improve quality and effectiveness, there is a well-known signal that a company has this overbureaucratic form of mountain. This signal is manifested when the CEO readily acknowledges the urgent need for improvement, but is always too busy to become more than superficially involved in the effort.

When a question arises about whether the CEO will become directly involved in given improvement activities, the answer is "Oh, no! The CEO is too busy for that!" This responsibility is delegated to someone else, such as a quality assurance department or a TQM focal point, so the CEO can be free to work on "pressing problems." Of course, the CEO will come to presentations and workshops on improvement, but will stay only long enough to express an endorsement of the undertaking. After a few comments, the CEO will leave the room to return to those pressing problems.

What are these pressing problems? Why don't the CEO and other senior managers have more time for the critical issues of improvement? The answer is that the pressing problems they must rush off to work out result from the mountain of bureaucracy they and their predecessors built. For instance, a senior manager is needed to sign a waiver to authorize skipping the company's lengthy review process so a customer can get a needed product sooner. Or a manager is needed urgently to authorize a deviation on certain inspection processes so a batch of products can be shipped on time.

If United States managers only understood the true meaning of leadership! If only they would patiently and systematically eliminate these mountains, then time would be available for them to work on the truly relevant issues that face their companies. Much more of their time could be spent on improving quality and increasing effectiveness. In most United States organizations, pressing problems are a never-ending series of fire-fighting actions in which the CEO and other senior managers attempt to prevent things from coming apart.

In companies with these mountains of problems, improvement is a long uphill struggle. There are no quick fixes. Managers' attitudes must change so that abuses to their most valuable asset, their personnel, never occur again. Furthermore, managers must become personally and deeply involved in improvement. They must be involved in improvement every day. Improvement must be the first item on the agenda at every staff meeting. Managers must be willing to work harder at improvement than anyone else. They must read and discuss the works of the quality philosophers. Their day-to-day work should continue along the lines summarized below. This work involves empowering everyone in the company to participate in satisfying the expectations of internal and external customers by continually improving the processes by which the organization's work is conducted. Continual improvement restores the organization with the competitive flexibility and vitality so critical in today's multinational competitive environment.

This book's TQM/MGEEM complete step-by-step implementation procedure satisfies each of the management requirements identified in this chapter. It works to remove the barriers and obstacles to improved quality and performance. TQM/MGEEM can be understood and applied by in-house personnel largely with in-house assets. There is little need to spend exorbitant sums on outside consultants. The actions required to develop TQM/MGEEM are significant, immediate enhancements to quality. After its establishment, TQM/MGEEM provides a means of measuring, monitoring, and enhancing quality which is highly cost-effective and acceptable to workers. TQM/MGEEM involves personnel from all hierarchical levels within a user organization. In addition, TQM/MGEEM is a procedure for systematically implementing any one or combination of the teachings of the quality philosophers.

A brief overview of TQM/MGEEM follows:

Making use of TQM/MGEEM in an organization requires the strong, visible, continuous support of the CEO who begins the undertaking by forming a quality council of senior managers. This council establishes policy to ensure that people are empowered to improve things; participates directly in continual education for improvement; and provides overall direction, coordination, oversight and reinforcement.

TQM/MGEEM requires the services of facilitators who are trained from among in-house volunteers. To implement TQM/MGEEM in the target organizations within a company (all divisions, all departments, all branches, etc.), facilitators work with Blue Teams and Gold Teams. A Blue Team is composed of the manager of a target organization, his/her immediate superior and immediate subordinates, and representative customers and suppliers.

Facilitators use consensus-building techniques to guide Blue Teams through a review of their target organization's mission statement and exercises to develop an appreciation for harmonious and cooperative relations with customers and suppliers.

Blue Teams are then guided to break target organizations' mission statements into measurable parts, called *key result areas* (KRAs). KRAs concern achieving performance and quality.

Facilitators then lead Gold Teams, formed of the target organization manager's subordinates and key workers, to consensus on ways to measure performance on the KRAs, called *indicators.*

To most users, an important benefit of TQM/MGEEM is that it makes possible the truly comprehensive measurement of quality. To many organizations, especially those in the service industry, the measurement of quality traditionally has been a difficult, if not insoluble, problem.

Gold Teams also build feedback charts, one for each indicator, which are used to track the indicator(s) performance through time and are the basis for periodic feedback on the KRAs progress. Feedback charts form the basis of the most powerful part of a TQM/MGEEM system.

On a monthly basis, members of each target organization, including management and workers, hold feedback meetings in which they review progress on their charts. Not only do workers receive highly motivational feedback on how well they are doing as a group, but their ideas are solicited about *how to improve the processes* by which work is accomplished, and how to eliminate unrealistic bureaucracy. In these periodic feedback meetings, every effort is made to strengthen group ties, promote cooperation, and tap workers' unrealized potential. Suppliers and customers regularly attend these feedback meetings where their expectations and ideas for improvement are solicited.

In TQM/MGEEM, the manager's principal job is to respond to the ideas of workers, customers, and suppliers by continually improving the processes by which work is accomplished. Often it is necessary to use simple statistical tools to determine exactly what is wrong with a work process. Feedback meetings are held in every target organization within a company every month and, across time, a company's quality and overall effectiveness continually improves. Quality and effectiveness advance through team building by improving the processes by which the company does business; by creating harmonious, cooperative relations with suppliers; and by satisfying changing and rising customer expectations.

It is not necessary for United States companies to take a back seat to any offshore competitor. It is not necessary for United States firms to produce products that don't work. It is not necessary for internal and external customers to suffer delays, errors, abuses, and insults. It is not necessary for United States firms to go out of business because they can't keep up with competition. Any organization — a two-chair barber shop, a multiregional service organization, a huge manufacturer, an aircraft carrier — can use the principles and philosophy of TQM/MGEEM to become highly effective through never-ending improvement. This book teaches how to make it happen.

CHAPTER
3

PREPARATIONS TO BEGIN

TQM/MGEEM is implemented in target organizations by two teams, a Blue Team and a Gold Team, who work with a trained facilitator. Before describing the work involved in implementation, five preliminary considerations must be addressed:

1. The key role of the CEO.

2. Selection of facilitators.

3. Selection of target organizations where the implementation will begin.

4. Selection of individuals to be members of the Blue and Gold Teams.

5. Description of facilities and materials to be used in the implementation.

The Key Role of the Chief Executive Officer (CEO)

The Iron Law of Organizational Development is that any initiative to improve an organization must have the strong, visible, and continual support of its CEO. If any of these three conditions is missing, the effort is doomed. This law is so important that many consultants will not accept engagements involving organizational development unless they are convinced the CEO is fully behind the effort. Any lack of interest by the CEO will be reflected in a corresponding lack of interest among middle managers. Consequently, even the best efforts of consultants and motivated other senior and middle-level managers, supervisors, and workers cannot save the undertaking. If the project fails, the consultants will be blamed and their reputations will suffer even though the real cause of the failure was a lack of sufficient support by the CEO. To ensure the proper development and survival of TQM/MGEEM, certain actions are recommended to demonstrate the CEO's support.

The most effective way for the CEO to demonstrate approval of TQM/MGEEM is to establish and support a quality council of senior managers. (See Juran for an unparalleled discussion of quality improvement councils.)[22] Such councils usually have the same membership as the top corporate management group.

When workers are unionized, it is important that senior union representatives be involved as members in council activities. Union education, cooperation, and involvement are an important part of any successful quality improvement effort.

In large organizations, or where physical facilities are separated from the headquarters, there should be a council not only at the headquarters, but also at each separate facility.

When there are councils at other than the corporate level, they should be linked vertically to the corporate council through a common member, the chairperson of the lower level council. For instance, a division manager who is the chairperson of a division-level council should be the vertical linkage and advocate to the group. Establishment of such councils and their subsequent continuing actions to promote quality sends a message to managers and others that the CEO considers quality a serious matter.

The responsibilities of the quality council parallel those of any high-level functional committee. Their most important responsibility is to study the meaning of quality and publish the company's policy with respect to its employees, customers, suppliers, investors, and community. A critical part of this policy is a statement of *commitment* to improvement. The council must show its understanding that improvement requires change and that only they have the authority to authorize these necessary changes. Unless the council takes the actions necessary to change the way business is conducted, little improvement will take place. (Anyone who doubts the truth of this is simply mistaken!)

The second most important responsibility of the council is to become *personally* involved in educating everyone in the company about improvement. This responsibility must not be delegated. The CEO, other managers, and union representatives must make presentations, live and on video, about improvement. For instance, the CEO may wish to make a presentation on one of Deming's 14 points. Other senior managers may either discuss another of the 14 points, or key ideas and concepts from other quality philosophers.

Such presentations must become a regular part of staff meetings and have a high priority for discussion any time personnel meet. Only through council participation in education will corporate culture change for the better. The council's responsibilities also include providing resources, reviewing progress, and assuring recognition for quality improvements.

At a meeting of the senior staff to announce the establishment of a quality council, the CEO should explain the decision to implement TQM/MGEEM. The theme of this presentation should be upbeat. It should not include references to problem areas or identify personnel or groups doing well or poorly.

The CEO should comment on the importance of employees in the work of improvement, the importance of quality in the face of stiffening competition, and the importance of anticipating and satisfying customers' needs. The CEO should emphasize that in contrast to other approaches to improvement, TQM/MGEEM encourages employee input about how the organization can improve itself. The CEO should make a supportive introduction of a facilitator who then gives a presentation on the plan to implement TQM/MGEEM, its use, and benefits.

The facilitator who gives this presentation should, of course, be familiar with this book's contents. The facilitator's presentation and the implementation plan will reflect the wishes of the CEO as developed in conversations with the facilitator.

Any staff member who hesitates to support the CEO's commitment to TQM/MGEEM should be encouraged to ask questions and express concerns. It is important that the CEO and facilitator take the time to fully answer all questions and resolve all concerns about TQM/MGEEM. At this point, to enhance commitment, many facilitators advocate the use of various team building exercises. Such exercises are discussed in French and Bell.[10]

Another opportunity for the CEO to express support for the TQM/MGEEM implementation is at a meeting of all employees and union representatives (if the organization is unionized) called especially for this purpose. (To encourage union support, the CEO may wish to make a separate presentation for senior union officials who are not company employees.)

If there are numerous employees, such a presentation could require use of a cafeteria or auditorium, or perhaps several separate presentations. The CEO must be present at these meetings to express an endorsement of TQM/MGEEM. The CEO must not make an appearance and then duck out to return to work. This conveys the wrong message. Use of a videotape for the CEO's presentation is strongly discouraged. Videos play an important role in training, but the initial endorsement of TQM/MGEEM by the CEO is too important for a video. The CEO shows support by his/her presence. The CEO, however, may rely on a facilitator to present a technical overview of TQM/MGEEM at these meetings.

There is nothing mysterious about TQM/MGEEM. Nothing about its development or use should be kept secret from anyone. Considerable experience shows conclusively that improvement with TQM/MGEEM greatly benefits all, including workers, supervisors, managers, stockholders, customers, suppliers, and unions. Consequently, the decision to implement TQM/MGEEM should be communicated to all interested parties with a sense of pride and enthusiasm.

At various meetings with employees the CEO and facilitator repeat essentially what they said at the earlier meeting with the senior staff. Again, it is important to allow sufficient time for questions. If the size of the audience makes it feasible, refreshments should be served at the end of the meetings, and both the CEO and facilitator should be available to answer questions. Some people prefer not to ask questions in a large group or before their co-workers. To accommodate them, both the CEO and facilitator should announce that they will be available later in their offices to answer questions. No employee should feel intimidated about expressing a viewpoint, raising an issue, or complaining. As will be seen later, leaders who have adopted the philosophy which underlies TQM/MGEEM view complaints as opportunities in the never-ending process of improvement.

Another opportunity for the CEO to show support is when the facilitator first meets with the Blue and Gold Teams that will develop TQM/MGEEM. The CEO's very presence at the start of these meetings will be sufficient to stress the importance of the work at hand, but a few comments which emphasize the value of quality would be an even stronger endorsement.

At these meetings, the CEO should discuss the significance of what each team is about to do and express appreciation for their efforts. Since team members will attend the CEO's address at the earlier meeting of all employees, they will have a good idea of what's going on and what is expected of them.

After these remarks, the CEO reintroduces the facilitator and may leave the room to return to work. The facilitator then begins to work with the teams, as will presently be described. It is important that the CEO remain in touch through facilitators with how the implementation is proceeding. Some CEOs demonstrate their interest by returning for brief visits as the Blue and Gold Teams are engaged in TQM/MGEEM work.

Another way the CEO can show support for TQM/MGEEM is to ask How goes it? questions at appropriate times throughout the implementation. Short question-and-answer exchanges should take place as an agenda item at staff meetings, or in casual conversations in hallways between the CEO and managers who are implementing TQM/MGEEM in their departments. These questions should not require detailed answers or be perceived as pressure on the managers, but should serve to remind them and others that the TQM/MGEEM project is a concern of the CEO. If it is known that TQM/MGEEM is on the CEO's mind, it will be on the minds of other managers.

As TQM/MGEEM develops through the organization, there is provision in the process for management review of the various stages of development. These reviews also serve as reminders to middle-managers and others of the CEO's continuing interest in TQM/MGEEM.

Another means of maintaining the visibility of the TQM/MGEEM project is via publishing periodic How goes it? reports from the CEO. The usual vehicles for communicating to various organizational interest groups should be used, including letters to union representatives; news releases, brochures, and posters to customers; quarterly earnings statements and annual reports to stockholders; memoranda to managers, supervisors, and workers; and the company house organ, a TQM/MGEEM newsletter, and posters to employees.

The level of detail provided to each interest group will vary and should be left to the discretion of the CEO with the advice of the public relations staff. The theme of these messages must stress that management is committed to the long-term effort of improvement. In no case should the theme exhort workers to do a better job. Every worker can be counted on to do his/her best if management will remove the senseless barriers to pride of workmanship. Banners and bumper stickers exhorting workers to put their backs into it should not be substituted for management's discharging its responsibilities for improving quality.

There are those who believe improvement efforts should be played close to the vest. As they see it, announcing commitment to a broad-scale improvement effort is tantamount to admitting that something is wrong with the organization, that things have not been going right. Nothing could be further from the truth. The correct perspective is that no organization should ever stop improving. Continual improvement is a way of life for organizations which survive and prosper. The correct perspective is that our management has always and will always look for better ways to do business.

The CEO must let it be known that he/she is personally responsible for improvement. This responsibility must not be delegated. If the organization has a reputation for poor quality, unresponsiveness to customer needs, and low morale, this is an opportunity to announce turning over a new leaf, introducing a new era, and adopting a new philosophy of dedication to quality.

Selection of Facilitators

There is a common expectation among many managers that there is an expert out there somewhere with the solution to the company's problems. As a result, through the years employees of most companies have endured a parade of experts and their programs.

At any given time, there are best-selling books, expensive speakers, and high-dollar consultants who offer programs on whatever happens to be hot. Consequently, many employees develop a foxhole complex. Their approach to each new program is to stay low in their foxhole, give the new system apparent support with lip service, and go through the motions. Employees learn from years of experience that senior management support will eventually weaken, and the program finally will fade away. They have learned over the years that senior management will eventually lose interest, despair of the project, or a new CEO will come in with another one. Many employees regard organizational life as an endless series of improvement programs. Since employees almost never have any input about the details of such programs, they are seldom permanently motivated by them, and often try to manipulate and *game* them.

This does not mean that much of what is offered by experts is not correct and useful. This means that an element usually missing in most organizational development efforts is sufficiently widespread employee involvement. It also means that there is no one-best solution to every organization's problems, quality or otherwise.

Organizations come in all sizes and shapes. They require solutions that are unique to their particular situations. An approach that works for an IBM or a Navy avionics repair department may not work as well for a CPA firm, grocery, fast-food chain, health-care facility, or university. Therefore, what is needed is an approach to improving quality that allows managers and employees to proceed in a systematic, thoughtful manner to develop the best solutions for them. This is how TQM/MGEEM works.

TQM/MGEEM is a procedure that allows organizations to develop their own unique approach, or combination of approaches, to the solution of their quality problems. In this spirit, facilitators should not be expected to have the final solution to the organization's quality problems. Rather, facilitators lead employees through a simple step-by-step procedure to develop TQM/MGEEM, which allows the employees themselves to use a variety of resources to identify and solve their own quality problems.

Solutions to the quality problems of a given organization are not developed by a facilitator, by this book's author, or by some expert, but by the people who work in the organization. Since the organization's personnel build the key features of the TQM/MGEEM quality improvement effort themselves, they are more likely to be motivated by it and less likely to manipulate it. They regard gaming as simply cheating themselves. This is why facilitators are called facilitators. They do not direct or mandate TQM/MGEEM, but facilitate its development through the people who know the organization best — its members. Therefore, it is important that facilitators only facilitate and in no way influence organizational participants in their development of their TQM/MGEEM. Their TQM/MGEEM belongs to them, not to the facilitator.

Facilitators should possess various skills, many of which are taught in this text. Among the most important is knowledge of the meaning of certain words used to discuss (1) the input-output approach, in which organizations are viewed as components of systems or processes (examples of the terms used in this approach are *inputs, outputs, value-adding activities, suppliers,* and *customers*); and (2) organizational measurement (examples of the terms used in this approach are *quality, effectiveness, efficiency,* and *timeliness*). Knowledge of these terms is easy to acquire (probably already known by most employees), and will be reviewed in the following pages.

Another important facilitator skill is ability to build consensus in meetings of as many as 20 people. This skill includes knowledge of how to get group members to speak their minds, and how to bring a group to agreement on various questions. There are a number of books (e.g., Delbecq, Van de Ven, and Gustafson)[5] and many magazine articles (e.g., see *Quality*

Progress or *Journal of Training and Development*) detailing how to achieve consensus, build teams, and conduct good meetings.

Most medium and large companies have personnel trained in these skills. Such people are likely to hold a behavioral science degree and work in the human resources area, as quality circle facilitators, or as human relations trainers.

Beyond some general aptitude for working with groups or teams, facilitators need only carefully follow and trust the step-by-step TQM/ MGEEM process laid out herein. The consensus-building technique advocated here is the nominal group technique (NGT), and it will be discussed in detail.

Two issues should be addressed immediately after facilitators are identified. If they are not addressed and resolved early in the effort, these issues will be the basis of unending facilitator confusion and questions.

The first question is, Is my involvement in TQM/MGEEM an extra duty? The answer to this is yes. At least 15 percent of the manager's time and as much as 100 percent of the facilitators' time will be required by TQM/MGEEM work, depending on the ratio of facilitators to number and size of the target organizations. Provisions must be made for supplying this extra time in facilitators' work schedules. It is unfair and highly demotivating to ask facilitators to maintain their usual work loads while devoting time to the improvement effort.

The second question is not asked by facilitators but by other workers in the company, and facilitators are expected to have the answer. This question is, As the company becomes more efficient, will I lose my job? The answer must be no. No one will lose his or her job. When manpower requirements are reduced as a result of this initiative (as they surely will be because TQM/MGEEM makes companies much more efficient), the policy must be that people who are displaced will be retained and reassigned into equally good or better jobs that become available through attrition and retirement. In fact, companies which use TQM/MGEEM come to brag that not a single person lost his or her job or an hour of pay even though there was a reduction in staff brought about because of greatly increased efficiency. More often, however, as TQM/MGEEM guides a company toward increased quality more customers are attracted. And as a company's market share increases, more jobs are created.

Some prior knowledge of a target organization's mission, hierarchical structure, existing information systems, unique language/acronyms, key personnel, suppliers, and customers is helpful to facilitators in implementing TQM/MGEEM. Of course, a facilitator who is employed in a selected target organization will already be familiar with it, but outside facilitators should read available internal documentation (e.g., statements of objectives, mission statements, organization charts, manning documents), and be escorted on an unobtrusive site visit through the target organization. The main benefit of this familiarization process is that the facilitator will better understand the comments of members of the Blue and Gold Teams as they work to implement TQM/MGEEM. Less clarification will be needed, and the work of the teams will go smoother and faster.

A final word of caution is necessary about the selection of facilitators. There are many ways to sabotage any organizational development effort such as TQM/MGEEM. Reasons why managers would want to be involved in such sabotage are mentioned throughout this book. The reasons vary from a belief that TQM/MGEEM is just another management program to the fear produced because TQM/MGEEM may have been introduced without sufficient education for an effective culture change.

Regardless of the many reasons, such sabotage does occur, and one way to accomplish it is through the selection of the wrong types of people as facilitators. For instance, let's suppose facilitators are selected from among employees who are about to retire. After these facilitators are trained and develop some experience, they are soon lost through retirement. What does this pattern of facilitator selection do for the TQM/MGEEM effort? It ensures that the cadre of facilitators is forever inexperienced.

Consider another method of sabotage. Suppose middle managers are allowed to select from their subordinates those who will be trained as facilitators. What kind of people will be selected by middle managers who do not support the TQM/MGEEM effort? Suppose some middle managers are convinced that TQM/MGEEM is just another short-lived management program. Will they identify their best personnel for facilitator training? Will they surrender 15 to 100 percent of the time of some of their critical employees for "this new nonsense?" The answer is no. Consequently, it may be a self-fulfilling prophecy that TQM/MGEEM won't succeed. The reason for its failure won't be that TQM/MGEEM is unsound, but that less critical employees were carefully selected by uncommitted middle managers to facilitate it.

The self-fulfilling nature of this sabotage becomes real when a new facilitator, known among his or her peers to be among the least critical employees, finishes facilitator training and returns to begin implementing TQM/MGEEM. How anxious will peers be to work with a person they know to be among the least critical? Selecting less critical people as facilitators sends a clear message to everyone about management's real level of interest in TQM/MGEEM. Everyone knows that high-status, effective people are selected to get behind important efforts. TQM/MGEEM facilitators must be these kinds of people.

A word of clarification is needed concerning the meaning of the term *least critical* employees. Who are these so-called least critical employees? These are employees who, through no fault of their own or perhaps of no one, are not seen as highly capable. For example, everything else being equal, which person from these pairs of employees would typically reflect greater management support if selected as a facilitator:

1. in the Army–a second lieutenant or a colonel?

2. in a company–a 24-year-old with eight months seniority or a 42-year-old with 12 years seniority?

3. in a hospital–a clerk from the medical records department or an assistant to the administrator?

4. in a university–an instructor or a full professor?

To be young, low in seniority, or low in occupational prestige or position certainly doesn't mean an individual is less motivated or willing. Other employees who understand the power structure, however, will regard the selection of such less critical persons as a weak endorsement of TQM/MGEEM by management. Therefore, great care must be taken to communicate the right message when facilitators are selected.

Selecting a Target Organization

TQM/MGEEM will work in any organizational component of a company. When TQM/MGEEM has not been fully successful, it has never been because of a difficult or unusual type of organization. TQM/MGEEM failure has almost always been because of a reluctant CEO. However, the list of areas where this program has been successful is long and continues to grow. (The list includes manufacturing, sales, food service, contracting, engineering, insurance, law enforcement, test and evaluation, research and development, health care, accounting, finance, education, and prisons.)

To understand how to select a target organization where TQM/MGEEM is to be first implemented, assume the hierarchical organization shown in Figure 3.1 arranged with a CEO and staff at the corporate level, three divisions below that, five branches in each division, and many sections or work centers in each branch. TQM/MGEEM eventually should be implemented in all parts of any organization, from small work centers with a few workers and one supervisor to the entire organization of many managers, supervisors, and possibly thousands of workers.

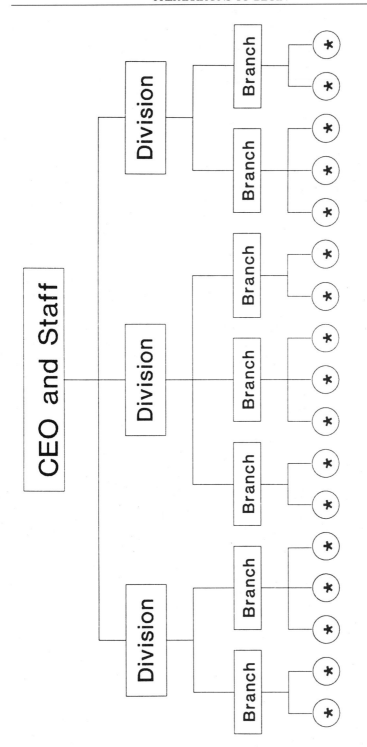

* Work Centers

FIGURE 3.1   Assumed Hierarchical Organization

Let's count the possible target organizations in Figure 3.1. The CEO and staff comprise one. The three divisions comprise three more. Therefore, the first two hierarchical levels make up four target organizations. The 15 branches are 15 more target organizations. Thus, for these three hierarchical levels, there are 19 target organizations: one at the corporate level, three at the division level, and 15 at the branch level. Work centers within each branch contain still more target organizations.

Implementing TQM/MGEEM for an entire multilevel organization raises the question of whether it is best to start at the top and work down, start at the bottom and work up, or initiate all levels simultaneously. The latter method results in a faster implementation, but requires a cadre of facilitators. If a cadre of facilitators is available, some managers believe it is best that they work simultaneously through the steps of TQM/MGEEM for various organizational components. For example, after training in the first step in TQM/MGEEM, all facilitators conduct this first step for parts of the organization at the same time. After this step is completed, all facilitators meet as a group with their trainer to review progress then begin training in the second step of TQM/MGEEM. The facilitators then implement the second step in unison followed by another group meeting with their trainer to review progress. This procedure continues through TQM/MGEEM's various steps.

Other managers believe it is best to implement TQM/MGEEM only at the work center level, not at the middle or top of the hierarchy. They contend that the greatest improvements in quality occur "where the rubber meets the road," where products are manufactured, or where customers are served.

Still others argue that improvement effort should not focus on the lower-level workers at all, but that the most important improvements arise mainly from continually improving all of the internal processes by which organizations conduct their business. They claim that making these improvements is management's responsibility.

This last viewpoint is supported by a wealth of evidence. Removing obstacles that stand in the way of workers' efforts to do a good job results in greater improvement than simply urging workers to work harder. With rare exceptions, workers want to do a good job. They want to feel a sense of pride and craftsmanship in their work. The obstacle that prevents them from doing a good job is some senseless work procedure, requirement, or other obstruction which management should remove. Remember that this is one of the mountains identified earlier. To encourage management to assume its responsibilities to improve work processes, some believe it is advisable to develop TQM/MGEEM at top- and middle-management levels, not at the work center level.

It is worth repeating that workers will do a craftsmanlike job if managers create an obstacle-free work environment where quality is possible. As will be presented in later chapters, TQM/MGEEM encourages the creation of this kind of environment.

Experience shows that most CEOs who contemplate use of TQM/ MGEEM first want to test its feasibility. For this test they usually identify a target organization within the company that has massive quality, political, or morale problems which they, their accountants, and engineers have been unable to solve. They say, "Well, if TQM/MGEEM will work in that department, it will work anywhere!"

It is gratifying to know that considerable evidence conclusively shows that TQM/MGEEM has never failed in such rigorous, acid-test target organizations. As CEOs have learned from TQM/MGEEM implementation in troubled organizations, the technique works regardless of any kind of quality, morale, political, or measurement problem. In fact, testing TQM/ MGEEM in a troubled target organization yields more spectacular improvements in effectiveness than in organizations where few problems exist. This is because larger gains are possible in organizations that are in trouble.

Performing a feasibility test of TQM/MGEEM will increase managers' confidence in the approach, and word-of-mouth communication tends to heighten the interest of other employees in "doing" their department. Managers will hear workers in other departments saying "When are they going to do us?"

It is important to point out that there are serious drawbacks to conducting feasibility tests of TQM/MGEEM in a troubled target organization. These drawbacks stem from the fact that troubled organizations usually are not typical of the rest of a company. Although it is true that such organizations have a greater potential for improvement, their implementation almost always requires more time and usually is much more difficult. Such organizations have all sorts of problems that must be solved. Personality conflicts often exist which require attention. There may be serious political issues that must be resolved. Consequently, when TQM/ MGEEM is tested in such an organization, management often gets an inaccurate picture of the effort required for the benefits achieved. Management may conclude, "Gee, TQM/MGEEM did improve effectiveness by 45 percent, but look how long it took!"

Another drawback to implementing TQM/MGEEM in a troubled organization may occur when employees sit in on such a feasibility test as part of their training to become facilitators. When trainees see the many problems and often gut-wrenching personal conflicts that must be resolved they may be reluctant to serve as a facilitator. They get the mistaken impression that all TQM/MGEEM facilitation is tough. Actually, the opposite is true. The typical TQM/MGEEM implementation goes smoothly, is a pleasant experience for everyone involved, and is fun for the facilitator. For these reasons, if a feasibility test is required, it is best to select a target organization that is typical of the company rather than the worst possible case.

It is not uncommon for CEOs to select the top-down method of implementation. They reason that there are various fabrics that hold companies together and help them coordinate their diverse activities toward common objectives. Among the most important of these fabrics are the written objectives or mission statements which should exist at every hierarchical level. These statements tie together in a cascading, unifying manner the objectives of each level so that the work of the entire company is coordinated.

More specifically, every company should have a mission. The divisions that make up a company should also have missions which direct them to accomplish activities which support the company's larger mission. Then, within divisions, branches should also have missions which direct them to accomplish activities that support the division which, in turn, support the company, etc.

Coordination of these various missions is an important method whereby companies seek and maintain constancy of purpose. In this manner, all parts of a company tend to work toward the same goals.

As explained earlier, the introductory work of implementing TQM/MGEEM is accomplished by Blue and Gold Teams for each target organization within a company, including the corporate level and at each division, branch, and work center. For each of these target organizations, a Blue Team ensures that there is a viable mission statement. This team then breaks the mission statement into measurable parts, called key result areas (KRAs). KRAs are the principal intended accomplishments of a target organization. As will be explained later, TQM/MGEEM also involves tracking performance on KRAs with indicators.

A key limitation that can occur with the bottom-up approach to TQM/MGEEM implementation is that personnel in higher-level target organizations often revise their mission statements as they go through the soul-searching required in the TQM/MGEEM development process. Because all of a company's mission statements are vertically tied together, changes in mission statements at the top usually produce changes in mission statements in the middle and bottom. Thus, in the bottom-up approach, TQM/MGEEM systems developed in lower level target organizations may require revision for changes made in mission statements at any higher level.

From this perspective, it is best to begin development of the TQM/MGEEM at the top and work down.

Another reason to start at the top and work down is that, astonishing as it may seem, many target organizations do not have mission statements. It is common to see a mission statement at the corporate level but none for middle- and lower-level organizations. In such cases, the top-down approach is necessary so that mission statements can be developed at the middle and lower levels which are consonant with that at the top. On the other hand, mission statements may exist for all organizational components, and they may have recently been satisfactorily reviewed. In such cases, there might be no danger of changes in the higher organizational levels mission statements, and taking a bottom-up approach could prove reasonable.

In addition to the requirement that a clear mission statement must exist for the organization above any organization selected for TQM/MGEEM implementation, there is another consideration to keep in mind in selecting target organizations. If two or more organizational components have a common mission statement and identical customers and suppliers, it may be possible to treat them as one target organization for purposes of TQM/MGEEM implementation. When an organizational component is distinct, however, with respect to mission, customers, or suppliers, it is best that it have its own TQM/MGEEM system. Undoubtedly, other factors, such as size, have a bearing on the selection of target organizations.

The preceding guidance should assist managers in deciding how to begin TQM/MGEEM implementation. Implementation in hundreds of organizations, however, suggests yet another strategy which I personally endorse. Because quality should be driven by customer expectations, it is important to consider implementing TQM/MGEEM horizontally (or sideways), rather than vertically (from top-to-bottom or bottom-to-top). In the approach I recommend, implementation in a company begins in the departments that deal directly with external customers and then continues into the departments that support the departments dealing directly with external customers.

As an example consider a hospital. The organizational components of a hospital that come into direct contact with customers (patients and their families) are the clinics or wards where medical care is provided and other organizations, such as admissions, billing, social services, and the cafeteria. It is in these components that TQM/MGEEM should be implemented first.

The next components to implement TQM/MGEEM are those that provide support (inputs or resources), those that deal directly with customers. For the clinics, these support departments include the laboratories, x-ray, in-house pharmacy, housekeeping, and security. (Identifying support departments is part of the TQM/MGEEM implementation process and will be explained later.)

Experience demonstrates that many of the most troublesome quality and effectiveness problems exist in two key areas: (1) in the organizations that deal directly with external customers, and (2) in the relationship *between* the departments serving external customers and other departments providing support to them. TQM/MGEEM is highly successful in harmonizing these relationships.

Consider a second example of this horizontal approach to TQM/MGEEM implementation. How should TQM/MGEEM be implemented in a military organization, say an Air Force base where several different airlift squadrons operate?

Airlift squadrons use cargo airplanes to transport troops and cargo. The first tier of implementation would be in the airlift squadrons themselves. These squadrons train, organize, and schedule aircrews to fly airlift missions. The process of implementing TQM/MGEEM in these squadrons identifies their key suppliers (as will be explained later).

These key supplier or support units are maintenance, aerial port, supply, command and control, ground transportation, intelligence, and weather. These organizations would form the second tier for implementation.

Yet a third tier may then be identified, the Air Base Group, composed of such other support organizations as the medical and dental clinics; billeting; accounting and finance; personnel; motor pool; civil engineering; security police; and morale, welfare, and recreation.

Consider a university as another example. Where should a TQM/MGEEM implementation begin? The answer is in the departments that interface directly with customers.

This raises a controversy common to most organizations including universities: Who are the customers? Some people believe students are the customers while others contend that students are the output (product) and that the real customer is society. (A methodology to work toward a solution to the question of who is the customer is presented later.)

For the sake of this illustration, let's assume students are the customers of universities. The first tier of organizations for implementation would, therefore, be the parts of a university that come into direct contact with students. These would include the academic departments (composed of professors), the registrar's office, the bursar's office, the library, the bookstore, etc.

The second tier would be the organizations that support the first tier. These would include the physical plant, housekeeping, reprographics, computer support center, and traffic and security.

This implementation approach should be considered as a general model.

For instance, certain tiers may not be discretely defined, but overlap with other tiers. Some professors, for example, may only do research and not have much or any student contact. Traffic and security, on the other hand, may have considerable student contact and should be defined as belonging to the first tier.

One other approach to selecting target organizations for TQM/ MGEEM implementation should be identified. This is called the drowning man approach because it often is used by companies to keep themselves from going under.

The organization(s) targeted for TQM/MGEEM implementation are those that are the critical areas of the company — the areas where the bleeding is taking place, the areas that absolutely must get turned around if the company is to survive. Sometimes these critical organizations can be identified through judgment by senior management, often newly hired to generate a turnaround. It is probably best, however, to supplement this judgment with results from one of a variety of diagnostic questionnaires designed to assess organizational strengths and weaknesses. Of course, the critical areas vary from company to company. In any case, a massive effort is focused in the critical areas and for some time other healthier parts of the company may only be affected by TQM/MGEEM as a by-product of the work with the critical areas.

The guidance presented herein on the alternative methods of selecting target organizations should be considered advisory and should be supplemented by the judgment of facilitators and managers who are knowledgeable of the organizations under consideration.

Selecting Participants for the Teams

For each target organization, two teams, a Blue Team and a Gold Team, are formed to work with a facilitator to develop TQM/MGEEM. Each team member is selected for his/her unique experience and perspectives. Let's examine both teams.

Each Blue Team is composed of a target organization's manager, the manager's immediate superior and immediate subordinates, and representative customers and suppliers. Consider the organization shown in Figure 3.1. If the target organization is a branch, the membership of the Blue Team would be the branch manager, the division manager, the work center supervisors, and judgmentally chosen representative customers and suppliers.

Identifying customers who are to be members of a Blue Team usually is easy when a target organization provides products or services to ultimate or external customers. As Juran suggests, for all target organizations, customers should be identified as persons or organizations that receive or are influenced by the organization's output or service.[22] It is astonishing that many target organization members, including their managers, do not know the identity of their customers. This is especially common in organizations whose customers are internal, i.e., other departments within the same company. Employees know that they provide support to these other internal departments, but often do not regard them as real customers. They consider customers as only those to whom the *company* sells its products or services, and not other departments that receive *their* products or services as customers. In fact, as stated earlier, internal customers are not only disregarded as customers, but are often thought of in a strictly competitive sense as rivals or adversaries. Of course, this is a serious problem which TQM/MGEEM works to correct.

To identify several representative customers to be members of a Blue Team, consider the following reasoning (further explained in Chapter 4). Target organizations perform certain value-adding activities, or work, on a day-to-day basis which results in their ouput, i.e., their goods or services. This output is input (resources) to either (1) customers internal to the company, or (2) customers external to the company.

Customers receive or are influenced by this output. They may eat it, sit on it, hang it on the wall, be healthier because of it, add a mark-up to it and pass it along to someone else, etc. In some way customers use this output to help accomplish their mission. They use product designs to help manufacture something. They use stenographic services to document an important meeting. They use consultation from engineers to identify or correct a problem. Hopefully, customers do better work because they receive this input. For instance, a target organization may have repaired the customers' air conditioning system, painted their walls, provided a new desk, or expedited hiring a needed employee. A customer is able to repair a jet engine because a target organization provided spare parts. People or organizations who benefit from the work of a target organization are its customers.

Several of these customers are needed as members of the Blue Team. Although target organization customers will be identified in a more systematic manner later in the TQM/MGEEM process, at this point their selection can be based on the judgment of the target organization manager using the reasoning just described.

Two or three people who work in supplier organizations also are invited to be members of the Blue Team. When suppliers are external to the company, target organization members have no difficulty identifying them, but when suppliers are internal to the company, there usually is some confusion. Therefore, it is helpful to again consider the same reasoning used previously to identify internal and external customers. As implied in the earlier discussion of customers, a supplier is any person or organization who provides a target organization with the inputs (resources) required to accomplish its mission, to conduct its value-adding activities. These inputs can include human resources, raw materials of all sorts, physical facilities, utilities, etc. Often these inputs are internal, i.e., they originate from another department within the same company. In any case, they are an internal supplier, e.g., human resources are provided to many target organizations by an internal supplier — the personnel department. A more complex example follows.

In a certain company, the commercial services department verifies the payment of debts and sends vouchers on them to the accounts payable department. Accounts payable writes checks, puts them into addressed envelopes, and takes them to the mailroom.

Who are the suppliers in this example? Commercial services is a supplier of inputs (vouchers) to accounts payable and accounts payable is a supplier of inputs (envelopes containing checks) to the mailroom.

Other suppliers to all three of these organizations are personnel, which supplies human resources; physical plant, which supplies a clean building with adequate climatic conditions; computer services, which supplies computer time; etc.

The second team which works with a facilitator to implement TQM/MGEEM is called the Gold Team. It is composed of the immediate subordinates of the target organization's manager and selected key workers. In other words, from the Blue Team remove the manager, the manager's immediate superior, customers, and suppliers. These people may return to work. Now add key workers.

For the branch in Figure 3.1, the Gold Team consists of the work center supervisors and key workers. Key workers should be selected for their experience and knowledge of the target organization. They should be opinion leaders among the other workers in the target organization. Their support of TQM/MGEEM will encourage its wider acceptance among the other workers. An ideal Gold Team includes eight to 10 participants, but it may be smaller or larger as required. Too few participants on a Gold Team results in failure to develop sufficiently broad support among other personnel, and too many participants make the team's work time consuming and slow. The risks of moving too slowly are that participants may become bored and labor costs of implementing TQM/MGEEM increase as personnel are kept away from their regular jobs.

Under no circumstances should anyone who should be on a Gold Team be prevented from participating. Excluding key people hurts feelings and is counterproductive to the process' objectives. If a Gold Team initially is too large, it can be broken into two or more groups on the basis of similarity of function or work. After these groups have achieved their results, a brief consensus-building meeting of the groups—or, better, their representatives—is facilitated in which results are amalgamated.

Although Blue and Gold Teams should constitute specific members, as previously suggested, there are occasions where modifications are appropriate. One of these occasions is when the manager of a target organization is fearful of exposing too much to his/her superior. Such a manager may feel insecure (often for good reason); the supervisor may be fearsome. The manager may wish to exclude the superior from the Blue Team and secure the superior's input later in the process of reviewing the proposed TQM/MGEEM system.

Another occasion for modification of team membership is when target organization members feel uncomfortable inviting their customers or suppliers. They may fear that customers or suppliers will be too difficult to work with because of strained past relations. A history of strained relations makes the use of TQM/MGEEM even more imperative. When it is felt that customers and suppliers should be excluded at this stage, it is not ideal but it is permitted. This does not mean that those individuals are excluded permanently. As explained in Chapter 10 they can get involved later in feedback meetings.

A third case for possible exception to the recommendations on team membership is when a manager of a target organization wishes to be a member of both the Blue and Gold Teams. This desire may suggest a lack of trust by the manager in members of the Gold Team. More often, however, it suggests that the manager is merely highly motivated and wishes to make a contribution to both teams. In any case, the facilitator must discuss this request for modification with the manager and be flexible about granting such requests. In many cases, conditions of fear and mistrust motivate the requests to modify recommended group membership, but these conditions eventually will be reduced and removed as the organization is gradually but surely strengthened through the use of TQM/MGEEM.

Necessary Facilities and Materials

Meetings of the two teams to develop TQM/MGEEM involve a certain cost because employees are kept away from their jobs for a period of time. Although meetings may require as little as four hours for a small work center, every effort should be made to ensure that the work of the teams goes smoothly and effectively so that employees are not detained unnecessarily. Therefore, having the right facilities and materials for the meetings is important.

The meeting room should be well-ventilated, with adequate lighting for participants to work comfortably. Restrooms should be nearby. The meeting room should be far enough from participants' offices or work areas to prevent participants return to them during breaks. It may be best to conduct the meetings at an off-site, perhaps at a nearby hotel or conference facility. There should be no telephones in the meeting room, and messages to participants, especially managers, should be limited. Perhaps a message board could be provided outside the door so participants may take messages during breaks. Fresh coffee, juice, and pastries should be available at the beginning and throughout the morning sessions, and soft drinks and fruit should be available at the breaks in afternoon sessions. If feasible, sessions should start 30 minutes earlier than usual working hours, and lunch can be catered so that participants remain in the room.

These deviations from normal, workplace practice create a heightened sense of importance about the undertaking, allow more time for the work at hand, and provide greater continuity of effort.

The room size should be sufficient to accommodate a long conference table or U-shaped arrangement of tables with comfortable chairs. There should be at least 25 linear feet of wall space free of windows, doors, drapes, and other obstructions. (The walls will be used to hang chart paper with masking tape.) The room should be arranged so that participants can exit to a restroom through a door at the opposite end of the room from where the facilitator is leading the work. No exit should be available at the end of the room where the facilitator is working. At the far side of the room, opposite the facilitator, there should be sufficient space for several participants to stretch their legs without losing touch with what's going on. Near the rear door there should be a table where refreshments are placed. If feasible, the room should be quickly cleaned after catered lunches.

A number of materials are essential to the work of the facilitator. These include at least one easel with a full pad of chart paper. A second full pad of chart paper should be available when the other is exhausted. The facilitator should be familiar with how to replace paper on easels. Markers of different colors should be available for use in writing on the chart paper, and masking tape should be on hand to hang pages of chart paper on the walls without damaging them. An overhead projector on a table and a screen are required at the front of the room. Having a spare bulb for the projector is advisable. The projector is used by the facilitator to display important information on transparencies. (These transparencies are identified later in this text and should be prepared prior to the meetings for the facilitator's use.) A large chalkboard or white board with appropriate marking instruments must be placed at the front of the room.

It is important that certain details of the team sessions be recorded. Participant comments need not be written down, but a record should be kept of the date of the sessions, names of participants, and everything the facilitator writes on chart paper.

It will be explained later that target organization members are free to revise the details of their TQM/MGEEM system after its initial development. In subsequent revisions, they will benefit from having a detailed record of the meetings' results. Suggestions initially discarded through consensus may later appear reasonable and be incorporated into the TQM/MGEEM.

To require that the facilitator keep these records will slow the process and keep employees away from their jobs even longer. It is suggested that a recorder be available to assist the facilitator. The recorder need not be in the room at all times, but must be present when results are being written on chart paper. (After some experience working together, the facilitator and recorder learn to plan and coordinate these times.) At other times, the recorder can be attending to other responsibilities, such as coordination of refreshments and lunch, setting up the message board, and assuring sufficient supplies. Within a week after completion of team meetings, results must be typed, reproduced, and made available for distribution to participants for a *sanity check* or *pulse* meeting.

Many organizations recognize the need to develop a cadre of trained TQM/MGEEM facilitators. An excellent opportunity for this training is to have the selected persons present when actual use of the TQM/MGEEM technique is occurring. If so, a trainee should act as recorder.

At each participant's place at the tables there should be a pad of lined 8½x11-inch paper, several pencils, and at least 15 3x5-inch index cards. Extra paper, pencils, a pencil sharpener, and index cards should be available in a cardboard box placed under a table at the front of the room. On each table there should be one marker and one 5x7-inch index card for each participant. At the beginning of a session, the facilitator should instruct participants to fold the 5x7-inch card in half so that it forms a tent on the table in front of them. Each participant should be asked to write on both sides of the tent card the name they wish to be called during the sessions. In this way correct names can be seen and used by all, including the facilitator who will find the use of participant names a valuable means of keeping the process moving. Some outside facilitators like to ask participants to designate with the letters, C, S, and T.O. on their tent cards whether they are customers, suppliers, or members of the target organization. Other facilitators learn and memorize this information by asking participants to identify themselves and their organizational affiliation at the session's beginning.

MISSION STATEMENTS, CUSTOMERS, AND SUPPLIERS

The first phase of TQM/MGEEM development involves reviewing a target organization's mission statement and conducting exercises to ensure understanding of customers and harmony with suppliers. This preliminary work is an extremely important part of the process and is requisite to the phases which follow (described in later chapters). For a number of organizations, this first phase requires considerable time and effort, but its importance cannot be overemphasized. The first phase is accomplished by a Blue Team made up of a target organization manager, the manager's immediate superior and immediate subordinates, and judgmentally selected customers and suppliers.

Experience shows that the efforts of facilitators to implement TQM/ MGEEM are much better received if participants have been exposed to several months of general training in the importance of quality and customer service. As emphasized in the Preface, senior managers must participate as teachers in this training if an organization's culture is to change. This training should take place at staff meetings and other meetings where videos of the quality philosophers are shown and discussed by senior managers. Senior managers should be encouraged to present and discuss each of Deming's 14 points.[7] Education in the culture of quality does not stop, however, when TQM/MGEEM begins. Learning about quality should never stop.

Kicking Off: The Work of the Blue Team

It is important that the work of a Blue Team be introduced by a CEO's brief appearance to demonstrate support for what the team is about to do. Comments by the CEO should be brief and include a statement of the company's commitment to improvement, the importance of suppliers and employees in the never-ending quest for quality, and the importance of understanding and satisfying customer expectations. Following these remarks, the CEO should introduce the person who will act as facilitator in a manner that shows confidence in that facilitator's abilities. The CEO then leaves the room, and the facilitator makes a few introductory remarks.

Facilitators learn which remarks work best for them, and successful introductory remarks vary from one facilitator to another. All members of Blue Teams, except for customers and suppliers, know what is expected of them because they were present at the earlier presentation on TQM/ MGEEM. They can be expected to be interested, motivated, and anxious to get started. After all, they are about to undertake an important and meaningful task. Many of the team members have spent their entire working lives in this company. Anything that has to do with improving it will be interesting to them. It is best, therefore, for the facilitator to keep the introductory remarks brief enough to orient customers and suppliers about what is to transpire and then continue with the work at hand.

TQM/MGEEM's value to the company, its customers, and suppliers should be explained to the customers and suppliers when they are initially invited to serve on a Blue Team. The role of TQM/MGEEM in the never-ending quest to improve products and services should have been stressed to them. Remember, it is only fair to observe that some members of Blue

Teams will be skeptical because they have seen programs come and go, and may suspect that the TQM/MGEEM is just another program. It is unlikely, however, that their skepticism will reveal itself this early in the TQM/MGEEM development process.

Several introductory remarks and transparencies for display on an overhead projector are suggested for use by first-time facilitators. As they become more experienced, facilitators develop introductory remarks that work best for their unique styles. It should be reassuring to them to know that if they stick to the basic steps described in this book, the TQM/MGEEM development process will go smoothly even if some of the words, or even complete transparencies, are inadvertently omitted. Experience shows that the TQM/MGEEM development process is rigorous. Its purpose is easily understood and, after experiencing the earlier briefing given to all employees, most Blue Team participants will understand what is expected of them. In many ways the TQM/MGEEM developmental process runs itself. Facilitators merely need to provide direction, keep things moving, and trust the process.

A facilitator should begin by addressing the issue of what is expected of team members during the course of the work. The facilitator should make a transparency to be shown on an overhead projector. The transparency should include the following points under the heading *Improper Team Participation:*

- Don't judge, argue, or correct someone else.
- Don't talk too much.
- Don't try to game the situation.

The facilitator should then discuss each of these points. The facilitator may wish to observe that there are no soap boxes in the meeting room, nor are there any axes to grind. Neither should team members seek to subvert the project's purposes. It should be explained how each team member's contribution is necessary if the work is to be a success. Participants should be told that they are to be personally involved in developing a system of improvement for their own use. The system will be theirs, and if that system is good, they will benefit.

A second transparency should then be made up to contain the following information under the title *Proper Approach to Team Participation:*

- Play manager for a day.
- Trust the process.
- Listen, observe, think.
- Contribute.

As this transparency is shown, the facilitator should stress the positive side of what participants should do. First, they are asked to play the role of manager for a day. They are to forget that they are customers, suppliers, subordinates, or the manager's superior. For this one day, they are to assume the perspective of the target organization's manager.

In addition, they are asked to trust the process. Trusting the process means appreciating that the TQM/MGEEM development process is hardy. If they work at the tasks set before them, the process will carry the team through to success.

When things seem to be stalled, going down the wrong path, or confused, team members and the facilitator need only patiently and faithfully follow the steps in the process. The process will set things right and, in due course, produce results.

It also should be stressed to team members that following the process does guarantee results, but the *quality* of the results depends on the team's efforts. If they collaborate, stay flexible, and are willing to learn from one another, the result will make an invaluable and lasting contribution by improving the quality and effectiveness of the target organization.

A third transparency should be made up of the following information under the title *Steps in the TQM/MGEEM Process:*

- Review mission statement.
- Identify customers and suppliers.
- Develop KRAs.
- Develop indicators.
- Create feedback charts.

The facilitator should explain to the Blue Team that the first step in developing the TQM/MGEEM is to review the mission statement. This transparency portrays the overall logic of the TQM/MGEEM process and is instructional for customers and suppliers who did not have the benefit of hearing the earlier presentation on TQM/MGEEM.

The facilitator reiterates how the five components of the TQM/MGEEM process fit together to achieve constancy of purpose for the organization:

1. The mission is to serve customers.
2. Customers and suppliers are identified.
3. KRAs are the measurable components of the mission.
4. Indicators demonstrate how well the organization is accomplishing its KRAs.
5. Feedback charts provide periodic information to managers and workers on how well they are doing on their indicators.

Reviewing the Mission Statement

It is incredible that many target organizations do not have a mission statement. A mission statement usually exists for a company as a whole, but seldom do all of the organizational components of companies have them. Occasionally, a target organization will have a mission statement, but no one can find it! Personnel search high and low, finally locating it in an old annual report stored in the basement.

Why isn't this vital document more accessible? Probably the best answer is that many managers simply don't appreciate its value.

Another, somewhat sinister explanation, however, runs like this: If the exact nature of the mission is not understood by workers, how can they know what to do when they face a situation not covered in their training, assuming they had any formal training in the first place? The answer is simply that they won't know what to do. They will have to ask the boss, and this helps maintain the boss' power.

Consequently, many bosses — perhaps subconsciously — aren't interested in sharing the valuable information in mission statements because it gives workers a degree of autonomy. With knowledge of the mission, workers have greater self-control. They don't need to keep running to the boss to ask what to do. They can solve problems at their level without using the hierarchy. Of course, workers like this autonomy. As business environments become more uncertain and changing, there is greater need for self-control, and greater need for a capacity at the customer-contact level for continuous adjustment through real-time problem solving.

Many organizations find that when knowledge of the mission among trained workers becomes complete, there is far less need, if any, for supervisors. Workers themselves assume the supervisors' valid function. The invalid functions of the supervisors, e.g., policeman and micro-manager, can be abandoned. These invalid functions are remnants of a management style that worked badly anyway, creating the most adverse, abusive, and pitiful of conditions.

If a mission statement does not exist, or is inadequate, the facilitator should work with the Blue Team to develop it. If there is a mission statement at the next higher level above the target organization, it should be used as a development guide to replace a missing or inadequate mission statement. Since the target organization manager's superior is a member of the Blue Team, this person can supply valuable information about how the target organization contributes to the mission of the next higher level. These contributions are the essence of the target organization's mission statement.

A good way to start thinking about the mission statement is to consider what would happen if the target organization did not do its job. The manager's superior can be given a heads-up by the facilitator to be prepared to answer this question. This answer confirms the value of the target organization and can be used to highlight the importance of each employee in the target organization as their work contributes to the mission. When target organizations don't do their jobs, examples of what doesn't happen include employees not receiving their paychecks, spare parts not being available to the component repair or assembly units, nonexistent sanitary conditions in the plant, security not provided for employees, toilets not flushing, mail service that is no longer available. Such information from the target organization manager's superior helps focus the mission and emphasize its importance, in a motivating manner, to members of the Blue Team.

When target organizations do not have mission statements, it is common for well-intentioned personnel to be working in opposite or, at least, inconsonant directions. Without a mission statement to guide them, people develop different ideas what is important. Not having mission statements or having mission statements that are incomplete, or not known and used, often combines with another condition to create an extremely serious organizational problem.

The other condition is the practice of moving managers through different supervisory positions in the interest of broadening their careers. What happens when a new manager takes over an organization that has no visible mission statement? The new manager often changes the direction of the organization in midstream from the direction which was followed under the previous manager. This change in direction may be small or dramatic.

Changing the direction of organizations because new managers do not have clear, up-to-date mission statements to follow has many negative consequences. The most serious problem is that an organization's mission frequently is not accomplished as originally planned. Each succeeding manager has a different idea about what should be done. Usually this involves doing what is best for each manager's own career. Managers learn to ask themselves How can I use my present position to advance my career? rather than How can I help this organization better accomplish its mission? Unfortunately, this attitude is disastrous because the mission (always to satisfy customer expectations) often is subordinated to advancing managers' careers.

A related consequence is that subordinates can become confused and disillusioned when a new manager with new ideas about the organization's direction fails to support their work with the vigor displayed by the previous manager. When mission emphasis changes, personnel and resources get transferred to the projects which the new manager considers important.

Just as workers begin to get the hang of a certain project they get pulled off of it and put on something new. After years of seeing a stream of new managers, each with different ideas about the organization's mission, personnel often cannot commit themselves to work which keeps changing. They become resigned to working largely for the money, especially if they can't find another job. What is needed, of course, is a viable mission statement for each target organization at every level throughout the company, and a culture which reinforces managers and others who accomplish their mission.

Often, what is termed a mission statement is merely a description of an organization chart expressing the functional relationships between a company's various components. Slightly more complete mission statements are commonly written by manpower personnel or industrial engineers and deal only with the most prosaic nuts and bolts descriptions of the work to be accomplished. This manner of thinking about mission statements is far from ideal.

Another problem with most mission statements is that usually they are considered to be set in concrete; they never change. This unchanging nature of mission statements represents a serious misunderstanding of the most important role of any organization, to serve its customers. This misunderstanding fails to take into account that customers and their expectations change. Therefore, organizations which serve customers who have changing requirements should also change, and this change should be reflected in their mission statements. Mission statements should be living documents. They must evolve as customers and their expectations change.

Mission statements should be written in a manner that helps employees. They should contain information that helps employees learn what they are expected to do when new on a job, and whether their abilities, interests, and philosophies are suited to the company where they are about to become employed.

An example which demonstrates this comes from my days as a baseball player. I fancied myself a pretty good ball player who could have made it to the majors if I had been four inches taller and 60 pounds heavier. In any case, I had played on and off for some semi-pro and other teams which paid their pitchers, best hitters, and best glove men $20 to $50 a game.

Graduate school forced me to place that experience behind me when I moved to a city where semi-pro ball didn't exist. I was, however, delighted to be invited to play in a church softball league. Since the time required wouldn't take too much time from my studies, I agreed to play. In the several practice sessions before the league began, I was recognized as a strong hitter and selected to bat in the fourth, "clean up," position.

In the first game, I hit a homer and a triple my first two times at the plate. I was filled with a strong sense of competitive joy as the game entered the final innings with the score tied. Then, a terrible thing happened. The coach, an assistant pastor, took out three or four players — including me — and substituted the team's weakest players from the bench! They struck out, made fielding errors, and the game was lost.

After the game, I discussed this disastrous decision, as I regarded it, with the coach. I said, "Coach, we were winning until you made those substitutions! How could you do that?"

He replied that it was the team philosophy to "let everyone play." He explained it isn't right to ask players to come out to a game and then not give them a chance to play. "Winning," he said, "is not as important as other considerations such as fellowship and having a good time."

This, however, was not my philosophy. I had grown up listening to the New York Yankees on the radio and playing ball every time I got a chance. Since I was a kid, I believed you are out there to win. If a guy could play shortstop better than you, he got the position. The best "sticks" hit at the top of the batting order. Subs knew they were there as learners and in case a regular got hurt. Some players would rather be a sub on a championship team than a regular on a team that never makes it to the playoffs.

In this example, who was wrong? The answer is no one. Neither the coach nor I was wrong. It was just a matter of believing in different mission statements for a ball team. In his way, he was right and, in my way, I was right. The problem was that I should have been informed of the team's philosophy, or mission statement, so that I could decide whether it matched my needs. The same is true for a company's prospective new employees. They should be informed of the mission statement so they can decide whether it is something they can support. Otherwise, something invariably will happen which will lead to disillusionment.

Another way mission statements help employees is by providing a rallying point to employees in their day-to-day work. An example of how a mission can be a rallying point comes out of military research and development organizations. Senior scientists in these organizations explain how motivated everyone working there was when their work supported our troops in Viet Nam.

After the war ended, they say that there was a perceptible lull in morale as the results of their work were then going on the shelf to develop the technology base, rather than directly benefiting troops. Later, however, when some of these organizations became involved in the effort to put a person in space and eventually on the moon, enthusiasm about the work returned to the high levels experienced during the war.

Mission statements should express unequivocal commitment to the never-ending improvement of the quality of a company's outputs to meet its customer requirements. These statements should not only overview the nuts and bolts of what is required to accomplish this (e.g., manufacturing fine furniture, providing unexcelled engineering services, or serving the best Southern fried chicken), but should also stress how employees, suppliers, the community, and investors join together for this objective in a spirit of teamwork and harmony.

Mission statements of company components should cascade from the overarching mission statement of the company itself. The mission statement of each underlying component should address how that component makes a unique contribution to the company's overall mission. Mission statements should strongly express the necessity for teamwork and harmony among employees and suppliers. (For an excellent discussion of the desirable features of mission statements, see Chapter 1 of Gitlow and Gitlow.)[12]

If a given target organization has no mission statement, a facilitator should proceed as follows to develop one. First, the manager's superior should be invited to review for the Blue Team the mission statement that exists at that manager's level, the level above the target organization. With or without this valuable input, the facilitator then moves directly to the step in the TQM/MGEEM development process of creating key result areas (KRAs). This step is explained thoroughly in Chapter 5, but is reviewed briefly here.

KRAs are the measurable components of a mission statement, an organization's principal intended accomplishments. Ordinarily, KRAs are developed by a Blue Team which has a satisfactory mission statement at its disposal. With the help of a facilitator, they break the mission statement into measurable parts — the KRAs. Thus, a mission statement is a cluster of KRAs.

Looking at this process another way, a facilitator can help target organization members develop their mission statement by leading them first to identify KRAs (as explained in Chapter 5), and then writing up a paragraph which summarizes the KRAs. That paragraph is the mission statement.

When a mission statement already exists for a target organization, it should be placed on a transparency and shown to the Blue Team on an overhead projector. The facilitator should ask members whether it accurately portrays their role. On this occasion, members of the Blue Team may learn for the first time what the framers of the mission statement think the company is all about. Often they realize that their mission statement is completely out-of-date or otherwise badly in need of revision. In such cases it is important that the facilitator lead the team through a session to revise it. This may unearth a need for strategic planning.

Before strategic planning takes place, however, team members should be provided with study materials on strategic planning and its relationship to the mission statement. A number of materials are available on this subject (Pierce,[33] Pierce and Davis,[34] and Fahey[9]).

Blue Teams must take the necessary time to modify and refine their mission statement. After management's approval of the new or refined mission statement, the future direction of the target organization is made more certain, and a much better understanding of the mission is achieved by organization members. The target organization now has a mission about which personnel can seek to achieve constancy of purpose.

The next transparency begins the Blue Team's work that leads to customer identification.

Input-Output Analysis

With a transparency made up to show the diagram in Figure 4.1, the facilitator introduces the Blue Team to what often is a new way for organization members to perceive themselves and their environment. This vision occurs through the use of input-output analysis.

The idea behind input-output analysis is that a target organization is one component in a system, just as the heart is one component of the human body, or a battery is one component of a car. All of the system's components must work together if the entire unit is to be successful.

A Blue Team is asked to think of their target organization as the large rectangle in the center of Figure 4.1. Under various laws, regulations, and customs, the target organization performs its day-to-day work, called *value-adding* activities.

To get a better feel for the meaning of these value-adding activities, the facilitator may wish to call on several team members who are employees of the target organization to explain some of the work they perform. For instance, the facilitator could read someone's name from his tent card and say, "Joe, could you describe some of what you were working on last week?" After acknowledging Joe's response, the facilitator moves on to two or three other employees for their comments on their value-adding activities.

Next, the facilitator explains that to perform these activities, the target organization must have various inputs (resources) which come from another component of the overall system — the target organization's suppliers.

Suppliers are upstream of the target organization and provide inputs

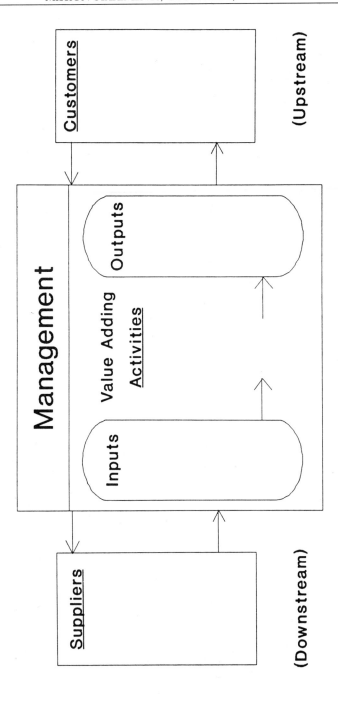

FIGURE 4.1 Input-Output Diagram

such as raw materials, personnel, computer paper, taskings, spare parts, physical facilities, empty boxes, and utilities. The target organization's inputs are the suppliers' outputs.

The facilitator stresses that the target organization must cooperate with its upstream suppliers to ensure that their output meets the target organization's requirements. Supplier outputs must be of sufficient quality so that they, in turn, can be used by the target organization to produce quality output for its customers.

No target organization can produce quality output for its downstream customers unless it receives quality inputs from its upstream suppliers. Requirements on the outputs of suppliers take various forms, including strength, durability, timeliness, brightness, texture, etc.

In using the inputs received from suppliers, a target organization's value-adding activities result in outputs which go out the door to their internal or external customers. Of course, these outputs are the target organization's products and services.

Just as a target organization has requirements or standards of quality for the inputs (resources) it receives from its suppliers, the target organization's outputs must meet the requirements or standards of quality set by its customers. Facilitators may wish to refer to Juran's excellent book, *Juran on Leadership for Quality: An Executive Handbook* (pp. 86-87) for more ideas on the importance of customers and suppliers.[22]

Customer Identification

Based on the above reasoning, facilitators should emphasize to Blue Teams that the best measure of the performance of any organization is the extent to which its outputs meet customer requirements. The reason all organizations exist is to fully and completely satisfy their customers' needs. As explained in Chapter 1, far too many organizations in the United States do not adequately satisfy the needs of their customers. Unless they have a secure monopoly, these organizations will sooner or later lose markets to competitors who are willing to do what is necessary to meet customer needs. In fact, countless organizations of this type go belly-up every day. (At this point some facilitators find it useful to show and discuss one of many videotapes available on the importance of customers.)

Facilitators should not attempt to force team members to accept "extent of customer focus" as the best measure of performance. The customer identification step in the TQM/MGEEM development process, however, does provide a forum in which team members are faced squarely with this issue.

Most team members immediately acknowledge the customer's key role. Unfortunately, others do not think for themselves and follow the often misguided direction of the team, the manager, or the manager's superior for cues for their attitudes.

A few will snidely, and occasionally actively, resist any efforts to reorient the organization toward fulfilling customer needs. Frequently these team members have benefited from the status quo (usually through promotion) and feel threatened by change. Their attitudes cannot be expected to change quickly, but they may become more trusting as they realize that TQM/MGEEM is not a threat to them, but is in everyone's best interest.

It is fair to observe that the attitudes of some personnel with many years of seniority never appear to change on this issue. It can only be hoped that their unchanging attitudes will not have such a strong influence that they will drive the company to ruin.

Considerable evidence shows that TQM/MGEEM dramatically improves organizational performance and creates a culture of quality improvement. Perhaps the most important measure of the success of any effort to use TQM/MGEEM is the extent to which it allows personnel to appreciate the utterly vital need to understand and satisfy customer expectations.

To examine the issues related to the interface between the target organization and its customers, facilitators ask Blue Teams the question, What is the definition of the term customer?

After consideration of different definitions, facilitators should suggest an approach from Juran's excellent approach that a customer is any person(s), organization(s), system(s), or processor(s) who use(s) or is affected by the target organization's output.[22] Following discussion of a variety of definitions, teams usually settle on a definition with which they feel comfortable.

Facilitators should lead this discussion so that team members come to realize that customers can be internal as well as external to the company. As discussed in Chapter 1, various departments support each other in the same company. For example, contracting supports engineering, repair supports sales, supply supports maintenance, etc. In other words, within a company, departments are customers of each other. Then there are external customers, outside of the company, who are commonly thought of as persons walking around on the street. It is, however, a serious error to focus exclusively on external customers. Facilitators should take pains to stress to Blue Teams the existence and importance of internal customers.

It also is important that facilitators explain (through discussion of the input-output diagram in Figure 4.1 if possible) that within every company each department, or target organization, is not merely a processor doing value-adding activities. Of course, it is true that each department is a processor, but team members should not be so concerned with that role that they fail to see the other roles played by each target organization. Each target organization is also a *supplier* because the outputs of their value-adding activities are inputs to either or both internal or external customers.

Many Blue Team members will not immediately understand this concept and should be given time to study a number of examples in the context of their own company. For instance, in the case of internal customers, the physical plant is a supplier that provides heating and air conditioning and other forms of support to their customers — everyone using the building; the computer center is a supplier that provides computer time and technical services to their customers — operational units; the print shop is a supplier that provides graphics and copy support to its customers; etc.

In addition to being processors and suppliers, each target organization also is a *customer* in the sense that other internal or external suppliers provide them with inputs (resources) in one way or another. As an example, the physical plant, computer center, print shop, and other internal organizations benefit as customers of the personnel department as it coordinates training, provides health and retirement plans, and administers payroll. It is important that Blue Teams, and eventually all members of target organizations, adopt an input–output way of perceiving themselves in each of these three roles: processor, supplier, and customer. Readers familiar with the work of Juran will recognize this as his famous triple role concept.[22]

At this point, it should be agreed upon in the discussion that various components of the company are customers of one another. Facilitators may wish to point out to Blue Teams that although customers are both internal and external, internal customers may be further subdivided. To explain this, facilitators should provide an example such as the following:

A physical plant (as a supplier) provides heating and air conditioning to other departments (customers) which use the company's physical facilities. Discussion should be conducted so that Blue Teams realize that each of the various components within the physical plant, called sections, branches, or work centers, are themselves processors, suppliers, and customers.

For instance, there may be a functional unit within the physical plant department called *receiving* that interfaces with physical plant customers to document requests for the services of the physical plant, such as "turn up the air conditioning" or "the heat isn't working." This unit, in turn, may task other functional units within the physical plant (e.g., the specialists in heating and air conditioning, carpentry, plumbing, etc.) with work requests. These functional units can be regarded as processors whose customers are both *receiving* and the organization which originally requested the work. The expectations of both customers must be satisfied. In turn, one of these functional units may require the assistance of another of the functional units within the physical plant. For example, plumbers might need carpenters to move a wall. When this happens, the carpenters are the suppliers to their customers — the plumbers. The point is that the functional units within the same department are at one time or another processors, suppliers, and customers of each other.

Many target organizations have only internal customers. They provide output only to other components of the same company who, in turn, may provide output to other internal and/or external customers. External customers are commonly thought of as the ultimate consumer and may be an institution, e.g., a jail, hospital, or monastery; a member of a channel of distribution, e.g., a wholesaler or retailer; or the so-called ultimate consumer, the person walking around on the street.

As facilitators help Blue Teams define the term *customer*, the question may arise as to how far down the chain of distribution a target organization should go in forming its definition.

As an example, suppose a target organization supplies products to wholesalers for redistribution further downstream to institutions as well as directly to ultimate consumers. Such a target organization has three external customers: the wholesalers, the institutions, and the ultimate consumers. All of these customers directly receive or are affected by the target organization's output. The institutions to whom the wholesalers provide output are not the immediate customers of the target organization, but should be considered as the target organization's responsibility. Of course, they are also the responsibility of the wholesalers. It should be clear that a target organization advances its own interests by assisting immediate customers (in this case, the wholesalers) to provide better service to their customers (here, the institutions).

Consider another example. Let's assume there is an internal target organization that produces an output, say wheels, which is input to another internal organization which uses wheels to assemble children's wagons. Yet another internal organization (a sales department) sells the wagons to an external customer (a wholesaler) who distributes them to other external customers (retailers) who sell the wagons to yet other external customers (the parents of children). Who are the customers of the target organization which produces the wheels? The answer is all of the customers who receive or are affected by the wheels. This includes the two internal customers (assembly and sales), the distributors (wholesalers and retailers), the parents, and the children.

The target organization should recognize all of these as customers and gather information about their needs so that every effort can be made to cooperate with intermediaries in satisfying them. For instance, what are the first internal customer's (the assembler) engineering requirements for the wheels so that they fit the wagons? What characteristics should the wheels have to make them meet the requirements of wholesalers and retailers? What do parents require in wheels on wagons for their children? What characteristics of wheels make them best from a child's perspective?

Despite the complexities involved in identifying customers, the essential contribution of asking the question Who is the customer? is that it provides a vehicle by which facilitators can get Blue Teams meaningfully involved in a number of issues related to the importance of customers. The desired result of this discussion and the next step in the process (actually identifying the customers of the target organization) is not to obtain a definitive list of customers, but to change or deepen attitudes about the customers' importance.

As mentioned earlier, personnel in too many organizations in the United States believe "this would be a great place to work if it weren't for the customers." Consequently, facilitators will accept any list of customers identified by Blue Teams in the customer identification exercise to be explained next. Any list of customers is a success as it is evidence that customers at least are recognized, and that the attitudes of key members of the target organization are changing or deepening.

It is a basic principle that appears throughout the TQM/MGEEM process that although precision of measurement is important, it is not as important as changing attitudes to create a culture of improvement. As will be shown, a precise list of customers is not as significant as bringing about a change of attitude about the customers' importance.

In many cases, the customers of target organizations are obvious, such as the internal customer down the hall. For other organizations, however, hundreds of thousands of dollars have been spent on research to identify customers, and members of Blue Teams can simply provide the names while the facilitator records them on chart paper. In fact, many organizations have formal, automated information gathering systems which periodically construct profiles of their often-changing customers and their requirements. Data for such profiles come from various parts of the product or service distribution system, including questionnaires completed by customers at the point-of-purchase.

Responsibilities for such information systems usually lie in the marketing department. However, even when customers are easy to identify, facilitators should ask for discussion about each customer name suggested. "Why is this department, organization, or individual a customer?" Every participant on a Blue Team should have an opportunity to raise an objection or voice a concern about why so-and-so is or is not a customer. Each team member should be given an opportunity to influence the group.

In situations where customers are not so obvious, especially in the case of internal customers, it is often necessary for a facilitator to employ a structured group process to organize the team's thinking. The nominal group technique (NGT) is well-suited for this purpose. The NGT is fully explained in the book by Delbecq, Van de Ven, and Gustafson and described below in sufficient detail for this use by a facilitator.[5]

Facilitators should indicate to Blue Teams that the TQM/MGEEM development process uses the NGT to help them reach consensus on a variety of important questions. It should be explained that use of the NGT provides a variety of benefits. It capitalizes on each participant's knowledge and experience. It prevents aggressive or high-status members from dominating the discussion. It allows various degrees of anonymous input, generates many new ideas, prevents participants from becoming stuck in one train of thought, and is a pleasant and satisfying experience for participants.

From the viewpoint of TQM/MGEEM, there are two especially important benefits in using the NGT. The first is that it increases participants' sense of ownership of TQM/MGEEM since they have a voice in its creation.

The second benefit is that the NGT empowers workers as it draws them into the decision-making process. Used in this manner, the NGT can establish an environment which emphasizes the importance of personal growth and brings employees toward their full potential.

A transparency outlining the steps in the NGT should be made up. These steps are:

1. Pose a nominal question.
2. Call for silent generation.
3. Conduct round-robin listing.
4. Lead discussion and clarification.
5. Call for voting.

The facilitator should then quickly walk the Blue Team through the steps in the NGT. To identify customers, the facilitator should say:

Here are the steps in the Nominal Group Technique (NGT) which we shall use to identify customers. First, I will pose the nominal question: "Who are the customers of [name of target organization]?" You will then be given 10 minutes to write down or silently generate your answers to this question. Next, without discussion, I will record your answers on chart paper as each of you, in turn, reads one of your answers to me. We will then discuss and clarify each answer.

With these introductory remarks, the facilitator begins the NGT process to identify customers.

Posing the Nominal Question

Before this session occurs, the facilitator should prepare a transparency which shows the customer identification nominal question with the name of the target organization. This question is "Who are the customers of [name of target organization]?" As this transparency is shown to the Blue Team, the nominal question is posed by the facilitator.

> We are now ready to use the NGT to help us identify customers. This transparency shows the question I want you to answer: "Who are the customers of [name of target organization]?" Remember that you are playing "manager for a day." You are to assume the point-of-view of the manager of [name of the target organization] for all of the work we do.

Silent Generation

> Please use the paper and pencil in front of you to silently generate your answers to this question. You have 10 minutes. Please do not talk to anyone during this time. OK. Begin.

During these 10 minutes, the facilitator should try to avoid requests for clarification and discourage discussion of any kind. Team members have just been briefed on input–output analysis and have agreed on a definition of the term *customer,* so they should share a reasonably common perspective in identifying the organization's customers. The facilitator should be quiet and unavailable as team members go through the silent generation step. No one should be moving around the room during this time.

On rare occasions, team members may still be confused and insist on further clarification of the definition of the term *customer* before they will try to identify who their customers are. The facilitator's reaction to this request should be to repeat key parts of the earlier explanation of input–output analysis. The input–output diagram shown in Figure 4.1 should be shown again as a transparency and the term *customer* defined again as the individual(s), organization(s), or process(es) that directly receive or are influenced by the output of the target organization. The facilitator should also remind team members that customers may be internal or external. Reiteration of the definition is almost always sufficient. If not, the Blue Team should be encouraged to again clarify the definition to suit its needs. After all, the TQM/MGEEM it is creating is for its own use.

If the team is unable to satisfactorily modify the definition, however, the facilitator may offer more comments which may sufficiently structure the definition so that the team can accept it and begin silent generation. As an example, for target organizations which serve ultimate, external customers, it may be helpful for the facilitator to observe that in the purchase of the product or service there are *influencers, actual purchasers,* and *users.* For instance, in a family, the mother may make the decision to purchase a certain breakfast cereal, the father may go to the grocery store and make the purchase, it may be served to a child, and the family dog may eat it.

In the case of internal customers, the facilitator might wish to observe that there are *requesters* and *users* (e.g., one internal department may define specifications and request a product or service while another internal department may actually receive and use it.) Often, however, the requester and user are the same department.

Occasionally, customers and suppliers may be the same person or organization. Thus, a given organization may be a supplier, as it provides a work request for a product or service, and a customer when the work request is received. Team members should be able to use this additional structure to agree on a definition of the term, customer, so that they can begin silent generation.

One suggestion occasionally made by members of Blue Teams is to complete the NGT process separately to identify internal and external customers. This suggestion is quite reasonable since the purpose of this exercise is to sensitize Blue Team members to the existence and importance of their customers. If a majority of participants believe this approach is appropriate, the facilitator should agree and lead the team through the NGT process twice. This is more time consuming, but usually worthwhile.

After approximately 10 minutes in the silent generation step, the facilitator moves the team to the NGT round-robin listing step by saying:

> It is now time to record your thoughts. I would like to go around the room asking each of you, in turn, to read the name of one customer from your list. As you read a name, I will write it on chart paper. The idea is to get your thoughts mapped out as quickly as possible, so we will not have any discussion as we quickly go through round-robin listing. You should say "pass" if your list is exhausted, but you may add to your list as we go along and suggest another customer when it is your turn.

The facilitator then calls on team members, by the names on their tent cards, to identify one customer. The facilitator writes numbers, beginning with 1, and records what team members have said to identify customers, word-for-word, at the top of a sheet of chart paper on an easel (or on a large white board). After a customer name is written, the facilitator asks its sponsor if the name is written correctly. If the name is correct, the facilitator moves on quickly to the next participant.

When a sheet of chart paper is filled with names, the sheet is carefully torn off the pad and hung with masking tape on the wall in everyone's view. It is possible that as many as five to 10 sheets of paper will be hung around the room when round-robin listing is finished. (The process will go smoother and faster if the completed sheets are torn off by the facilitator and then taped to the walls by someone else. This allows the facilitator to concentrate on interaction with team members during round-robin listing.) Round-robin listing ends when every team members says "Pass." It is permissible, however, for team members to add other customer names if they think of them during the process' next phase.

Discussion and Clarification

To introduce the discussion and clarification phase, the facilitator should say:

> Now we want to conduct a review of our efforts so far. I will go back to the first customer name and ask its sponsor to share with us the thinking that led to its identification. The sponsor will be asked why this person, organization, or company should be considered a customer. We shall go around the room in this manner. The purpose of this review is to improve the clarity and accuracy of customer names and to remove any overlap. This is not a time for arguments. You may ask a question about a customer name when it is under review. You may state how you disagree that a name is a customer when it is under review. The sponsor may answer your disagreement. Please direct all of your remarks to me, not to other participants. The point is we want to get all viewpoints on each proposed customer name out in the open. There is no need to argue because we will vote in a few minutes. Merely express your viewpoint.

Team members often see overlap among customer names and wish to combine several into a single category. It is a ground rule that the sponsor of a customer name "owns" it. This means that only a sponsor may agree to combine, modify, or delete a customer name which he or she proposed.

Notice that at this stage customer names can never have more than one sponsor. This is because the earlier NGT round-robin listing step permits only one sponsor per customer name.

The facilitator documents on chart paper how customer names are combined or broken up. For instance, suppose customer names No. 4 — Jones & Son, No. 13 — ABC, Inc., and No. 24 — Steinborough and Norton, are all wholesalers. The sponsors of each of the three names may decide to combine them into a new, larger customer grouping, say No. 25 — Wholesalers. If so, the facilitator should draw a line through the three individual customer names to show they are deleted, write an encircled 25 beside each number (Nos. 4, 13, and 24) to show that they were moved to No. 25, and write the old numbers (Nos. 4, 13, and 24) beside the new No. 25 — Wholesalers, to show which names were combined to create the new category. This is important because team members who originally proposed Nos. 4, 13, and 24 will want to be assured that their proposed customer names are not entirely lost. This combined name now has three sponsors.

When combinations of customers' names are suggested and are agreeable to all sponsors involved, it is important that the facilitator determine with a direct question whether all team members are in support of the proposed combination. Someone may prefer that a given customer name be left out of the combination and, unless it is left out, they will not vote for the consolidated item in the upcoming voting stage. Sponsors must hear of any such lack of support to help them decide whether to proceed with the consolidation.

Notation should also be made on the chart paper if a too-broad item is broken up. For instance, suppose the customer name "Wholesalers" is considered too broad. Team members may prefer to list the specific wholesalers with whom they directly provide input. Such a change must be approved by the sponsor and documented with numbers on chart paper. New numbers should be assigned to the new wholesale customers who formerly were clustered into No. 25 — Wholesalers. The facilitator should then draw a line through No. 25 — Wholesalers, and add to the chart paper the new numbers and names of the new wholesalers. Beside each new name should be written an encircled 25 to show that the old cluster was broken up into these specific customer names. Also, beside the lined-out No. 25 — Wholesalers, is added to the encircled numbers of the new customer names.

The discussion and clarification stage should produce a list of customers with which the team, as a whole, is satisfied. If an objection is raised to a customer name, the sponsor of the customer name is asked by the facilitator to again explain why the name was proposed. "Why is this person, department, or organization a customer?"

The objection should be resolved at this point by discussion between the facilitator, the objector, and sponsor. No argument should be involved, merely expression of opinions to the facilitator.

Whether or not the disputed customer name is accepted will be settled on the basis of the definition of what a customer is. It is important to remember that the ultimate decisions in the discussion and clarification stage, about whether disputed customer names are or are not customers, rest with their sponsors. If sponsors are not persuaded that names should be removed, the names remain.

Team members who object to customer names have an opportunity to voice their opinions, but must abide by the sponsors' decisions. Members who objected must be content to vote against the customer names when given the opportunity during the upcoming voting stage.

Remember that there are two purposes of the customer identification phase of the TQM/MGEEM process. The first is to bring members of Blue Teams to the realization that customers are the focal point of their organization's activities. The second is that customers must be sufficiently identified so that they can be invited to attend feedback meetings. (Exactly how customers participate in feedback meetings is discussed in Chapter 11.) Facilitators should not urge Blue Teams to reduce their list of customer names. The number doesn't matter. What matters is that organization members are discussing their customers. What matters is that team members are placed in the position of realizing that their customers are the center of their universe, that knowing and serving the customer is of utmost importance.

First-time facilitators often are amazed that Blue Team members don't know their customers' identity. A dramatic illustration of this comes from the following incident, which repeated itself in a number of sessions with different Blue Teams for which I was the facilitator.

During round-robin listing, certain team members may identify only one customer, the target organization manager! First-time facilitators often are confused by this because the term *customer* has been defined as the person(s)/organization(s) who receive the output of the target organization. The facilitator wonders why someone would name the manager as a customer? How does the manager receive or become influenced by the output? During the discussion and clarification phase, the facilitator asks the sponsor how the manager is the customer. Without thinking twice the sponsor says:

> You see, every Monday morning we have a staff meeting where Mr. Jones [the manager] has a checklist from which he tasks me with the work I am to accomplish for the week. Then, there is another staff meeting every Friday afternoon where he asks me if I did what he told me to do. We go down his checklist for compliance and noncompliance. So, you see, I spend the entire week working for my customer, Mr. Jones. So, Mr. Jones is my customer. He gets my output.

Of course, there are at least two serious problems with identifying the manager as the customer. The first problem is that the team member who works for the manager may resent any real customer's request for service. A real customer's request for service may be seen as an intrusion on the member's time. The member is motivated to please the manager. But, wait, you may think that the manager will ensure that members of the target organization take care of their real customers. You're right. This is what should happen, and it does in healthy organizations. However, what often happens is that a manager's thoughts are focused on *using* the target organization to get promoted. Many managers do not care in the least about the real customers. Their careers are all that matters. Think of the damage this does to an organization. When a career-first attitude is common among managers it can lead to a company's ruin.

Facilitators should assist Blue Teams in understanding several important concepts related to their customers. One concept suggested by Juran is that there are the "critical few" customers and the "important many" customers.[22] This means that a few customers contribute more to the target organization or company, in terms of sales, profits, or mission criticality, than all the others combined. This concept usually can be made clear to team members if they are asked to vote for the customers they regard as critical.

Facilitators should allow participants to decide for themselves what is meant by "critical." If discussion of the definition of the term *critical* is needed, or if the team feels it needs to reach a consensus on the definition, the facilitator should agree and lead this discussion. This discussion probably will focus on factors such as sales, profit, or mission-criticality, as a definition of critical.

In order to vote, team members are asked to use 3x5-inch index cards to write the names of the customers which they regard as critical from the list they just developed. If the original list has 15 to 20 names, team members should be asked to select five. If the list is over 20, they should be asked to select seven or eight. After team members have selected their critical few, they are given a 15-minute break while the facilitator tallies the vote and writes (in red) the total number of votes each customer received beside their names on the chart paper, which still hangs on the walls in the meeting room.

Review of these results invariably shows that a small percentage of customers is critical, while a large percentage is merely important. If appropriate, the facilitator may wish to display this information in a Pareto chart. This is not to say that the so-called important customers are not valuable. Remember that they, too, make a contribution to profit, sales, or mission-criticality. As will be explained in Chapter 10, target organizations should remain in continual contact with their critical few customers to ensure the understanding, anticipation, and satisfaction of their ever-changing expectations.

A recorder should make a copy of the list of all customer names generated, note which were combined and broken up, and record the vote's results. After the customer identification and voting phase is completed, facilitators should involve Blue Teams in a similar exercise to identify and prioritize suppliers.

Identifying Suppliers

It is important that Blue Teams also go through an NGT exercise to identify and prioritize their upstream suppliers. As in the case of identifying customers, the objective is not to obtain a definitive list of suppliers, but to build a better understanding of the critical role of suppliers in the never-ending efforts of the target organization to provide quality products and services to its customers. Here it is advisable to make a presentation to the Blue Team on Deming's fourth point on ending the practice of awarding business on the basis of price alone.[7] Elaboration on this point by Gitlow and Gitlow,[12] Scherkenbach,[37] and Walton[44] may be useful. Hopefully, education throughout the company on Deming's philosophy will have been underway for at least several months, and participants need only be reminded of the importance of their suppliers.

Referring again to the input–output slide, facilitators should preface this NGT exercise with several relevant examples of how a lack of support from suppliers can reduce the ability of target organizations to satisfy their customers' expectations.

One such example occurred when I was invited to make a TQM/MGEEM awareness presentation to the 450 supervisors of a certain company. Because the presentation was two hours in length, I wanted to liven it up by getting the audience involved. I requested that a two-page handout be reproduced for each member of the audience so that during the presentation they could write the answers to certain thought-provoking questions about quality, which I planned to ask. To impress an audience with the importance of mission statements, I would ask them to write on the handout several parts of their own personal mission statement.

The company print shop delivered 450 beautiful reproductions of the handout, but they were a day late! The lack of quality (here in timeliness) in the support of one of my suppliers (the print shop) caused the quality of my output (my speech) to my customers (the 450 supervisors) to be less than it could have been.

As was true in the exercise to identify customers, it is important that Blue Teams regard suppliers as both internal and external. Some suppliers are departments in the company; others are external to the company. Any definition and subdivision of suppliers is acceptable as long as it helps Blue Teams recognize that the quality of their output is directly affected by the quality of support from their suppliers.

The identification process and subsequent voting, as was demonstrated in identifying customers, provides a way for facilitators to enter a discussion of the need for harmony and cooperation with suppliers. The nominal question should be Who are the suppliers of the resources (inputs) which you use to accomplish your mission? The input–output diagram may again be used for clarification. In the voting phase, facilitators may wish to suggest that participants vote for those suppliers whose inputs are most critical to their work. Critical suppliers should be thought of as those who, if they do not produce high-quality outputs, cause the target organization to have greater difficulties satisfying its customers or accomplishing its mission.

Blue Teams may ask to conduct an NGT exercise separately for internal and external suppliers. Facilitators should support this recommendation. The voting step of the NGT should again result in an appreciation that there are a "critical few" and an "important many" suppliers.

Once a Blue Team has accepted the idea that there are a few critical suppliers, the facilitator should emphasize the importance of building and maintaining harmony and cooperation with these suppliers in the interest of better satisfying the requirements of the target organization's customers.

Usually it is easy to get suppliers to appreciate the importance of harmony and cooperation in their relations with a target organization. External suppliers represented on the Blue Teams normally understand that if a target organization, their customer, prospers by satisfying its customers, then the external suppliers, in turn, also will prosper.

Internal suppliers represented on Blue Teams also usually are interested in learning about harmony and cooperation. They realize that they will soon be involved in building a TQM/MGEEM system for themselves as its development expands throughout the company.

Remember that all internal target organizations have heard a presentation on the subject of TQM/MGEEM and, therefore, should be in a receptive frame of mind toward its implementation. In fact, depending on where TQM/MGEEM is first implemented in a company, it may be that the internal suppliers of the target organization already will have begun to develop their own TQM/MGEEM. Thus, they will be sensitive to the need for cooperation with their customers (one of whom is the target organization).

Most users of TQM/MGEEM are convinced that many benefits result when the critical few suppliers complete the exercises with a Blue Team to review the target organization mission statement and identify its customers and suppliers. As members of a Blue Team, suppliers develop a better understanding of the requirements of the target organization, and how the success of the target organization will benefit them. They come to better appreciate their roles in helping target organizations satisfy their customers' expectations.

In encouraging target organizations to improve their relationships with suppliers, facilitators should be aware that existing relations are seldom based on cooperation and harmony. In fact, relations often are adversarial. Feelings may be so intense, especially with internal suppliers, that target organization members may resist including them on Blue Teams for fear they won't agree to participate or that, if they do, their presence will be disruptive.

In rare cases, it may be necessary for a facilitator to request a meeting between the manager of the target organization implementing TQM/ MGEEM and the managers of key internal supplier organizations, in the presence of their common higher level manager, to discuss the philosophy of harmony and cooperation.

An example of the importance of full support by senior managers follows. The purpose of this meeting is, of course, coordinated with and supported by the higher level manager.

When internal supplier representatives finally show up for their first Blue Team meeting, they often sit together on a far side of the meeting room and look wary, as if they expect a fistfight to break out at any moment with target organization personnel. This is indicative of years of disagreement, confrontation, and hard feelings. This level of fear underscores the need for all parties to commit themselves to a continuing effort to bring harmony and cooperation to the relationships between target organizations and their suppliers.

Much of the problem of friction with internal suppliers arises from the fact that they usually have a monopoly. If you want a toilet fixed, you must get the physical plant people in the company to fix it. If you want copies reproduced, you must do business with the company's print shop. Before you can get a piece of new equipment, you must go through the company's procurement office. You can't go downtown to hire a plumber, get a quick-copy shop to do your repro work, or buy new equipment directly. Since internal suppliers know they have captive customers, over the years they gradually begin to make operating decisions on the basis of what is best for themselves, such as what makes their costs look good to their boss, rather than on the basis of what is best for their customers.

Like everyone else, internal suppliers probably don't have a mission statement which focuses on their commitment to their customers. An example of this problem resulted from a memorandum that was sent from supply to all department heads in a certain company:

> In accordance with companywide cost reduction efforts, we have changed our hours. Instead of being open from 8:00 A.M. to 4:30 P.M., we will now provide counter service only in the afternoons from 1:30 to 4:30 P.M. Our people will benefit from the additional time to catch up on paperwork and maintain inventory. Please explain to your people that they must confine their requests for supplies to our new hours.

Rather than saving money, when a support organization fails to fully serve its customers, overall company costs actually rise! How can this happen?

When a secretary runs out of typewriter ribbon in the early morning she knows that the typewriter cannot be used until a ribbon is secured from supply at 1:30 P.M. This typewriter cannot be used all morning, so required work on this typewriter is delayed half a day.

In every department, people in this company without needed supplies lose productivity. How do you suppose employees react to such a restriction of hours by a supply department? Every conscientious employee who doesn't want to be delayed in his/her work builds up a secret inventory of job-essential supplies. The secretary in question starts keeping two or three typewriter ribbons and also creates a backup of other essential supply items.

As a result, the inventory of supplies in the company doubles or triples. The investment to carry this additional inventory correspondingly doubles or triples, and these funds are not thereafter available to managers for other uses.

Even worse, employees have been taught a habit that is difficult to break, hoarding supplies. Even if the hours of supply return to a full day, many employees will remember the inconvenience of scarcity and continue to hoard supplies because they need them to do their job. (Note that their motive is not selfishness or malice but to do their work.)

The monopoly problem of internal suppliers is so bad that some companies solve it by forcing support functions to compete for business against outside suppliers. In this approach internal customers are given the choice of spending their money (budget) with internal or external suppliers. This has resulted in many support functions literally going out of business and being replaced by contractors and outside suppliers. Consequently, the support once provided by such internal suppliers as the company cafeteria, print shop, and maintenance gets farmed out. Working through the TQM/MGEEM process usually awakens internal suppliers by dramatically streamlining their operations and maximizing their service to customers.

Much of the basic problem with external suppliers, on the other hand, is said to originate from purchasing departments' insistence on awarding business solely on the basis of price. Anyone familiar in even the slightest way with the procurement function knows the blame for this problem does not lie with what professional purchasing agents are taught or wish to practice. Virtually every textbook on purchasing written in the past 40 years contains strong assertions on the price-quality relationship. For instance, Lewis (p. 141)[24] stated over 40 years ago that "contrary to the opinion of a great many people, no reputable purchasing man takes the position that only price is a matter of first importance. Technical quality and service are of equal importance[1]. . ."

Lewis referred to a survey of the membership of the National Association of Purchasing Agents to the effect that 85 percent of all respondents named quality first as compared with other key purchasing factors such as price, service, the financial responsibility of the vendor, reciprocity, etc. Another example of the sensitivity of purchasing agents to the price-quality issue is by Heinritz and Farrell (p. 143[17]):

> No honest purchasing man will deny a keen interest in the prices of the material he buys, but he will be just as honest in declaring that price is generally the last factor to be considered, for price is meaningless unless it is predicated on adequate quality, assured delivery, reliability and continuity of supply, and satisfying commercial relations.

If statements on the price-quality relationship are so clearly stated in the purchasing textbooks, why is there such a common practice that business be awarded on the basis of price alone? Is it that purchasing agents don't practice what they preach? Is it because, for lack of better measures, higher level managers evaluate purchasing departments on the basis of the frequency with which procurement actions go to the lowest bidders? Is it because governmental and other regulations require buying from the lowest bidders?

Worrying about the cause of this problem is important only if it contributes to finding a solution. Correcting the problem, however, means to take the necessary action through education and changing regulations, policies, and laws to put into practice what textbooks on purchasing have been saying for decades, that price is merely one factor in selecting a supplier. Organizations must go far beyond price considerations to identify their critical suppliers who can learn to appreciate that it is in their own best interest to enter into a close, long-term relationship of harmony and cooperation with their customers. More will be said in Chapter 10 about establishing and maintaining such relationships.

CHAPTER

5

DEVELOPING KEY RESULT
AREAS (KRAs)

The second phase of TQM/MGEEM implementation is the development
of key result areas (KRAs) for a target organization. The concept and use
of key result areas and their subsequent measurement with indicators was
initially proposed at the Human Resources Directorate by Tuttle,[42] and
further developed by Tuttle and Weaver,[43] and Weaver and Looper.[46] In
this phase, a facilitator works with a Blue Team to develop these KRAs.
Many managers find KRA development so educational that they invite
new employees and selected others as observers. These observers will learn

much about the mission of the target organization, but must be cautioned that they are observers and should not get involved in the discussion. Their questions or comments can be considered during breaks.

The facilitator should speak briefly to the Blue Team about the logic of the TQM/MGEEM process: The organization's mission is to serve customers, and KRAs are the measurable components of this mission. The facilitator should stress that following the logic of the process keeps the organization on track in its focus on satisfying its customers' needs. The mission statement should stress continual improvement of the quality of products and service to meet customer needs. The facilitator then begins the process of helping the Blue Team identify the measurable parts of its mission statement — their KRAs — using the NGT.

Posing the Nominal Question

The facilitator should explain to the Blue Team that they are about to use the NGT to reach a consensus on the principal intended accomplishments of the target organization. The facilitator should prepare a transparency of this nominal question: "What results or categories of results is [name of organization] expected to accomplish?" With this transparency displayed on an overhead projector, the facilitator rephrases the nominal question: "What do the stockholders [or top management, U.S. Navy, or other owners] pay [name of target organization] to accomplish?

Before inviting team members to silently generate answers to the KRA nominal question, the facilitator should show a second transparency with information about what makes a good KRA. The transparency should be titled "Characteristics of Good KRAs" and should list the following characteristics:

1. Breaks the mission into measurable parts.
2. Must succeed, make-or-break areas.
3. Outputs, not inputs.
4. Ends, not means.
5. Results, not activities, processes, or tools.

The facilitator should stress that KRAs break the organization's mission statement into its measurable parts. Some team members will be better able to accept this concept if it is explained as an equation in which the mission is the sum of all of the KRAs. The facilitator explains that KRAs can be regarded as separate parts of the mission that can be combined to form the entire mission.

The facilitator should then stress two other points. The first point is that the organization has many important KRAs, but what is wanted here are the most important among these. KRAs are the critical, must succeed, make-or-break areas of the mission. Unless they are accomplished, the organization will not survive.

Second, in terms of input-output analysis, the facilitator should stress that KRAs are outputs. They are the results of value-adding activities. They go out the door to internal and/or external customers to satisfy their expectations. KRAs are *not* inputs or value-adding activities. They are not the resources used in value-adding activities. They are not the day-to-day processes or tools used to create outputs.

Regardless of stressing that KRAs are not processes, some team members invariably will suggest processes as KRAs during the round-robin listing step of the NGT. Fortunately, however, such errors usually are identified and removed by other team members during the discussion and clarification step of the NGT.

After this explanation, the Blue Team should be prepared to hear the KRA nominal question, "What results or categories of results is [name of target organization] expected to accomplish?" and view it on an overhead projector. At this point, it is helpful to distribute a copy of the revised mission statement. The facilitator should then pose the nominal question in these words:

> Now we are ready for the nominal question. "What results or categories of results is [name of target organization] expected to accomplish?" Remember that you are to answer this question as if you are the manager of the target organization. What is this organization paid to accomplish? What goes out the door to customers?

Silent Generation

The facilitator then asks for the silent generation of answers in the following words:

> I would like you to take 10 minutes to write as many answers as you like to this question. While doing so, please don't talk to anyone. Write brief statements or phrases.

After saying this, the facilitator should be quiet and unavailable for questions. After 10 to 15 minutes, or when everyone has stopped writing, the facilitator moves on to the round-robin listing step.

Round-Robin Listing

Just as the NGT was used to identify customers and suppliers (Chapter 4), the round-robin listing serves to record the team's thoughts on chart paper as quickly as possible without discussion.

> Now I want to get your thoughts down on paper. I want to map your thinking. You'll have time later to explain your thoughts, but now let's go around and around the room, each time getting one answer from each person, just as we did before with customers and suppliers.

The facilitator numbers and writes each KRA on the chart paper without discussion as they are suggested by participants. Each KRA is double-checked for accuracy and completeness with its sponsor (the participant who suggested it) before the facilitator moves on to the next team member for another KRA. When everyone says "Pass," the round-robin listing step is complete.

Discussion and Clarification

This part of KRA development is educational for new employees who are occasionally present as observers. To begin discussion and clarification, the facilitator returns to the first KRA and invites its sponsor to explain the thinking that contributed to the decision to recommend it. After the sponsor has had time to fully explain the suggested KRA without interruption, others are invited, in turn, to express their support or argument against *this* KRA. Team members express themselves directly to the facilitator, and not to one another. This is essential to the NGT.

Speaking to the facilitator and not to each other prevents arguments between team members and keeps the facilitator in control of the discussion. The facilitator should explain to team members that there is no reason for them to argue during the discussion and clarification step because they will soon have the opportunity to vote on their choices. At this stage they merely need to express their viewpoint. The facilitator also should tell team members to listen carefully during the discussion and clarification step so that they can decide which KRAs to vote for and against in the upcoming voting step of the NGT.

The facilitator should take great care to obtain everyone's input on each KRA, especially those who don't speak up voluntarily. Looking at a name on a tent card, the facilitator should say, "Mary, I think KRA Number 19 belongs to you. Would you please tell us why you think it is a KRA of this organization?" Participation should be as broad as possible. This builds support for the results.

Remember that the purpose of the discussion and clarification phase is to improve clarity and accuracy, and to reduce overlap and redundancy among the KRAs. The discussion and clarification step usually results in reducing the original list of KRAs by as much as 50 percent.

Reduction of the number of KRAs during discussion and clarification occurs in several ways. It is common, for instance, for participants to realize that a KRA they suggested is really an input or value-adding process. If a sponsor doesn't realize this about his/her suggested KRA, another participant almost always will bring it to the sponsor's attention. For instance, someone might propose in the round-robin listing step that "to keep personnel fully trained" is a KRA. Others may suggest, however, that "personnel" is an input (resource) needed to accomplish the work and that "keeping personnel fully trained" is a value-added process by which organizations produce KRAs. Trained people produce KRAs. Neither the people nor the training are KRAs. As a result of this discussion, the suggested KRA, "to keep personnel fully trained," may be simply struck from the list on the chart paper without fanfare and especially without embarrassing its sponsor.

The facilitator politely asks the sponsor, "Bill, if this is an input (or process), as Mary Jo suggests, is it OK with you if we strike it from the list?" A line is then drawn through the item and an encircled capital P is placed beside it to show it was struck from the list because it is a process. If Bill disagrees with Mary Jo's suggestion, the KRA remains on the list. He owns it, and only he can agree to strike it.

Another reason KRA lists become smaller during the discussion and clarification step of the NGT is that KRAs often get combined when their sponsors hear the reasoning behind other similar KRAs. For example, Malcolm may say, "You know, KRA Number 19 is so much like my KRA that I am willing to allow mine to be struck if the word 'timely' is added before the third word from the end in KRA Number 19."

The facilitator's response is to ask the participant who "owns" KRA Number 19 to identify himself or herself. When the sponsor acknowledges ownership, the facilitator asks, "Is it OK with you, Larry, if we add the word 'timely' to your KRA?" If Larry's answer is "Yes," the word is added, and Malcolm's KRA is struck with an encircled 19 to show where it went.

Before the two KRAs are combined, the facilitator should ask whether anyone else on the team has advice to the two owners. Someone may have liked Malcolm's KRA and won't support it in the upcoming vote if it's combined with Larry's KRA. Malcolm and Larry must hear such objections in deciding whether to combine the two KRAs. If Larry's answer is "No," both KRAs stay on the chart paper, and clarification and discussion continues. In fact, several similar KRAs can, with the agreement of their sponsors and usually some modification of wording, get grouped into a common KRA. One of the similar KRAs survives with modifications, and the others are struck. If the original list is not substantially reduced during discussion and clarification, the facilitator should not despair. The next step in the NGT process, voting, will reduce it. A recorder should document the original list of KRAs, as well as those combined, expanded, and eliminated.

The facilitator should be sensitive to several concerns during KRA identification and discussion. Many KRAs are dropped in the discussion and clarification step because they are reassembled into clusters. The facilitator should be concerned, however, that too much reassembly is undesirable because, if carried to an extreme, it results in the re-creation of the mission statement itself.

Remember that KRAs are the measurable components of the mission statement. It stands to reason, therefore, that their sum *is* the mission statement. In fact, it was explained in Chapter 4 that a mission statement can be created by using this process to identify KRAs. The resulting KRAs can be written up in one or two paragraphs as a mission statement. In any case, some reassembly of KRAs is desirable, but reassembly should not be encouraged to go too far. The key is to focus on developing a set of KRAs which arranges the measurable parts of the mission into discrete, nonoverlapping units.

Although the facilitator should be concerned about too much or too little reassembly of KRAs, the result will be successful, though possibly awkward, regardless of how it turns out. This is a testament to the rigor of the TQM/MGEEM process. As an example, suppose a mission statement has 10 KRAs and two indicators (measures of how well each KRA is being accomplished) for each KRA. (Indicators are discussed in detail in Chapter 6.) If no reassembly takes place, the TQM/MGEEM will have 10 KRAs and 20 indicators, two indicators per KRA. This is a successful TQM/MGEEM system. If the original 10 KRAs are reassembled into five KRAs, the TQM/MGEEM will have five KRAs and 20 indicators, four indicators per KRA. This, too, is a successful TQM/MGEEM system. If all 10 KRAs are reassembled into one KRA, there will be one KRA (the mission statement itself) and 20 indicators. This, too, is a successful system.

Regardless of the extent of reassembly of KRAs, the TQM/MGEEM system in question could have the same number of indicators. Only one KRA or too many KRAs, however, tends to be awkward. In other words, both extremes are undesirable. Probably five to seven KRAs is optimum, but the more important issue is whether the resulting TQM/MGEEM system covers the most important dimensions of the organization's mission statement.

There is a second concern for the facilitator to consider during discussion and clarification. What will team members do when they realize that the upcoming vote to select critical KRAs may eliminate a KRA which they sponsored? A team member may attempt to save a weak KRA by making it a *rider*, that is, vigorously seeking to merge it with another, stronger KRA. Such merging is healthy as long as the two KRAs are similar, i.e., as long as both involve the same output.

If the two KRAs are not similar, their merger will be harmful to the TQM/MGEEM process. The facilitator's role here is to point out to team members that what is desired is a set of discrete KRAs. It should be stressed to them that KRAs can be merged, but only if they are similar. The facilitator should urge team members not to suggest mergers unless the KRAs involved are similar.

Sponsors of stronger KRAs should be urged to reject merger with weaker KRAs (riders) if they are not similar. In addition, when sponsors of two or more KRAs have agreed to merge them, other team members should be encouraged to voice objections if they see any incompatibility among the KRAs involved. Remember, the objective of discussion and clarification is to create discrete, nonoverlapping KRAs which cover the mission statement. This should be fully explained to team members so they understand the need to resist efforts to piggyback incompatible KRAs.

After discussion and clarification, the facilitator leads the Blue Team through a voting process to further reduce the number of KRAs. A large number of KRAs is not desirable because the organization should concentrate on only the most important aspects of its mission. As Tom Peters observes, it is critical that managers measure what's important and keep the system simple (Chapter S-1).[30] Furthermore, using KRAs that are not of vital importance raises their visibility and tends to attract resources to areas that are not mission-critical. The measurement system should be small enough for easy operation and should not create additional, unnecessary paperwork. KRAs beyond five to seven should be added only if their value justifies the cost of collecting and managing the extra data.

Voting

There are two methods by which voting can take place, and the facilitator must choose between them before the voting process to be used is explained to the Blue Team. Let's consider both voting methods. The first voting method is by a show of hands. A show of hands for and against each

KRA usually reveals that everyone agrees on the importance and unimportance of most KRAs. The KRAs that receive the vote of all or a majority of team members are declared "selected" as part of the TQM/MGEEM system. Those that do not receive any votes or only a very few votes are declared "not selected." KRAs that are in doubt because they receive only a few votes, the so-called "marginal KRAs," should be considered further on a case-by-case basis.

To accomplish this, a team member who voted for a marginal KRA is invited to explain why he/she did so. Similarly, a team member who voted against the same KRA is invited to explain why it was not supported. The facilitator should not allow argument, merely individual expressions of support or lack of support. Other team members are then invited to speak for or against the marginal KRA under consideration. When everyone has expressed an opinion, a second vote on the KRAs in doubt is conducted by another show of hands. The learning that occurs during the additional discussion usually brings about sufficient agreement on the marginal KRAs. If not, there is further discussion of remaining marginal KRAs, and a third show of hands is required.

It is hoped that team members will not be afraid to speak and vote their minds, but if fear exists it may be necessary to use secret voting rather than a show of hands.

There is an even more important reason to use secret voting. A particular kind of secret voting provides a considerable amount of information to participants about how the team as a whole evaluates and prioritizes the KRAs. Unfortunately, this voting process requires more time than a show of hands, but the secrecy and additional information usually is worthwhile. (Incidentally, if even more secrecy is needed in the NGT process, the earlier step of round-robin listing can be done by team members anonymously writing suggested KRAs on 3x5-inch cards. The facilitator would write each of them without attribution on chart paper. Team members are then arbitrarily called on to discuss the KRAs so that no one knows who sponsored the KRAs. This is recommended only in cases of fear in the target organization because it demands much more time. Unfortunately, many U.S. managers mistakenly believe "a little employee fear is a good thing," so occasionally this approach is required. The facilitator leads the team through this secret voting process with the following words:

Now that you have discussed and clarified KRAs, it is time to prioritize them. Take five 3x5-inch index cards from the stack of such cards available at your table. Look at the KRAs that have not been crossed out on the chart paper on the walls. Think about the original question, "What results or categories of results is this organization expected to accomplish?" and, remember that you are playing "manager for a day." Which of these KRAs would you, as manager, think are the most important? Identify the five KRAs that are the most important. Write the *name* of each of the KRAs in the center of a different 3x5 card, and write the *number* of each KRA in the upper left-hand corner of its card. [Remember that the KRAs are numbered consecutively as they were written on chart paper in the round-robin listing step. These are the KRA numbers. The facilitator may wish to draw a red circle around the numbers of the KRAs that are eligible for voting.] When you are finished, you should have five cards with the names of each of the five KRAs which you think are the most important written in the center of the cards, one KRA per card, and the number of each KRA from the chart paper in the upper left-hand corner.

At this point, the facilitator draws a large rectangle on the chalkboard or on chart paper to represent a 3x5 card and says:

If you select KRA Number 4, "Provide technical services to wholesalers," as one of your five most important KRAs, you would write "Provide technical services to wholesalers" in the center of the card and a "4" in the upper left-hand corner.

Here, the facilitator should write "Provide technical services to wholesalers" in the middle of a large rectangle drawn on a chalkboard and write a "4" in the upper left-hand corner.

After you have completed writing five KRA names and numbers on cards, place each of the five cards face up on the table in front of you. Has everyone done that?

The facilitator pauses to check that every team member has placed each of the cards face up on the table. A bit more time usually is needed to ensure that everyone has finished selecting and writing up the five cards.

Now let's do the next step together to prioritize your selection. Let's do this together. Make sure you can see all five cards. Look at the five cards on the table in front of you and select the one KRA which you, as manager for a day, consider *most* important. If you could have only one KRA, which would it be? Write a "5" in the lower right-hand corner of this card and turn the card over on the table. OK. Has everyone done that? Now look at the remaining four cards. Choose the KRA that you, as manager, think is *least* important. If you had to do without one KRA, which would it be? "Write a "1" in the lower right-hand corner of that card, and turn it over. OK. Has everyone completed that? Let's stay together now. OK. Look at the remaining three cards, and select the *most* important KRA from among these three. Write a "4" in the lower right-hand corner, and turn the card over. OK. Is everyone finished? Now look at the two remaining cards. Select the *least* important KRA, write a "2" in the lower right-hand corner, and turn the card over. Now write a "3" in the lower right-hand corner of the remaining card, and turn it over. I have to tally the vote now, so give your cards to the recorder at the back of the room. We'll take a 15-minute break.

The facilitators could have asked for any number of cards (KRAs) to be selected. Instead of five, any number (3, 4, 6, 7, 8, 9, or 10) would have worked equally as well. Regardless of the number of KRAs to be selected, the assignment of weights for importance works the same way. Start with the most important. Take least important next, etc.

To tally the vote, the facilitator and assistant divide the 3x5-inch cards into stacks according to the numbers in the upper left-hand corners. This groups the cards by KRA. All the cards for "Provide technical services to wholesalers" go in one stack; all the cards for some other KRA go in another stack, etc.

Three types of analysis are then performed on the stacks. First, the cards in the stacks are counted. This gives the *number* of team members who select a given KRA as among the five most important. Second, the cards in the stacks are arranged in numerical order from lowest to highest by the numbers in the lower right-hand corner. The number in the lower right-hand corner is the *weight* each KRA received in the voting. Third, the weights in each stack are summed. This sum of weights gives the *importance* of each KRA. The results of all three analyses should be summarized and illustrated on chart paper.

An example of the result of this voting process appears in Figure 5.1. Every KRA that received a vote is listed in numerical order in column one under "KRA Number" by the numbers in the upper left-hand corners of the cards. In other words, each row in this table represents a KRA that received a vote, even if a stack for a given KRA has only one card in it. For KRAs that didn't receive any votes, there is no stack, and they are not shown on this table.

In the second column, "Voting Pattern," are the individual weights each KRA received, as written in the lower right-hand corner of the cards and arranged in numerical order from low to high in the analysis' second step. Each of the weights is recorded in this column from low to high.

The third column, "Voting Summary," is a fraction representing two sums which are the results of the first and third analyses: The numerator is the total number of team members who voted for a given KRA (the first step in the analysis), and the denominator is the sum of the weights each KRA received (the third step in the analysis). For example, consider the voting results in Figure 5.1. Column 1, "KRA Number," lists eight KRAs: numbers 4, 9, 10, 11, 13, 21, 22, and 24. If the team originally identified 34 KRAs in the round-robin step, what happened to the other 26 KRAs not in Column 1? The answer is that they either were combined with other KRAs or did not receive any votes in the voting step. These other 26 KRAs, therefore, are no longer considered.

The second column, "Voting Pattern," shows that KRA No. 4 received

(Voting instructions to eight group members: "Vote for the 5 KRAs you think the manager feels are the most important.")

KRA Number	Voting Pattern	Voting Summary
4	2, 4, 4, 4, 5, 5, 5, 5	8/34[a]
9	1, 1, 1, 2, 2, 3	6/10
10	2, 2, 3, 4	4/11
11	1, 1, 1, 1, 2, 3, 3, 4	8/16
13	3, 4, 5, 5	4/17
21	2, 3	2/5
22	1	1/1
24	1, 3, 3, 4, 4, 5, 5	7/25

[a] Indicates that all eight participants voted for KRA #4 and the sum of the votes assigned is 34 (2, 4, 4, 4, 5, 5, 5, 5).

FIGURE 5.1   Example of Voting Results

the votes of all eight members of the Blue Team which are 2, 4, 4, 4, 5, 5, 5, and 5. These are the weights recorded by team members in the lower right-hand corners of their 3x5 cards.

The fraction 8/34 in column three, "Voting Summary," shows, by the numerator, that all eight team members voted for KRA No. 4 and, by the denominator, the sum of the weights assigned is 34 $(2 + 4 + 4 + 4 + 5 + 5 + 5 + 5)$.

Team members return to the room after their break, and the facilitator explains how to interpret Figure 5.1, the results of their voting to prioritize the KRAs. The facilitator explains the meaning of the fraction in "Vote Summary" column and says that the maximum fraction any KRA could get is 8/40. This would mean that if all eight team members voted for a KRA, its numerator would be 8. It would also mean that each voter gave the KRA the highest weight possible (5). Therefore, the denominator would be 40 (8 votes × the highest weight of 5).

The facilitator continues the explanation by pointing out that KRA No. 4 received the strongest support (8/34), KRA Nos. 9, 10, 11, 13, and 24 received moderately strong support (6/10, 4/11, 8/16, 4/17, and 7/25), and KRA Nos. 21 and 22 received weak support (2/5, 1/1). The facilitator then observes that only two team members voted for KRA No. 21, and neither gave it a high priority, as shown by the weights of 2 and 3, shown in

Column 2. KRA No. 22 received only one vote, and the team member participant who voted for it gave it the lowest priority possible, 1, again shown in Column 2.

Now the facilitator is ready to lead the team to further reduce the remaining KRAs to a manageable number. The facilitator may wish to approach this further reduction by seeking consensus on two extremes, first on KRAs that received so few votes that the team agrees they can be dropped and, second, on KRAs that received so many votes they can be declared accepted. This will leave only the in-between, marginal KRAs for discussion.

Before dealing with the marginal KRAs, it is not uncommon for a participant to ask the team to reconsider a KRA that was not crossed out on the chart paper during discussion and clarification, but which received no or only a few votes.

A participant making such a suggestion senses that the KRA in question is about to be dropped and proposes to make it a rider on a strong KRA. One may wonder why the sponsor of the weak KRA didn't try to make it a rider in the discussion and clarification step. The answer is the KRA in question is important to the sponsor, and it was hoped that it would garner enough votes to stand on its own. Realizing that the KRA didn't gather enough votes, the sponsor now wants to save it. Is it too late? No, not if the merger will improve the list of the KRAs.

In TQM/MGEEM, we are not driven by rules, but by the continuing desire for improvement. In TQM/MGEEM, continual improvement is a way of life. To bring about a merger after any vote, the discussion and clarification step of the NGT is used. The sponsor of the strong KRA, with which merger of a weak KRA is suggested, listens to the advice of any team member who has anything to say about the merger and then decides whether to accept the rider. The sponsor of the strong KRA now has an additional piece of information about the proposed rider than was available in the original discussion and clarification step, namely how many votes the proposed rider received. Getting none or only a few votes doesn't usually persuade a sponsor of a strong KRA to accept a proposed rider. The important issue is whether the weak KRA really is similar to the strong KRA. If not, the weak KRA should be dropped.

After the issue of merging weak KRAs is resolved, the facilitator should begin working to further reduce the list. The facilitator should say, "Is there any problem with dropping KRA Numbers 21 and 22?" Here team members who sponsored or voted for these two weak KRAs will see that the team, as a whole, does not support them. Ordinarily, they will not object to dropping the two weak KRAs. In almost every instance, dropping

KRAs in this manner will be accepted because team members appreciate that the TQM/MGEEM is a group process.

After the few KRAs that received weak support, in this case KRA Nos. 21 and 22, are dropped, the facilitator deals with the strongly supported KRAs by asking if there is any problem with accepting them as part of the target organization's TQM/MGEEM system. The KRA with the most votes or greatest weight is considered first. It almost will certainly be accepted. Then, the second strongest KRA is considered, etc. Although it is unlikely to happen, if there is any question about accepting strong KRAs, or if a dispute cannot be resolved through discussion, the unresolved KRAs are added to the KRAs that received marginal support. To deal with the marginal KRAs, the facilitator sets the stage by explaining to the team that they have rejected the weak KRAs and accepted the strong KRAs. It is now time to decide what to do with the KRAs that received marginal support.

The numbers identifying the marginal KRAs on the chart paper on the walls should be clearly identified (e.g., with a green asterisk) so that team members know which KRAs are currently under consideration. With a brief comment on the benefits of having a small TQM/MGEEM system based on five to seven KRAs, the facilitator calls the team's attention to each of the marginal KRAs in turn. For each KRA, the facilitator asks for a volunteer who voted for it to explain why he/she did so. The facilitator can point to the numerator in the fraction in Figure 5.1 to determine how many participants voted for the KRA under consideration. Those who voted for this KRA are encouraged to explain why they did so.

Next, the facilitator asks for someone who did not vote for the KRA under consideration to explain why he/she did not. Again, any others who did or did not vote for this KRA may explain their decision. After each of the marginal KRAs is discussed in this manner, the facilitator asks the team to vote on all of the marginal KRAs as a group using a smaller number of 3x5-inch index cards than was used in the first vote.

The number of cards to be used depends on how many marginal KRAs are under consideration and how many KRAs have already been accepted. If 10 to 15 KRAs are under consideration and the number thus far accepted is small, say one or two, the facilitator will allow five 3x5-inch index cards, because many more KRAs are needed to produce a system of five to seven KRAs. On the other hand, if four, five or six KRAs have been accepted, the facilitator will allow only a small number of 3x5-inch index cards, because not many more KRAs are needed to produce a system of five to seven.

The voting and the analysis of the results are conducted as described earlier in the discussion of the first vote. A team member may suggest that this vote be taken by show of hands. If there is any possibility for consensus by this less time-consuming method of hand vote, the facilitator should agree. Analysis of this vote should lead the team to agreement about which of the marginal KRAs to accept.

Occasionally team members want a system based on more than the suggested five to seven KRAs. When the team is discussing the results of their voting, they may want eight, nine, or more KRAs. In such cases the facilitator should remember that it is their system. If team members want 10 KRAs, they should have 10 KRAs.

In this situation, the facilitator should make two comments to the team. First, the team should be reminded that the larger the number of KRAs, the greater the effort involved in developing and maintaining the system. Second, it should be explained that the TQM/MGEEM system is not set in concrete. Like everything associated with the philosophy of continual improvement, the TQM/MGEEM system itself should change and improve as target organization personnel see ways to make it better.

Thus, if the Blue Team builds a system that turns out to be too large, with too many KRAs, it can later be reduced. Or, if some of the KRAs selected by the Blue Team are later determined to be insufficiently important to include in the system, they can be dropped.

Similarly, some KRAs that the Blue Team considered unimportant may later be discovered to be important. If so, they can be added. (Therefore, it is vital that the recorder keep an accurate record of everything written on chart paper. Later, members of the target organization may wish to remember a certain KRA that was suggested in their KRA development session. They may realize that a KRA initially discarded is important to their system's success.

After the Blue Team comes to consensus on the KRAs, their work in building the TQM/MGEEM system is finished and, with the exception of the manager's subordinates, they are thanked for their participation and excused. The manager's subordinates are retained because they are also members of the Gold Team. They provide a necessary linkage between the Blue and Gold Teams.

Universal Value of Key Result Areas

The value of KRAs extends far beyond their use in work organizations. In fact, every form of human endeavor can benefit enormously from developing and using KRAs. When I give a presentation on TQM/MGEEM, I often challenge my audience to take two minutes to silently generate their own personal KRAs. I pose the nominal question as, "What are the main things you are trying to accomplish with your life?"

After the two minutes of silence ends, I give examples of personal KRAs, e.g., "To be a good spouse," "To be a good parent," "To care for one's health," "To care for an aged parent," and "To continually improve." I then tell the group that when I give this exercise as part of my speech, members of the audience often approach me afterward to say that they were moved by the question about personal KRAs. They say they couldn't think of any KRAs for themselves. They comment that, in response to events, their lives seem not to have any KRAs; that their lives appear to go first in one direction and then another. They remark that they plan to sit down in some quiet place and try to figure out what their lives are all about.

I tell audiences that this is what target organization members do when posed with the KRA nominal question. They try to determine what is really important to them as an organization. Hopefully, this exercise gives the audience a better feel for the importance of KRAs. Perhaps they come to better appreciate how necessary it is for the members of any organization to collectively decide what is important. Without this, how can anyone have constancy of purpose, as called for by Dr. Deming?[7] It is their KRAs that pull them together for constancy of purpose.

I also offer my audiences another, even more compelling, challenge about KRAs. I know that the majority of them believe that people in most organizations understand what those organizations are trying to accomplish. They believe that most organization members are in agreement about their group's KRAs. This seems reasonable to them because one would think that membership in an organization, especially over a period of time, would bring knowledge of that organization's KRAs. To these people I offer a challenge. I challenge them to call a meeting of an organization which is near and dear to them (i.e., their own family) to discover whether members of this congregation are in agreement on their KRAs. The next requirement is that all family members must remain together for about two hours. (For some families, that is a serious enough challenge.) The family should sit together somewhere, e.g., around the kitchen table.

Imagine the scene. Standing at the head of the table is the person from my audience. Sitting around the table is the person's spouse, their teenage daughter, their eight-year-old son, Aunt Molly, and one of the spouse's parents who lives with them. I suggest that members of the audience tell their family that they heard something in a speech which should be of interest to them.

I ask them to pose to their families this nominal question, "What are the main things our family is trying to accomplish? They should write this question in large letters on a sheet of paper and tape it to something, say the refrigerator, for all family members to see.

It should be stressed to family members that they should look at the question from the standpoint of the head of the family, not just from their own personal perspective as an individual family member. Each member must answer the question as if he/she is the head of the family. Each family member should have several sheets of paper and a pencil and be given 10 minutes of silent generation. In silent generation, everyone is asked to write down as many answers to the question as they wish. During these 10 minutes there should be no discussion. Participants should be encouraged to think and write. The family member "facilitator" who posed the nominal question should also write answers during this time period.

After the time is up, the family goes through the round-robin listing step of NGT. One KRA is voiced by each family member, in turn, and written in large letters on paper and taped to the refrigerator or wall. This continues until all KRAs from everyone are on that paper. There is no discussion at this point, merely listing of KRAs. The paper used can be simple 8½x11-inch notebook paper. The sheets should be positioned on the wall so that everyone can see the answers from their seats.

Next, the facilitator goes around the room inviting each family member to, in turn, explain what he/she had in mind in each of their KRAs. Take only one KRA from each person. Discuss that KRA fully, then, go to a KRA from the next person. Again, discuss that KRA fully. No one should be allowed to explain all of his/her KRAs at one time. This is the discussion and clarification step of the NGT.

Unless a family is unusual, it will be clear that family members are not in agreement about the family's KRAs. In this session, much will be learned by everyone about their family. What a teenage daughter in high school thinks is important often is different from what a parent, grandparent, or aunt thinks is important.

Of course, prior to this exercise everyone imagined that the family was pulling together for the same KRAs. This exercise shows that, even with the best of intentions, members usually have been pulling in different, even contradictory, directions. Such a result suggests the need for family members to reach a consensus on what is important to them. If desired, such a consensus can be reached with the remaining steps in the NGT, as explained in this chapter.

This exercise usually is an eye opener to family members. It becomes clear that a KRA to get one's teenage daughter into college, or to pay off medical bills is more important than buying a new set of golf clubs or taking an extra vacation next summer.

Benefits of consensus are enormous. A family with consensus has direction. Such a family knows what is important and what is not important. Obviously, a family's chances for success are much greater when all the members are pulling in the same direction. Feelings of goodwill and harmony increase as family members work together toward common goals. For instance, the daughter realizes how important she is, and that everyone is making sacrifices, doing without things to save money for her college education. This should have beneficial effects on the daughter's study habits. The parents should feel more appreciated for making these sacrifices.

The value of identifying and discussing KRAs obviously extends beyond these examples involving oneself and one's family. KRAs are beneficial to all organizations, including Cub Scout troops, church groups, hospital clinics, baseball teams, school and training classes, aircraft carriers, departments, and companies. You name it, KRAs are important in every form of human endeavor.

DEVELOPING INDICATORS

After KRAs have been developed, the next step in the TQM/MGEEM process is to develop indicators. Indicators show how well KRAs are being accomplished.

To some people, the need for indicators is not obvious, so, several examples usually are needed to convince them. It is my viewpoint that if people in an organization have determined what they are trying to accomplish, i.e., they have KRAs, but do not have indicators, they are simply dreaming. At the very least they are reactive, instead of proactive.

The need for indicators not only applies to organizations, it also applies to individuals. To understand how important it is to have indicators to accompany KRAs, consider this example. Suppose you want to lose some weight. That would be your KRA. Suppose further that you don't have any indicators. You are not measuring anything. You don't get on the scales every week. If you don't measure, how do you know how well you're doing? You don't know. You are just dreaming about losing weight. You are not really managing your weight reduction effort. In such a situation you have no way of knowing how well you're doing.

Consider another example. Suppose your family has a KRA to get your daughter into college, but you're not measuring anything. You don't monitor her grades in high school or the money in your savings account. If not, what are you doing to prepare? You're just dreaming about getting her into college. You are not aggressively managing to achieve this KRA.

Similarly, if an organization wants to get its products to its customers on time but doesn't monitor timeliness, it, too, is dreaming. Without measurement an organization can never know how bad or good it is with on-time deliveries. Such an organization is simply dreaming about being on time.

Everyone should realize that the days of dreaming about becoming more effective and improving quality are gone. A new period of competition has arrived. Today, success requires that organizations become proactive about improvement. Improvement is too important to be left to dreamers.

Among the most attractive features of TQM/MGEEM is that it makes possible the measurement of outputs, or KRAs, of organizations, even where such measurement was previously difficult if not impossible. For each KRA developed by a Blue Team, at least one indicator is developed by a Gold Team. Indicators are the measurement tools used to know how well KRAs are being accomplished. Organizations that make products, like cars or sandwiches, usually have a fairly easy time with measurement. Consider organizations, however, whose output is less clear, e.g., corporate headquarters or staff, support functions (comptroller, maintenance, personnel, security, safety, information systems, finance, and production control), research and development, testing and evaluation, and the countless companies in the service and knowledge worker industries. To them, measurement beyond the only partially satisfactory tools of accounting and manpower is difficult and often given up as impossible. With TQM/MGEEM, however, the measurement of the output of any organization is possible. In the TQM/MGEEM approach, output may be conceptualized in any number of ways, including efficiency, effectiveness, performance, quality, improvement, or whatever. It doesn't matter. Regardless of its definition, output can be measured with TQM/MGEEM.

An important philosophical point about TQM/MGEEM should be

stressed. Although TQM/MGEEM is a powerful tool for measurement, it must be remembered that the level of measurement required need only be good enough to provide a foundation for improvement. The main goal of TQM/MGEEM is improvement, not precision of measurement. Managers must be concerned about improvement, not about the precision of measurement. For improvement to be correctly initiated, monitored, and directed, measurement of some sort is necessary. Measurement's most important objective, therefore, is to provide a foundation for improvement. Thus, managers should not micro-manage the measurement side of TQM/MGEEM. They should not be worried about whether a given value is 14.1 or 14.2, but should ensure that measurement is sufficient to provide a basis for improvement. Any level of measurement can be satisfactory. For instance, sufficient measurement can be expressed in terms such as excellent, good, fair, and poor, or A, B, C, D, and F.

Measurement need not be precise enough to satisfy a rocket scientist. In fact, satisfactory measurement for the basis of improvement often is based on perceptions and judgment. When a manager complains to me that a given measure in a TQM/MGEEM system is based on judgment rather than on more objective considerations, I have an answer that cannot be denied. "What are we trying to do here, measure or improve?" Our purpose is improvement! If measurements from which improvement grows are based on judgment, what difference does it make? Good judgment is among the most important requisites for a manager's success. Why not use judgment here? The bottom line is that measurement is important, but don't become obsessed with it. Remember that what really counts is improvement.

Preparation to Develop Indicators

It is important that the CEO or other representative of senior management be present at the start of the meeting of the Gold Team, composed of the manager's subordinates and key workers. This person's presence demonstrates support for what the Gold Team is about to do. Remembering that members of his team heard the CEO and facilitator speak at the earlier briefing to all employees, the CEO will want to keep his/her remarks to a minimum, perhaps 10 minutes. Beyond comments of support, there is need to stress the key role of employees in improvement and the importance of measurement so the target organization will realize how good they are. The facilitator is then reintroduced in a supportive manner.

In every TQM/MGEEM implementation, facilitators hear expressions of pessimism about whether it is possible to measure the work accomplished in the target organization. These forebodings are usually expressed in terms such as:

I know it's posssible to develop indicators for manufacturing organizations, but the work we do here is so unique that it simply can't be measured. Our results are indirect and intangible. Our outputs don't occur reguarly; it may take us months or even years to produce an output.

There is no need to worry about this. The TQM/MGEEM has never failed to measure the output of any of the hundreds of organizations where it was attempted. In fact, the problem usually is not one of whether it is possible to measure, but that, over the years, there has been too much measurement in the interest of control and compliance.

As managers come and go, each adds a bit more to what can become such a large number of measures that they choke an organization. The widespread misuse of computers has made this problem even worse. So, the problem isn't an inability to develop measures; it's usually too many measures. In such cases, it eventually will be shown how TQM/MGEEM helps by prioritizing the existing measures so that those that really count are the only ones used.

Measures not selected for use in the TQM/MGEEM system, unless needed to satisfy mandated requirements, such as tax reports, should be considered for elimination. (Some companies using TQM/MGEEM establish a cross-functional committee to identify and recommend the elimination of unnecessary measurement data.)

In the face of the comment "You can't measure what we do here," facilitators should take comfort in the fact that all target organizations have customers, some internal, some external. Therefore, at least one measure of any organization's output is always available — customer satisfaction. Hopefully, members of the Gold Team will realize that customer satisfaction is the best indicator, and that it can be measured satisfactorily.

One way to measure customer satisfaction is with one question answered monthly by customers through a questionnaire. This question can be worded as follows: "On the whole, how satisfied are you with the products and service you receive from [name of target organization]?" The answer should be recorded on a scale ranging from 4 for "very satisfied," 3 for "somewhat satisfied," 2 for "a little dissatisfied," and 1 for "very dissatisfied." If the customer is an internal organization, the questionnaire can be completed by that organization's manager after conferring as needed with subordinates.

Members of Gold Teams often believe that one question about customer satisfaction is not adequate. They may want to use a questionnaire that gets into the various components, or facets, which make up customer satisfaction. These facets may be defined as a team sees fit, but usually include dimensions of quality and timeliness. Examples of such questionnaires appear in most marketing research books available in any public library. Of course, such questionnaires should be periodically reviewed as customers and their needs change, and customers should not be asked to complete questionnaires until all target organizations in a company have developed their TQM/MGEEM systems. The reason is that several target organizations within the company may serve the same customers. One target organization may provide customers with products while others provide service and technical support. It would be an unnecessary imposition on customers to ask them to complete questionnaires from several or many target organizations. To avoid this, the questionnaires of each target organization should be coordinated, perhaps through a cross-functional committee, so that customers are asked to complete only one questionnaire each month. This one questionnaire should address the concerns of all involved target organizations.

Instead of using a questionnaire, some organizations prefer that target organization managers secure the required feedback by contacting customers by telephone or in person at customers' work sites. This approach has the advantage of demonstrating to customers and to target organization personnel that the management of the target organization is sincerely interested in understanding and satisfying customer needs. If this feedback takes place at customer work sites, personnel from the target organization should routinely be invited to accompany the manager or, as a small team, take the manager's place. While at the customer work sites, the manager or team should become familiar with customer operations to better appreciate how the target organization's products or services are used. Better products and service to customers will almost certainly result through improvement and even innovation as target organization personnel better appreciate customer needs and expectations. The most effective way to get feedback from customers when a TQM/MGEEM system is in place, however, is to invite customers to participate in the feedback meetings in a target organization. This use of feedback meetings is explained in Chapter 10.

Another measure available in almost every organization is timeliness. It is a rare organization that does not monitor whether its work is accomplished or delivered on time. Such time quotas are commonly called *deadlines* or *suspense dates*. Systems that establish and control these quotas usually are operated by someone in management or on the staff who determines how much time it should take to complete given work. Unfortunately, those assigned to perform the work often are told that results are expected by a given time — the deadline or suspense date.

If the Gold Team decides to incorporate a timeliness measure into their TQM/MGEEM system, they may wish to modify the measure so it becomes a negotiated deadline or negotiated suspense date. This means that those assigned to do the work are periodically invited to discuss with the manager or staff the proper amount of time to be allocated to the work about to be assigned. In these meetings, employees come to appreciate how work must be prioritized to meet various requirements.

Negotiation of the time to complete given work is recommended because it gives employees a greater sense of control over their work and encourages their sense of craftsmanship. On the other hand, managers and supervisors should not regard negotiation over deadlines and suspense dates as a limitation on their prerogatives to manage because they, of course, retain the final decision about when the work is to be completed. They should view the negotiation as an opportunity to develop better relations with their subordinates. Better two-way communication will result, and managers and supervisors can seek to revise their roles from disciplinarian, timekeeper, and judge to teacher, coach, and colleague. More will be said later about how managers should modify their roles.

Other measures which the Gold Team may wish to recommend as indicators can come from whatever the target organization is currently using or has used to assess its performance. This may be any of a number of accounting, engineering, or manpower measures. In other words, the facilitator should make the Gold Team aware that the TQM/MGEEM can accept as indicators measures currently used, once used, or entirely new ideas which they originate.

Introducing Indicators

The facilitator should begin the session to develop indicators with a brief overview to remind the Gold Team of what the TQM/MGEEM process is all about. Here the facilitator should refer to Juran's excellent concept of the customer as those internal and external persons, organizations, or processes receiving or affected by the output of the target organization.[22] The importance of the customer should be discussed. A copy of the revised mission statement should be given to each member of the Gold Team as the facilitator points out that the mission statement stresses satisfying the customer's requirements. The facilitator should then show a transparency on an overhead projector of the KRAs developed by the Blue Team. The term KRA should be defined and the role of KRAs as the measurable components of the target organization's mission should be explained.

It is important to remember that some members of the Gold Team, the manager's subordinates, were members of the Blue Team where the KRAs were developed. The facilitator may wish to call on them to assist in clarifying the meaning of the KRAs which they helped develop. Other members of the Gold Team should be encouraged to ask questions to ensure their complete understanding of the KRAs.

Next, the facilitator should make up a transparency with the characteristics of good indicators to display on an overhead projector. These characteristics are:

1. Important.
2. Easily understood.
3. Controlled by the function's actions.
4. Evaluate change.
5. Use existing data.
6. Measure both efficiency and effectiveness.

The facilitator should acknowledge that there is a variety of ways to evaluate how well any organization is doing on its KRAs, but the indicators selected should be the most important one(s). Furthermore, it should be noted that indicators must be easy to understand, not complex equations. The logic and relevance of indicators should be apparent.

Perhaps the most important characteristic of indicators is that they be under the target organization's control. This means that when an indicator goes up or down it should be a reflection of the performance of the target organization, not of a supplier or support organization. It is a serious mistake to select indicators of performance over which target organization members have only partial or no control. For instance, a repair shop should not have indicators that reflect the delivery performance of a warehouse which provides spare parts. If so, when the warehouse is late with a delivery, the indicators of the repair shop go down.

Another characteristic of good indicators is that they must be sensitive to change through time. When an organization's performance improves, the indicator should go up and vice versa. It also is important that indicators be based as much as possible on data that already exist. There is no need to add unnecessarily to an organization's paperwork burden.

Despite this admonition, it often is necessary and proper for a Gold Team to suggest an indicator for which no data currently exist. In such cases, the facilitator accepts the indicator, and the manager of the target organization will have to decide later whether the indicator is important enough to justify the cost of collecting the data. Usually it is the case that such indicators are worth the effort involved in their collection because the Gold Team members are knowledgeable of the work and know what they are doing when they suggest indicators. Finally, the facilitator should suggest to the Gold Team that two kinds of indicators should be included in their TQM/MGEEM system: efficiency and effectiveness.

Referring to the transparency prepared earlier, the facilitator should define efficiency as the relationship between outputs and inputs, or how well the organization uses its inputs (resources) to produce its outputs (goods and services). Efficiency usually is represented as an equation in which outputs (goods and services that go out the door to customers) are divided by inputs (resources such as manpower, capital, or material in dollars). It is easy to develop at least one good efficiency measure by asking team members to define the target organization's principal output. "What goes out the door to customers?" Wagon wheels, vouchers reviewed, engines repaired, teeth filled, orders processed, hamburgers sold, or whatever. This output is simply counted for a measurement period, say a month, and divided by some easily measured input (a resource) used to produce the output, such as manhours expended, for the same time period.

Effectiveness, on the other hand, is the extent to which an organization accomplishes its mission. It has been quipped that "Efficiency is doing things right and effectiveness is doing the right things." In any case, there is a variety of effectiveness measures, but probably the most useful are customer satisfaction, quality (measured by return rate, errors, complaints, and accuracy), and timeliness (such as average response or delivery time). Was it provided to the customer on time? Did it work as expected? Did the customer like it?

The facilitator might wish to show team members examples of actual indicators before they develop their own. Examples of indicators include percent of late reports, payroll processing time, number of open items, credit turnaround time, hours lost due to equipment downtime, number of off-specs approved, number of suspense dates met, morale, sick leave used, improvement in opinion surveys, percent errors in forecasts, accidents per quarter, sales made per call, percent of changed orders, and number of safety violations. For an extensive list of indicators arranged by functional area, see Harrington (pp. 95-106).[16]

Steps to Develop Indicators

It is now time for the facilitator to lead the Gold Team in the development of indicators for each KRA. It is recommended that the NGT be used to develop indicators for at least the first KRA. It may be that the NGT will be necessary to achieve consensus to develop indicators for all KRAs.

After developing indicators for one KRA, however, team members usually will have learned to work so well together that a simplified version of the NGT can be used. In the simpler version the facilitator still poses the nominal question, completes silent generation, round-robin listing, and discussion and clarification, but uses a show of hands or voice vote rather than time-consuming 3x5-inch cards for voting. First-time facilitators may feel more comfortable using the full NGT process to develop indicators for all KRAs, but as they become more secure with their abilities and better able to sense the capabilities of team members for consensus, they may want to use the less time-intensive version of the NGT. In any case, the facilitator begins the development of indicators by asking the Gold Team to select the easiest KRA for measurement. The facilitator says:

> Our task now is to develop a set of indicators that will allow the manager to determine if the organization is achieving the results described in the list of KRAs. I would like to begin with the KRA that is easiest to measure. That will help us become more comfortable with the indicator development process. Which KRA do you suggest?

Members of the Gold Team who were members of the Blue Team have had time since the earlier meetings to think about indicators. Generally, they will begin the discussion of which KRA is easiest to measure. It can be expected that they will have a number of indicators already thought out for the KRAs they sponsored when they served on the Blue Team. After a few minutes of discussion, a reasonably easy KRA will be identified for measurement and the work will have begun.

Posing the Nominal Question

The facilitator next writes the selected KRA on chart paper and states the indicator nominal question as follows:

> Throughout this meeting, I want you to play the role of "manager for a day." In that role, consider this nominal question: If you were the manager of [name of the target organization], what efficiency and effectiveness measures would you want on a monthly basis to know how well this particular KRA is being accomplished? Let's take 10 minutes to write your answers. Please don't talk to anyone while you silently generate.

Silent Generation

A team member may ask for clarification of remarks made earlier about the characteristics of good indicators or types of indicators. Such questions should be answered, and silent generation begins.

Round-Robin Listing

The next step is to map the Gold Team's answers to the indicator nominal question. The facilitator's task here is again to move around the team, getting one performance indicator from each member's list and writing on chart paper exactly what was said. The sponsor of each indicator is asked to verify that the suggested indicator is recorded correctly. This continues until everyone says "Pass."

Discussion and Clarification

After all indicators are listed for the KRA under consideration, the facilitator leads the Gold Team through a review process. The purpose of the review is to assure that the meaning of each indicator is clear and that redundancies have been removed. Team members are again called on, in turn, to explain their suggested indicators. In the ensuing discussion, the facilitator should seek to clarify each indicator as fully as possible. For instance, a team member may suggest "customer inquiries processed" as an indicator of the KRA "customer satisfaction." This suggestion may stimulate the facilitator to raise several questions for the indicator's sponsor. First, what is a *customer inquiry?*

The facilitator should be indirect with these questions of clarification to avoid making the sponsor look bad or feel embarrassed. The facilitator could ask "Does everyone understand the meaning of the phrase 'customer inquiry'? How is a customer 'inquiry' defined?" The team member who suggested this indicator may wish to explain its meaning. If not, someone else can.

Second, the facilitator may ask "Is the organization to simply count the number of monthly inquiries? Is the number of customer inquiries the indicator?" The indicator's sponsor may respond that the indicator would be more meaningful if "number of customer inquiries satisfied" is divided by "number of customer inquiries received."

The measure now begins to take on more meaning. The indicator is recognized to be a measure of effectiveness. Out of all customer inquiries received for a month, how many were satisfactorily processed? It is beneficial for the facilitator to elicit as much information as possible from each sponsor about the actual measurement to be made for a suggested indicator. Is it a mere count? How? Is it an equation? If so, what is the numerator? What is the denominator? Who will gather the information? Does it currently exist? Occasionally, a participant will merely have an idea for an indicator, but no suggestions about how to measure it. The facilitator should encourage ideas by recording them on chart paper. Another participant may subsequently see the value of the idea and be able to furnish the means of measurement.

Another consideration for performance indicators, such as the one about customer inquiries just discussed, is whether it should be expressed as a proportion or a percentage? If a percentage would be better (and it usually is because a percentage is understood by more people than a proportion), it is recorded on chart paper that the proportion is to be multiplied by 100. After such clarifications, the facilitator asks the permission of an indicator's sponsor to write the appropriate equation under the words that describe it. For instance, for the indicator "customer inquiries processed":

$$\frac{\text{Number of Customer Inquiries Processed}}{\text{Number of Customer Inquiries Received}} \times 100$$

Other team members are then invited, in turn, to clarify their suggested indicators for the KRA under consideration. Any overlap between them is identified, discussed, and eliminated.

Voting

As explained earlier, voting with 3x5-inch cards is recommended to reach consensus on the indicators for the first KRA. After indicators for the first KRA have been selected, the Gold Team probably will have learned to work well together, and it will be possible to omit the use of the cards in favor of voting by show of hands or voice. The latter methods of voting speeds the process considerably, but the facilitator must be sure that high status or aggressive team members do not dominate and bias results to their liking.

Hopefully, the Gold Team will come to consensus on one or a few important indicators for the KRA under consideration and then repeat the process for each of the other KRAs. The question of how many indicators to develop for each KRA involves balancing two different concerns: (1)

developing a system that measures each KRA well, and (2) the problem of too much paperwork.

It is recommended that the facilitator make a short presentation at this point on Tom Peters' excellent chapter "Measure What's Important," in which he stresses the need to use a small number of measures of what's really important.[30]

There are several checks which assure the value of all indicators. First, the manager of the target organization eventually will review the entire system. He/she will decide whether each indicator is worth the paperwork burden it requires.

Second, direct evidence that some indicators are not worthwhile results from the use of the next part of a TQM/MGEEM system — feedback charts. As will be explained in Chapter 7, feedback charts show the relationship between each indicator and organizational effectiveness. If the graphic shape of that relationship is flat, it means that the indicator it reflects is relatively unimportant because doing better on the indicator has little or no impact on effectiveness. Such a result raises a question about whether the indicator in question should be included in the TQM/MGEEM system.

Third, operational use of the TQM/MGEEM system may demonstrate that certain indicators are not worthwhile.

The last step in developing indicators is to refine them. The purpose of refinement is to make the next and final phase of the TQM/MGEEM development process, developing feedback charts, go more smoothly.

Refining Indicators

While the meaning of each indicator is still fresh on the minds of the Gold Team, the facilitator should lead them to consensus on the *feasible best, feasible worst,* and *indifference point* of performance for each. The facilitator should explain that this step is preliminary to the team's development of charts which will be used to periodically provide feedback to the manager and personnel of the target organization about how well they are doing on the indicators. Since they heard a presentation on the entire process when it was presented to all employees, the Gold Team should be reasonably familiar with this stage of the development process. The facilitator then leads the team through discussion and consensus on three questions for each indicator.

The first two questions to refine an indicator are as follows:

1. If everything goes right for a given measurement period [usually one month], what is the *feasible best* the target organization can do on this indicator?

2. If everything goes wrong for a given measurement period, what is the *feasible worst* the target organization can do on this indicator?

The facilitator should ensure that the Gold Team understands that feasible best and feasible worst are not the same as absolute (arithmetic) best and worst. The pair of feasible values are the best and worst considering real world restraints and circumstantial peculiarities. A practical example should be offered by the facilitator to get this point across. Consider an example from baseball:

Suppose the Gold Team is trying to establish the feasible best and feasible worst performance for a baseball team's weekly batting average. The first question they must answer is What is the baseball team's feasible best batting average? In other words, What is the team's best batting average if everything goes right with no injuries, proper equipment, sufficient batting practice, reasonable pitching, and good weather. Would the team batting average ever be the absolute (arithmetic) best of 1.000? Could every batter get a hit every time he came to the plate for a week?

Gold Team members will understand that an average of 1.000 is out of the question. After discussion, they may agree that an average of .280 might be the feasible best for a week if everything went right. Next, what would be the team's feasible worst batting average? What is the worst batting average if everything goes wrong, such as many injuries, illness, tough pitching, insufficient equipment, and cold weather. Could it ever be .000? Could every batter fail to get a hit every time they came to the plate for a week? Unlikely. Perhaps .120 might be a reasonable team feasible worst. The feasible best and worst are based on the Gold Team's best judgment, but can be revised later.

The third question asked by the facilitator to refine each indicator is:

Between the feasible best and worst, what is the level, point, or zone of performance on this indicator that is not good or bad, i.e., the "break-even," or "don't rock the boat" point?

The facilitator should tell the Gold Team that this is called the indifference point. It is at this point that the manager will not become concerned that performance is too low and commit more resources to it. Nor will the manager feel that performance is so good that the organization is recognized for outstanding effort. In the baseball example, it is the team batting average that isn't so good or so bad that the team is written up in the newspapers for being the best or worst team in the league. The team batting average is not leading the league, nor is it so bad that the coach is requiring extra batting practice, making team members run laps, or contemplating replacing the batting coach.

Members of the Gold Team may believe that the indifference point for certain indicators is not one point at all, but a series of points, or a zone. For example, indifference for a baseball team's batting average may not be one point (say .240), but a zone of say, .230 to .250. If the team batting average is in that zone, it is not bad, or good. Things just roll along.

The facilitator should lead the Gold Team to consensus on answers to all three of these questions for each indicator, one after another. It is advisable to show the three questions on an overhead screen and explain them with examples. Besides the example of the baseball team's batting average, other examples could be an individual's weight, cholesterol level, blood pressure, monthly contributions to a savings account, or hours of study per week by a student. Personal examples without curves are best. ("Without curves" means that less is always worse and more is always better, or vice versa).

To begin the process of answering these three questions about the feasible best, feasible worst, and indifference point, the first indicator is considered. The facilitator may wish to call on the sponsor of this indicator to suggest a feasible best. Often this is a good way to get things started. Others are then invited to voice their opinions about the suggested feasible best.

Members of the Gold Team have now been together enough that they probably can come to agreement through discussion rather than through a structured consensus-seeking technique, such as the NGT. After the feasible best is decided, feasible worsts and indifference points or zones are suggested, again possibly by the indicator's sponsor. These suggestions are discussed, and consensus is reached on their values. Then, the team moves on to consider the three questions for the other indicators.

It is important to remind team members that they have two opportunities later to fine-tune or conduct *sanity checks* or *pulses* of the system they are building. The first such fine-tuning occurs as soon as the results of their meeting have been typed up or keyed into an automated system. The second is when the first month's results are posted on their feedback charts. (Feedback charts are discussed in Chapter 7.) If a feasible best, feasible worst, or indifference point needs to be modified, it can be taken care of at that time.

Team members may wish to examine existing records on indicators before they attend sanity check meetings so that the most accurate feasible bests and worsts can be defined more realistically.

There is, however, a more important message underlying the facilitator's statement that there will be sanity check meetings to refine the system. The message is that the feasible bests and worsts, indifference point or zones, as well as other characteristics of the TQM/MGEEM, need only be the team's best current estimates. Although they should be seeking to develop the best possible answers, they should not struggle too much or spend too much time with their answers, because each element of the TQM/MGEEM will be reviewed later to make it more realistic and better suited to their needs. TQM/MGEEM, like the entire organization, is constantly and forever being improved. Continual improvement should become a way of life.

CHAPTER
7

DEVELOPING FEEDBACK
CHARTS

Many organizations have management information systems (MISs) based
on concepts such as KRAs and indicators. In my experience, however, few
of these systems routinely focus their KRAs and indicators through their
mission statements on customers' expectations to create constancy of
purpose. Furthermore, many managers have told me that, despite their
many advantages, MISs based solely on KRAs and indicators have a
number of inadequacies.

Consider the first inadequacy of most MISs based solely on KRAs and indicators. It is well understood that indicators rarely are of equal importance, yet few organizations have a systematic method of determining differences between them and ways of making decisions relative to their importance. To treat all indicators as if they are equally important obviously leads to less than optimum decisions. For instance, one indicator may be "products sold" while another is "participation in company recreation programs." Participation of employees in recreation programs is important, but not a matter of organizational survival like sales. Thus, for many important management decisions, e.g., the allocation of resources, indicators should not be considered equally important. To be useful, indicators should show that accomplishing some part(s) of the mission is more important than accomplishing another part(s).

Knowing which indicators are of critical, moderate or low importance is valuable to managers who must prioritize and allocate resources. Managers want to allocate resources to areas that are mission-critical. They want to worry only about what is important. To do this they must be able to distinguish between their indicators on the basis of their significance.

Consider an example from the military of how some indicators are more important than others. Commanders of Air Force flying squadrons have a number of indicators which help them determine their performance level. One indicator is *sortie production rate*, which demonstrates how many aircraft can be gotten into the air in a surprise exercise. Another indicator is *dental appointments missed.*

Are these two indicators of equal importance to commanders? Of course not. Ensuring that personnel keep their dental appointments is important and commanders will watch this indicator, but it is not nearly as important to the mission as getting aircraft into the air. Getting aircraft into the air is a matter of national security.

A second inadequacy of having an MIS composed only of KRAs and indicators is that many managers would like to be able to aggregate or roll up indicators into one number. Individual indicators illustrate how well an organization is doing in a specific area of the work, such as sales or absenteeism, but a number that is gathered from all individual indicators demonstrates how well the entire organization is doing across all indicators. Some managers find the ability to roll up measures a desirable feature of an MIS.

Perhaps the most serious inadequacy of MISs based solely on KRAs and indicators is that when in operation they seldom involve workers, other than those who manage the MIS itself. Lack of worker involvement in an MIS is a problem for at least two reasons:

First, there are many research studies which show that feedback to workers on the results of their performance is a powerful motivational influence. Everyone likes to know how well they're doing; they like to know the score. Therefore, it is important that information on how workers are doing, the indicators, is fed back to them.

Secondly, if workers are informed periodically about how the organization is doing on its indicators, their expertise can be tapped (1) to identify barriers that stand in their way of doing an even better job, and (2) to identify opportunities for improvement in the basic procedures and processes by which work is accomplished.

For these reasons, it is important that feedback on indicators be provided not only to managers but to workers as well. In Chapter 10 it will be explained how indicators can be given to workers in periodic feedback meetings, and how the events in these meetings motivate workers and provide a basis for continual improvement. At present, however, it is important to explain how facilitators lead Gold Teams to develop feedback charts, the final and most powerful part of any TQM/MGEEM system.

What Is a Feedback Chart?

The conceptual basis underlying feedback charts was proposed in an excellent book by Naylor and his associates concerning a theory of behavior in organizations.[27] These concepts were further developed at the Human Resources Directorate by Pritchard *et al.,* and Weaver and Looper.[36, 46]

Feedback charts are used in a TQM/MGEEM system to periodically display information about how well a target organization is doing on its indicators. The Gold Team develops one feedback chart for each indicator. (The general form of a feedback chart is shown in Figure 7.1.) The vertical axis of each feedback chart shows what we are trying to increase, usually organizational effectiveness, measured on a scale running in increments of 10 from -100 through $+100$.

The horizontal axis of each chart has an indicator (a different indicator for each chart) scaled from the feasible worst on the left to the feasible best on the right. The curve or slope on a feedback chart shows the judgment of the Gold Team about the impact on effectiveness (on the vertical axis) of different levels of performance on an indicator between its feasible worst and feasible best (on the horizontal axis).

The first step in developing feedback charts occurs immediately after a Gold Team finishes developing indicators. In this step, the facilitator leads the team to consensus on the feasible worst/best and indifference point

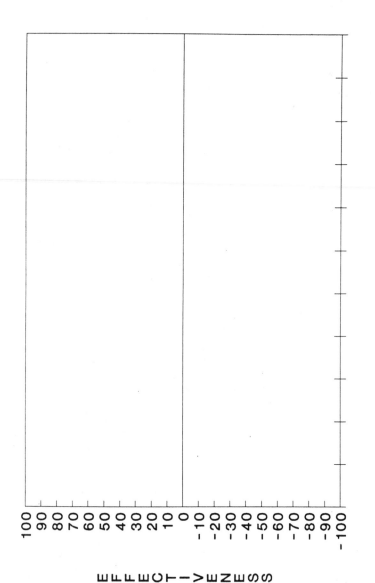

FIGURE 7.1   General Form of a Feedback Chart

(or zone) for each indicator. (This procedure was explained at the end of Chapter 6.)

Weighing Indicators

After agreement has been reached on the feasible best/worst and indifference point (or zone) for each indicator, the facilitator should suggest to the Gold Team that their indicators may not be of equal importance. Gold Team members can be convinced of this suggestion's truth by several examples, such as the previous example concerning the commander of the Air Force flying squadron.

For other examples, the facilitator could ask "Which of these indicators is of more interest to a manager of a baseball team: number of home runs hit *or* number of bats broken?" Or, "Would a manager of a computer support shop be more concerned about the number of customer requests satisfied *or* number of employees involved in shop-sponsored recreational activities?" Or, "Would a manager of an airport's avionics repair shop be more concerned about radios and radars returned from customer aircraft for failure to work properly after repair *or* unauthorized employee leave taken."

All of the indicators in these examples are important and deserve management attention, but obviously a baseball manager would be more interested in home runs, a manager of a computer support shop would be more interested in customer requests satisfied, and an avionics repair shop manager would be more interested in the failure rate on recently repaired equipment.

Making judgments about the relative importance of indicators is made easier by using an *Indicator Weighting Table,* which the facilitator presents to the Gold Team on a white or chalkboard. An indicator weighting table is composed of rows and columns. The facilitator writes in the rows the KRAs and indicators developed by the Blue and Gold Teams. In the first and fourth columns the facilitator writes *feasible best* and *feasible worst* for each indicator (as developed by procedures explained in Chapter 6 in the process of refining indicators). The facilitator should remind the Gold Team that these feasible bests and worsts are their judgments and are different from the absolute (arithmetic) worsts and bests.

Consider the information shown in Figure 7.2. There are four KRAs, six indicators, and six corresponding sets of feasible bests and worsts in Columns 1 and 4. Let's assume the Gold Team decided in the indicator refinement stage (explained in Chapter 6) that the feasible best they can do in satisfying customer inquiries (Indicator No. 1 in Figure 7.2) is 95 percent. They believe some peculiarity always will prevent the achievement of 100 percent, and they decided that the feasible worst is 50 percent.

On Indicator No. 2, the best and worst numbers of customer complaints are, respectively, 0 and 5, and so on for the feasible best and feasible worst for the other four indicators.

All feasible values are shown in columns 1 and 4. To save time, it is best for the facilitator to write this information in the Indicator Weighting Table format on a chalkboard during a break.

Columns 2 and 5 of the Indicator Weighting Table are used by the facilitator to record the judgments of the Gold Team to *rank* the relative importance of doing the feasible best and feasible worst on the indicators. To secure judgments about the ranks of the feasible best values for Column 1, the facilitator says:

> Suppose everything goes right for this organization for a given measurement period. You are staffed at 100 percent. Little sick or annual leave is taken. Other organizations you work with are cooperative. Because of these and other positive influences, your organization performs at its feasible best on *all* indicators. You perform at 95 percent on customer inquiries satisfied, 0 on customer complaints, and so on. If this were true, which of the six feasible bests would have the greatest *positive* effect on your overall performance (mission)?

The Gold Team discusses alternative answers to this question and reaches a consensus that the answer is Indicator No. 1. At this point, agreement almost always can be reached through discussion. If not, an alternative that includes structured discussion and voting is used. Indicator No. 1 is ranked 1 and a "1" is entered in Column 2, as shown in Figure 7.2. If there are ties of two or more indicators, the tied indicators receive the same rank. For example, if two indicators are believed to have the equally greatest positive impact they both receive the rank of 1. The facilitator continues:

> Now that you have identified the indicator whose feasible best has the greatest positive impact, which indicator's feasible best has the *second* greatest positive impact on the overall performance of this organization?

Following discussion and consensus, this indicator is ranked 2 and a "2" is marked in the appropriate row of Column 2. (This is Indicator No. 2 in Figure 7.2.) The process continues with the Gold Team ranking the importance of the feasible bests of the remaining indicators.

After the feasible bests have been ranked as shown in Column 2 in Figure 7.2, the facilitator asks the Gold Team to change these ranks to

	Best			Worst		
	Feasible (1)	Rank (2)	Effect. Points (3)	Feasible (4)	Rank (5)	Effect. Points (6)
KRA #1 Customer Satisfaction						
Indicator #1 No. of customer inquiries satisfied / No. of customer inquiries received × 100	95	1	100	50	1	-90
Indicator #2 No. of complaints received	0	2	90	5	2	-80
KRA #2 Timely Completion of Projects						
Indicator #3 Projects completed on time / Projects completed × 100	90	2	90	70	2	-80
KRA #3 Personnel in Training						
Indicator #4 Core mission personnel in training / Core mission personnel assigned × 100	25	4	65	0	3	-40
Indicator #5 Support personnel in training / Support personnel assigned × 100	40	3	70	10	3	-40
KRA #4 Community Service						
Indicator #6 No. of personnel who contributed to United Way / No. of personnel assigned × 100	100	5	40	98	4	-35

FIGURE 7.2 Example of an Indicator Weighting Table

effectiveness points which are recorded in Column 3. To accomplish this, the facilitator says:

> If the feasible best for indicator No. 1 is automatically given 100 effectiveness points, how much less is the impact on overall performance of the indicator whose feasible best is ranked second?

In Figure 7.2 this is Indicator No. 2. If its impact is almost as important as the impact of Indicator No. 1, it would have 98 or 95 effectiveness points. If its impact is half as important, it would have 50 effectiveness points. This process continues until all indicator ranks in Column 2 have been transformed to effectiveness points and recorded in Column 3. For the indicators shown in Figure 7.2, Indicator No. 1 with the rank of 1 automatically received 100 effectiveness points. Indicator No. 2 with the rank of 2 was judged to have 90 percent as positive an impact on the organization's effectiveness as Indicator No. 1 and was assigned 90 effectiveness points. Indicator No. 3 is tied with Indicator No. 2, so it also received 90 effectiveness points. Indicator No. 5 was ranked 3 because it was determined by the Gold Team to be much less important to the mission than Indicator Nos. 2 and 3. Indicator No. 5 was judged to receive only 70 effectiveness points. Indicator No. 4 was ranked 4 and was determined by the Gold Team to be almost as important as Indicator No. 5, so it was assigned 65 effectiveness points. Indicator No. 6 was ranked lowest at 5th and thought to be much less important than Indicator No. 4, so it was given only 40 effectiveness points.

The same process is then repeated to secure the ranks and effectiveness points of the feasible worsts. The facilitator begins this by making these comments to the Gold Team:

> Suppose everything goes wrong for this organization for a given measurement period. Your manning level is very low. There is a big snowstorm. There is an unexpected fire drill that keeps people away from their desks for half a day. The moon is full. Morale is low, and the organization operates at its feasible worst on all six indicators. If this were true, which of the feasible worsts would have the greatest *negative* effect on overall performance? Which low score would hurt you the most?

The feasible worsts are ranked in Column 5 with "1" for the indicator whose feasible worst is judged to have the most negative impact on organizational effectiveness; again ties are possible. Considering the feasible worsts, Indicator No. 1 is again thought by the Gold Team to have the most negative impact, Indicator Nos. 2 and 3 again tie as having the second most negative impact, Indicator Nos. 4 and 5 are also tied as the third most negative, and Indicator No. 6 is the fourth most negative. These ranks are shown in Column 5 of Figure 7.2. The next step is to transform these ranks to negative effectiveness points for Column 6.

Contrary to automatically assigning 100 effectiveness points for rank 1 of the feasible best, the automatic assignment of -100 is not necessary to transform to effectiveness points the indicator with the feasible worst rank. Often the feasible worst will receive -100 effectiveness points, but it is not required. It can be less than or greater than -100. For instance, in the case of Indicator No. 1 in Figure 7.2 (which was ranked 1 for feasible worst), the Gold Team may believe that the feasible worst is simply not as bad as minus 100. They saw a difference in the impact on the organization's effectiveness between the feasible best and worst on this indicator. They believe that -90 is the impact of the feasible worst. So, -90 is recorded in Column 6 for Indicator No. 1. The process continues with the Gold Team coming to consensus that the tie for second feasible worst indicator (Nos. 2 and 3) gets -80 effectiveness points, and the tie for third feasible worst indicator (Nos. 4 and 5) receives -40, and the fourth feasible worst indicator (No. 6) gets -35.

Note that the effectiveness points for the feasible bests are always positive (100, 90, 90, 65, 70, and 40), and the effectiveness points for the feasible worsts are always negative (-90, -80, -80, -40, -40, and -35). It should also be noted that in the unlikely event that an organization has only one indicator, its feasible best is assigned 100 effectiveness points, and its feasible worst is assigned the appropriate negative effectiveness points relative to -100.

This completes the discussion of how to weight performance indicators. The role of feasible bests, feasible worsts, indifference points (or zones), and effectiveness points in constructing curves on feedback charts will now be explained.

Specifying Curves on Feedback Charts

After refining and weighting indicators, the facilitator proceeds to the final step in the development of feedback charts: leading the Gold Team to develop curves or slopes for each feedback chart. For this work, it is recommended that the facilitator make a transparency of a feedback chart (like the one in Figure 7.1) for use on an overhead projector.

The facilitator should begin by presenting the Gold Team with a transparency of a feedback chart shown against a white or chalkboard, or other surface that can be written on. (If such a surface is unavailable, the transparency can be shown on a screen or wall, and the facilitator can write on the feedback chart transparency itself with an audiovisual pen. The markings of such pens can be removed easily from a plastic transparency with a damp tissue.) The same transparency will be written on for each feedback chart, but a recorder should be available to take careful notes on the construction of each feedback chart.)

The facilitator should explain to the Gold Team that the feedback charts they are about to complete will be the vehicle for periodic feedback to management and workers on the performance of the target organization. It should be explained that the values plotted on a feedback chart show the relationship between different levels of performance on an indicator (on the horizontal axis) and impact of those levels on the effectiveness of the organization (on the vertical axis).

Members of the Gold Team should be reminded that they made several important decisions about the development of the slopes of their feedback charts, e.g., for the first indicator they completed its horizontal axis when they defined its feasible best and worst. With these words, the facilitator should label the horizontal axis on the image of a feedback chart on the chalkboard with the name of the indicator in question, mark the feasible best as the next-to-the-highest point on the horizontal axis, and mark the feasible worst as the next-to-the-lowest point on the horizontal axis. (The feasible best and worst can go in the extreme lowest and highest points on the horizontal axis, but leaving a space at either end of the axis makes a more readable presentation.) On the horizontal axis, the feasible best always goes on the right, and the feasible worst always goes on the left. Next, the facilitator fills in intervals on the chalkboard along the horizontal axis between the feasible best and worst.

When under pressure to keep the meeting going, the facilitator may be concerned about how to precisely scale between the two extremes, but team members should be understanding and satisfied with a series of approximations. Later, when completed feedback charts are automated or typed, an exact horizontal scale can be developed. Such a scaling of the horizontal axis of Indicator No. 1 customer satisfaction, from Figure 7.2 is shown in Figure 7.3.

Next, the facilitator should explain to the Gold Team that they have already developed three points for a curve that will show their judgment about the impact on overall effectiveness of various performance levels on the indicator. These points are the indifference point (for customer satisfaction, it is a zone) and effectiveness values for the feasible worst and best.

Team members should then be shown Figure 7.4 and reminded of their earlier decision that the manager is indifferent if 75 to 85 percent of customer inquiries are satisfied. This is the indifference zone where

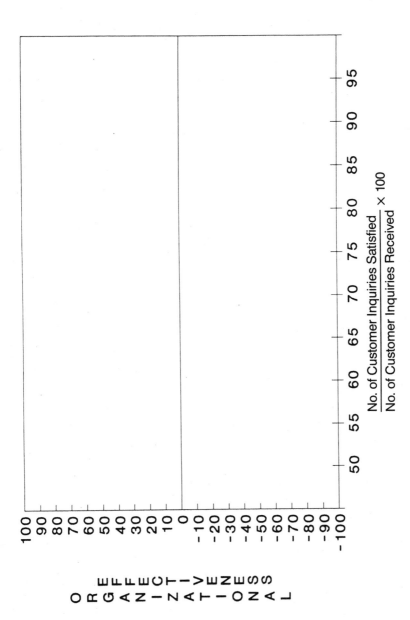

FIGURE 7.3 Customer Satisfaction Feedback Chart with Horizontal Axis Scaled

performance on this indicator has no positive or negative impact on the overall effectiveness of the organization. Thus, the effectiveness point for this zone of indifference of 75 to 85 on the horizontal axis is 0 on the vertical axis.

The team should be further reminded that they also made decisions earlier with the indicator weighting table about the comparative contribution to overall organizational effectiveness of the feasible best and worst for each indicator. For customer satisfaction, the feasible best of 95 percent was judged to be worth 100 effectiveness points, and the feasible worst of 50 percent was judged to be worth − 90 effectiveness points. These two points (for the feasible best, 95 on the X-axis and 100 on the Y-axis; for the feasible worst, 50 on the X-axis and − 90 on the Y-axis) are posted on a feedback chart as shown in Figure 7.4

Finally, members of the Gold Team are asked to complete the feedback chart shown in Figure 7.4 by connecting four points: first, the effectiveness point at the intersection of − 90 for 50 has to be connected to the intersection of 0 for 75. Second, the effectiveness point at the intersection of 0 for 85 has to be connected to the intersection of 100 for 95.

One option available at this point is to connect these points with straight lines. Later, after the system is in operation, another meeting of the Gold Team can consider whether the straight lines should be curves. The option of using straight lines may be exercised when there is pressure to get critical Gold Team members back to their jobs or when the facilitator feels additional learning about feedback charts through experience with them is needed. If this option is exercised, the charts are put into use and, after several months, the question of the benefit of using curves is raised in a feedback session.

Before asking the Gold Team to complete its first feedback chart, the facilitator may wish to use a chalkboard to draw and interpret several examples of curves on feedback charts. Figure 7.5 shows two such examples. The dashed-line curve suggests that a very broad range of performance on the indicator has little impact on effectiveness. From 55 to 94 percent on the indicator, the effectiveness impact is minute, only from − 10 to 10.

Performance on the indicator of less than 55 percent or greater than 94 percent, however, has substantial impact on effectiveness: A dramatic reduction at 50 percent to − 90 effectiveness points and a dramatic increase at 95 percent to 100 effectiveness points.

The solid-line curve in Figure 7.5 shows that when performance on the indicator falls below 75 percent the impact on effectiveness becomes severe, falling to almost − 90 effectiveness points for performance of 70

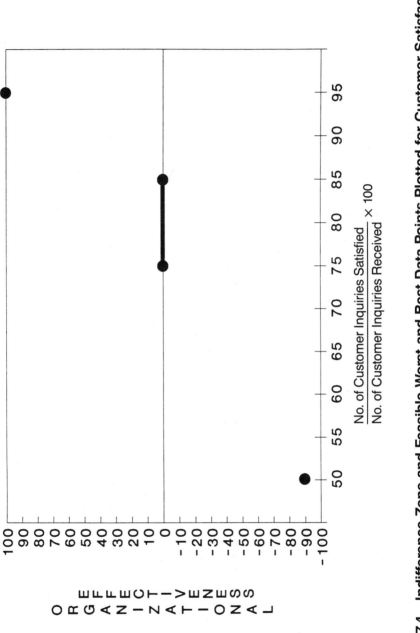

FIGURE 7.4   Indifference Zone and Feasible Worst and Best Data Points Plotted for Customer Satisfaction

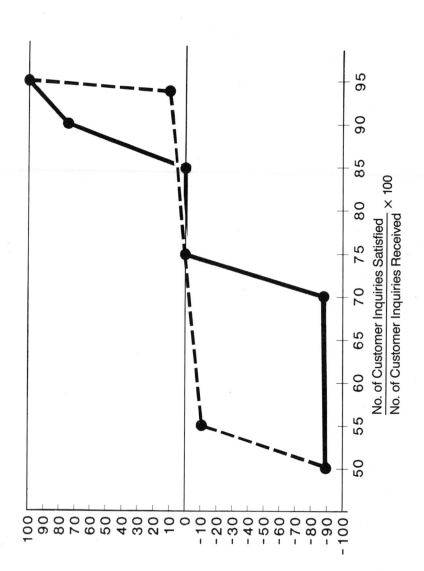

FIGURE 7.5 Examples of Slopes to Connect Feasible Worst, Feasible Best, and Indifference Zone

percent on the indicator. Below 70 percent on the indicator, the impact on effectiveness is already so low that it can get only slightly worse.

On the positive side, when the indicator's performance rises above 85 percent, the positive impact on effectiveness is dramatic. An increase from 85 to 90 on the indicator produces an increase in effectiveness from 0 to almost 75. Above the 90 percent level on the indicator, the impact on mission effectiveness is positive, but not as great as from 85 to 90. The facilitator should stress to the team that the curve is an expression of their policy about the impact on organizational effectiveness of various levels of performance on indicators. The steeper a curve, the more important the indicator. The flatter a curve, the less important the indicator.

The Gold Team should then be led through completion of the feedback charts. Team members quickly learn how to reach a consensus about the shape of curves for feedback charts, but the facilitator may wish to begin developing the curve of the first chart by asking questions such as these with respect to the example shown in Figure 7.4:

If the impact on overall effectiveness of 75 to 85 percent inquiries satisfied is zero effectiveness points, how much better is it to have 90 percent of inquiries satisfied? Ninety-five percent satisfied? How much worse is it to have only 70 percent satisfied? Sixty-five percent satisfied? Sixty percent satisfied?

Answers to each question form a data point which, when connected, result in the construction of a feedback curve.

Curves on feedback charts can have an unlimited variety of shapes. Usually they run from low on the bottom left to high on the upper right, but this is not always the case. Facilitators see all kinds of strange shapes in feedback curves. They must always remember that the main purpose of feedback charts, and for that matter the entire TQM/MGEEM system, is improvement. They must not allow themselves or the Gold Team to become overly concerned about the precision of measurement. An unusually shaped feedback curve should not surprise or concern anyone. Measurement in TQM/MGEEM only needs to be good enough to serve as a basis for improvement. Remember that improvement is what really counts.

For the sake of illustration, consider a feedback curve that does not follow the usual pattern of going from low on the bottom left to high on the upper right. Here is the situation. In a certain test and evaluation center, two types of employees are needed: engineers with college training in mathematical and theoretical issues, and technicians (recruited from the field) with plenty of practical experience. It was considered that a work force of about 50 percent engineers and 50 percent technicians is best.

Too many of either profession was considered bad. Too many technicians produce evaluations that lack sufficient mathematical and theoretical support.

If the indicator to monitor this mixture is "percent of engineers on staff," what would be the shape of the feedback curve? As shown in Figure 7.6, the curve does not go from low on the bottom left to high on the upper right. Instead, the feasible percent of engineers on staff ranges on the horizontal axis from 25 to 75. The feasible best is 50 percent engineers. There are two feasible worsts, 25 and 75 percent, and there are two indifference points, 30 and 70 percent. (Perhaps the indifference areas should be called zones, say from 30 to 35 and 65 to 70, in which case the curve would be flat in two places at indifference points.) Figure 7.6 shows that too few or too many engineers and, correspondingly, too few or too many technicians is bad while having a good mixture is best.

In the preceding example, should the facilitator be concerned that the greatest number of effectiveness points is at the middle of the horizontal axis rather than at the bottom right side? Should the facilitator be concerned that there are two indifferent points, or zones, rather than one? The answer to both questions is no. Instead, the facilitator should be concerned that the curve adequately captures the policy of the Gold Team toward the issues at hand. The facilitator should be concerned that when values of an indicator are posted on the curve (explained in Chapter 10), it means something. For instance, suppose 28 percent of the center's staff are engineers. Does posting 28 percent on a feedback chart help one evaluate whether that percentage of engineers is good or bad? Yes, it does. We locate 28 percent on the horizontal axis and read up to the curve and then read to the left to the vertical axis to -75 effectiveness points. Minus effectiveness points are bad. To correct this situation we need to do something with recruitment to get higher on the curve by moving to the right on the horizontal axis. This means finding more engineers.

Sanity Checking Feedback Charts

Before the TQM/MGEEM system is submitted to management for review, the Gold Team should conduct two sanity checks or pulse checks of their feedback charts. The first check should come immediately after the charts are put into the form in which they will be used for feedback to workers and management. This form can range from simple typed copies to a fully automated procedure on a computer. In either case, the Gold Team should convene a meeting to review their charts to determine if they were recorded and reproduced as originally specified. Did the facilitator, typist, or data entry clerk inadvertently make an error?

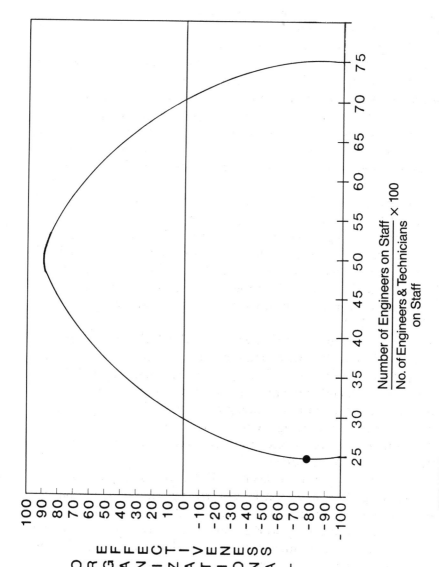

FIGURE 7.6 Feedback Curve for Percent of Engineering Staff

A second sanity check should occur when performance results on indicators are available after the first measurement period. (Some users suggest that this sanity check requires data from two or three measurement periods.) At this meeting, the Gold Team receives copies of their feedback charts together with performance levels plotted on each feedback chart. There is an "X" shown on the curve on each feedback chart to denote the level of performance for the past month.

The second sanity check is important because seeing real performance data may cause the Gold Team to rethink its judgment about the nature of the feedback charts. It is not unusual, for example, for actual performance on a feedback chart to be lower than the feasible worst or higher than the feasible best. This means that the organization did worse or better than the Gold Team thought possible. No value judgment should be made by the facilitator or others about such an occurrence. The team merely revises its estimate of the feasible worsts or bests, and the curves on the feedback charts involved are redrawn.

The Gold Team should feel free during sanity checks to modify their feedback charts through consensus in any way. Doing sanity checks offers the additional advantage of getting team members into the habit of meeting to discuss their charts. When the TQM/MGEEM is in operation, holding monthly meetings of all target organization personnel to review performance on their feedback charts is among the most powerful features of TQM/MGEEM.

After the Gold Team is satisfied with its feedback charts, the complete system of KRAs, performance indicators, and feedback charts is briefed to the appropriate higher level of management. Although TQM/MGEEM supports management's authority, the facilitator should ensure that four cautions are observed in this approval process. First, the facilitator should prebrief the higher level manager who is about to review the system. This briefing should reaffirm a key point emphasized in the decision to implement the TQM/MGEEM.

The basic philosophy of TQM/MGEEM is that significant gains in organizational performance come from increasing worker motivation and self-control, restoring or increasing workers' pride in their work and sense of craftsmanship, and getting worker input to identify obstacles to better performance and how to improve work procedures and processes. The manager conducting the review should be reminded by the facilitator that workers must feel a sense of ownership of TQM/MGEEM if vital feedback is to work. Workers buy into TQM/MGEEM by contributing to its creation.

The manager must appreciate that the central issue is not whether TQM/MGEEM measures with absolute precision, but that it provides a vehicle for motivation and continual improvement. For instance, whether a feasible best is 65 or 70 percent, or whether an indifference point is 25 or 30 is unimportant. What is important is that workers *accept* feedback from the feedback charts and are willing to use them to identify better ways of doing business. Thus, for the reviewing manager to disagree with and ask questions about a system is appropriate and reasonable as long as workers are allowed to maintain a sense of ownership.

Management interest is, in fact, stimulating to workers. In the proper environment, namely one devoid of fear, workers generally like to interact with the boss. They especially like to interact with the boss when they are given a chance to talk and give input. About the only time they see the boss is when he/she is running down the hall to "put out a fire" or when the boss directs them to do something.

The manager must be assured that the TQM/MGEEM system is measuring the important components of the organization's mission. For instance, if the selected indicators do not capture the important components of the mission, time and resources will be channelled into less important areas of work. That must not happen, and management should work with the Gold Team to ensure that some inappropriate feature of the system doesn't cause it.

If, however, the manager changes the system unnecessarily, say merely to show who is boss, workers will lose their sense of ownership and become resigned to business as usual where they do what they are told without much enthusiasm. They will be less willing to make suggestions about improvement. They will not have confidence that management will seriously consider the changes they suggest. This, of course, means that a main purpose of the TQM/MGEEM project has been defeated.

A second concern the facilitator needs to consider in coordinating a completed system with higher management is that the higher level managers should not expect to routinely monitor feedback charts developed at lower levels. Managers above the level of the target organization manager may wish to receive aggregated or rolled up results of performance for use as a management tool (see Chapter 8). These managers need to appreciate that feedback charts are intended for use by the workers and supervisors of target organizations as tools to improve performance.

Feedback charts should not be part of any reporting requirement to higher management except inasmuch as they form the basis for roll-up. Managers at each successive level can implement TQM/MGEEM systems at their own level and they should not be micro-managed by managers above them. They, too, should have self-control.

A third concern in coordinating with higher management is that members of the Gold Team often fear that the higher manager will not approve of the TQM/MGEEM system when it is submitted for review. This disapproval should be expected, at least with respect to some details, and is one of the most valuable parts of the TQM/MGEEM process. Disapproval requires that the higher manager, the manager of the target organization, and representatives from the Blue and Gold Teams conduct a meeting or series of meetings in which they talk to each other. Here they will discuss the system's details. After reflection, most team members will welcome these meetings because the higher level manager is expressing an interest in their work. Many workers believe most managers are interested only in getting the work out for the sake of selfish interests (i.e., for their own promotion), and care little about workers and their opinions. Actually, few managers give workers any credible reason to think otherwise. So, workers are pleased to see that managers are willing to listen, that managers may not be as self-seeking as is widely believed. Workers will see the required coordination meetings as a once-in-a-lifetime opportunity to present their viewpoint to management, but remember they will be suspicious because they have seen programs come and go. Privately, the workers believe TQM/MGEEM is simply another program the manager is using to get promoted. They believe that, in time, it will fade away.

Once higher-level managers overcome their concern that TQM/MGEEM will somehow subvert their authority, they also welcome meetings to discuss the features of TQM/MGEEM. Note that the key issue underlying this worker-management dialogue is continual improvement. Managers, specifically those with engineering, mathematics, finance, and accounting backgrounds, must resist the impulse to insist that everything about TQM/MGEEM be precise.

Remember that measurement need only be good enough to provide a foundation for continual improvement. It is a serious error to take measurement to the extreme by attempting to make everything about TQM/MGEEM highly precise. Continual improvement should be of genuine interest to all managers. In these meetings considerable discussion and education occurs and results in both sides, especially the managers, conceding to some degree so agreement is reached on the features of the TQM/MGEEM system to be used.

A fourth point to remember in coordinating TQM/MGEEM with higher management is that TQM/MGEEM does not undermine the traditional prerogatives of management. Management maintains the right to approve or modify the TQM/MGEEM system. Consequently, facilitators should be careful to represent TQM/MGEEM to workers as an opportunity to make *suggestions* about the best way to measure and enhance organizational performance and quality. Experience shows that most workers' suggestions will be accepted by management, especially since the manager of the target organization and his/her superior were members of the Blue Team. Workers, however, should *not* be allowed to believe that what they suggest will automatically be accepted by management. If a facilitator allows workers to believe that will occur, even minor changes in the TQM/MGEEM system by management are likely to surprise them. Instead of workers being interested and motivated, they will be disillusioned and dispirited.

ROLLING UP
FEEDBACK CHARTS

The TQM/MGEEM possesses a technical capability which makes it possible to roll up effectiveness scores from several feedback charts into one number. By adding effectiveness scores from different indicators, such as sales, training accomplished, and attendance, it is possible to obtain one number to measure the overall performance of a single target organization. It also is possible to roll up the indicators of several unlike target organizations into one number, e.g., a sales department and a service department.

Experience shows that only about 5 percent of the organizations that implement TQM/MGEEM will initially be interested in this roll-up feature. After an implementation has been in place for a year or so, however, another 10 percent will begin its use. While roll-up apparently is not interesting to all organizations which implement TQM/MGEEM, approximately 15 percent of them are highly interested and enthusiastic about it. Consequently, the reader may wish to browse through this chapter with the understanding that roll-up is not a necessary or critical part of a TQM/MGEEM implementation, but may be added as needed. Readers not interested in this roll-up feature should skip this chapter and continue with Chapters 9 through 12. The decision about whether to use roll-up rests, of course, with management. The powerful management tools and climate for improvement provided by TQM/MGEEM function perfectly with or without roll-up.

There are several different organizational settings in which roll-up can be useful. One of these settings is within a single target organization.

Rolling Up Within a Target Organization

Roll-up can be important to managers who wish to have a single measure of a single target organization's overall performance. Consider, for example, a sales department with two KRAs and three indicators. Its feedback charts, one for each indicator, are shown in Figure 8.1. Members of the Blue and Gold Teams have been through the TQM/MGEEM development process to review the mission statement, identify customers and suppliers and develop KRAs, indicators, and feedback charts. They have agreed on the feasible bests, worsts, indifference points (or zones), and relationships to organizational effectiveness of various levels of performance on each of three indicators. Suppose last month's performance of these indicators or the sales department was $920,000 in sales, 56 hours of training, and 96 percent attendance of personnel. With these indicators measured in different ways (dollars, hours, and percent), how can the sales manager assess the performance of the department as a whole? The manager can't simply add together $920,000, 56 hours, and 96 percent. Such an answer is uninterpretable.

The Feedback Chart Solution

The TQM/MGEEM answer to assessing the performance of a target organization is to use feedback charts to change the values on several indicators into a common scale—organizational effectiveness. Consider the

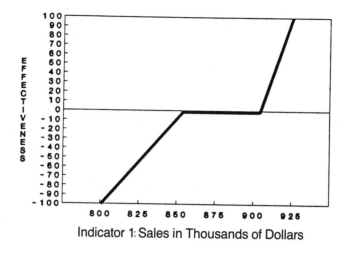

Indicator 1: Sales in Thousands of Dollars

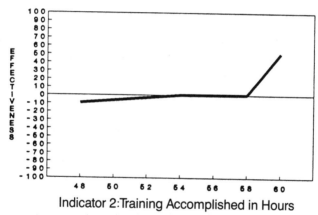

Indicator 2: Training Accomplished in Hours

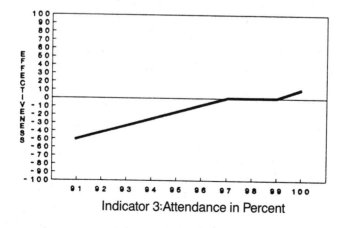

Indicator 3: Attendance in Percent

FIGURE 8.1 Feedback Charts for a Sales Department

example in Figure 8.1. For each value of each indicator (920,000, 52, and 96) on the three horizontal axes, read up on the three respective feedback charts to the curve and then to the left to the corresponding values in organizational effectiveness points on the vertical axes. On Indicator No. 1, the 920 in sales in thousands of dollars translates to 75 effectiveness points. On Indicator No. 2, the 56 hours spent on training translates to zero effectiveness points. On Indicator No. 3, 96 percent attendance translates to −15 effectiveness points. These three effectiveness values (75, 0, and −15) can then be summed to a value of 60 (the roll-up score), which represents the sales department's overall performance for the measurement period. This is possible because the levels of performance on the indicators ($920,000, 56, hours, and 96 percent) have been changed to the common scale of organizational effectiveness.

The TQM/MGEEM roll-up procedure has many advantages. First, it takes into account that indicators almost always vary in importance. The importance of an indicator is, of course, judged by the steepness of its curve. The steeper a curve, the more important the indicator; the flatter the curve, the less important the indicator. Indicator No. 1 in the example in Figure 8.1 is the most important of the three because its slope is the steepest.

Accomplishing either the feasible best and worst results in 100 and −100 effectiveness points, respectively. High sales mean great performance; low sales mean poor performance. The slopes of the other two indicators are not as steep, e.g., training (Indicator No. 2 in Figure 8.1) is believed beneficial when much of it is accomplished, but won't be too damaging when only a small amount takes place.

When attendance is between 54 and 58 percent, its slope indicates that performance is neither good nor bad. When attendance is less than 54 percent, however, performance begins to suffer. When attendance is between 97 and 99 percent (Indicator No. 3, Figure 8.1), there is no impact on effectiveness. When attendance is over 99 percent, there is a small positive benefit. When attendance falls below 97 percent, however, the situation deteriorates quickly.

A second advantage of the TQM/MGEEM roll-up procedure is that overall performance can be measured with any set of indicators, regardless of their diversity, because feedback charts convert all types of measures to a common effectiveness scale. This provides a considerable amount of freedom and flexibility of measurement.

A third advantage is that this entire procedure is unaffected by the common occurrence of non-straight-line relationships between performance on indicators and organizational effectiveness, as in the case of the three indicators in Figure 8.1.

Summing effectiveness points to a rolled-up score can be highly useful in assessing the overall organizational performance of a single target organization. This is especially true if the rolled-up scores are compared at different points through time, say monthly. It is recommended that rolled up scores be monitored through time by the manager at the next higher level above the target organization with a roll-up chart.

The Roll-Up Chart

Roll-up charts permit the graphical display of rolled up scores; the sum of organizational effectiveness scores from feedback charts. The use of roll-up charts is easy to understand, and they are useful to the manager at the next higher level. Their use involves simply plotting the roll-up score for any measurement period as the baseline. (The baseline may be for any period or can be an average for several periods [three months, six months, or more].)

Consider the roll-up scores for the sales department in the previous example. For the month in question, say October, the roll-up score of 60 (75, 0, and − 15) is simply plotted on a roll-up chart (see Figure 8.2). This requires no formula or calculation. Each succeeding month's roll-up score is also plotted on the chart, and the points for the various months connected with a straight line.

The vertical axis of organizational effectiveness is scaled to accommodate the expected range of rolled-up values. To continue the example with Figure 8.2, suppose the roll-up score for the sales department increases from 60 in October to 75 in November. The roll-up score of 75 is simply plotted for November on the roll-up chart in Figure 8.2. If the roll-up score increases again to 90 in December, then 90 is added to the chart.

As mentioned, the baseline on a roll-up chart can be determined in ways other than using the first month's roll-up score. If the TQM/MGEEM system is developed using data that already exist in the information system of the target organization, it may be possible to back into a baseline period roll-up score by taking the average for several months prior to the month of the TQM/MGEEM implementation.

If sufficient historical data do not exist, another option is available. After the TQM/MGEEM has been in operation for a period of time, the baseline can be defined as the average roll-up scores for any period of time, say six months or a year after the TQM/MGEEM has been in place.

It must be remembered, however, that a baseline should represent a typical or average period of performance. If a baseline is set in a period that is not typical of performance, subsequent percentages will be unrealistic.

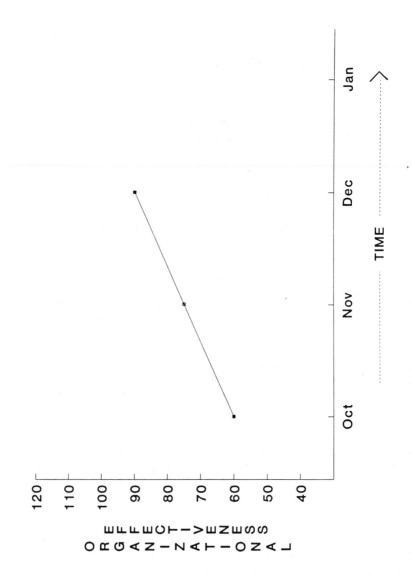

FIGURE 8.2 Example of a Roll-Up Chart

For instance, suppose the baseline is set below typical or average performance. Any subsequent improvement above this too-low baseline will look good superficially, but, in reality, will merely be movement from below average toward the average. On the other hand, suppose the baseline is inadvertently set at above-average. Any subsequent performance slightly below this too-high baseline will be regarded as comparatively poor, when in reality it probably is above average. If it is necessary that the baseline be atypical, this must be considered when interpreting current period performance data. When sufficient data points are available, statisticians may be interested in the use of control charts to determine, as Deming suggests, whether a system exists for the organization's performance.[7]

Essentially the same procedures apply to rolling up *across* target organizations, but an interesting problem must first be recognized and solved.

Rolling Up Across Target Organizations

A manager of two or more target organizations may wish to have one number with which to measure the organizations' combined performance. This could be for a branch, composed of work centers, for a division composed of branches, or for a corporate headquarters composed of divisions. As an example, consider Figure 8.3 which shows the branch of a high-tech company composed of two departments, a sales department with three feedback charts and a service department with five feedback charts. (The labels and values of the horizontal and vertical axes are omitted for simplicity.)

Assuming the sales and service departments have each developed TQM/MGEEM systems, how does the branch manager who supervises both branches obtain one number as a measure of how well the entire branch is doing? An obvious but incorrect answer is to simply add together the effectiveness scores from the eight feedback charts as was done in the previous example of roll-up within a single target organization.

To explain why this would be a mistake, suppose the roll-up scores for the high-tech company illustrated in Figure 8.3 for a given month are 75, 0, and −15 for the sales department and 90, 50, 50, −10, and 22 for the service department. (Note that these are *not* the effectiveness scores for the feasible bests or worsts as shown in Figure 8.3, but the effectiveness scores for actual performance.) Why would it be incorrect to add the

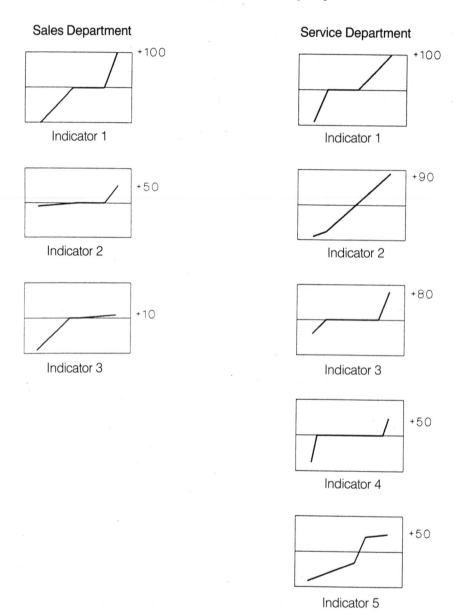

Branch of a High-Tech Company

FIGURE 8.3   Rolling Up Across Target Organizations

roll-up scores for both departments together for a total of 262 (75 + 0 − 15 + 90 + 50 + 50 − 10 + 22) and post the total for the branch on a roll-up chart? Let's explore that problem.

# The Unequal Contribution Problem

It is an error to roll up across target organizations by adding their roll-up scores. Consider that both departments, shown in Figure 8.3, do their feasible bests. The sales department contributes 160 (100 + 50 + 10) effectiveness points, while the service department contributes 370 (100 + 90 + 80 + 50 + 50). Assume further that the branch manager regards the contributions of both departments equally important to the branch's mission.

Alternatively, assume the branch manager considers the contribution of the sales department to be twice as important as the contribution of the service department. In either case, it is inaccurate to allow the service department to contribute a potential maximum of 370 effectiveness points while the equally or twice as important sales department contributes a potential maximum of only 160 effectiveness points. This is the problem of *unequal contribution* and arises when the maximum effectiveness scores of target organizations to be rolled up are not proportional to management's assessment of their relative contributions to the mission.

The Roll-Up Correction Factor

The solution to the unequal contribution problem involves use of a roll-up correction factor used *only* for purposes of roll-up across target organizations. It is important to stress that all of the information on feedback charts which was developed by Gold Teams is unaffected by the computations used to roll up across target organizations. In addition, within each target organization across which a roll-up is to take place, roll-up charts are unaffected and used as described earlier in this chapter.

Determining the roll-up correction factor requires that the facilitator meet with the manager of the target organizations across which the roll-up is to occur. The manager is asked to make judgments about the relative contribution of each subordinate target organization to the mission of the next hierarchical level.

In the example illustrated in Figure 8.3, the facilitator would meet with the branch manager to ask which of the two departments, sales or service, contributes most to the accomplishment of the branch mission. The answer must be that the two departments contribute equally or unequally. If the branch manager believes they contribute unequally he/she is asked to assign ranks, 1 for the most important department, 2 for the second most important, etc., for the number of departments.

Next, the branch manager is asked to assign percentages to the ranks, with rank 1 automatically set to 100 percent. In Figure 8.3, suppose the sales department is ranked 1 and the service department is ranked 2. The sales department automatically is set to 100 percent. If the branch manager believes the service department is only half as important as the sales department, the service department is assigned a value of 50 percent. On the other hand, if the two departments are considered by the branch manager to be equally important, they are both assigned 100 percent. If there were three departments, one could be at 100 percent, and the others could be tied at 50 percent. All kinds of combinations are possible.

To illustrate the roll-up correction factor, assume the branch manager believes the service department is only half as important to the branch mission as the sales department. Since the maximum effectiveness score for the feasible best of the sales department is 160 (100 + 50 + 10), the maximum effectiveness score for the feasible best for the service department should only be half of 160, or 80. This is half of 160 because the branch manager regards the service department as only half as important as the sales department.

To make the service department half as important as the sales department, a roll-up correction factor is used to create two modifications.

The first modification is to adjust the maximum effectiveness scores for the departments so they reflect their correct proportional contributions to the branch mission as judged by the branch manager. Since the service department is only half as important as the sales department, when the service department is doing its feasible best, its maximum effectiveness score should be half of the maximum effectiveness score when the sales department is doing its feasible best. Because the maximum effectiveness score of the sales department is 160, the corresponding maximum effectiveness score for the service department of 370 should be reduced to half of 160, or 80.

The second modification is to adjust the roll-up score of the service department which (after adjustment) will be added to the roll-up score of the sales department to attain the branch measure for a given period. For instance, suppose the indicator values on the horizontal axes of the five feedback charts of the service department in Figure 8.3 translate into five effectiveness scores (90, 50, 50, – 10, and 22) which sum to a roll-up score of 202. Before the 202 can be added to the corresponding roll-up score from the sales department, the 202 must be adjusted to reflect that the service department is only half as important as the sales department. The formula for this adjustment is

$$\frac{\text{Roll-up score before adjustment}}{\text{Roll-up score after adjustment}} = \text{Roll-up correction factor}$$

In this case, the maximum effectiveness score of the service department before adjustment is 370 (100 + 90 + 80 + 50 + 50) and after adjustment is 80 because the service department is only half as important as the sales department. Remember the sales department's maximum effectiveness score is 160. Thus, 370/80 = 4.63 is the roll-up correction factor. The roll-up score of 202 (90, 50, 50, −10, and 22) for the actual performance of the service department is divided by this roll-up correction factor (4.63) to adjust for the service department's being half as important as the sales department. The result of 43.6 can then be added to the roll-up score for actual performance of 60 (75, 0, and −15) for the sales department to arrive at the branch roll-up score of 103.6 (43.6 + 60).

For another example of the use of the roll-up correction factor to solve the unequal contribution problem, assume the branch manager considers the two departments in Figure 8.3 to make *equal* contributions to the branch mission. In that case, the maximum effectiveness score of 370 for the service department needs modification to equal the maximum effectiveness score of 160 for the sales department. It stands to reason that the maximum effectiveness scores for both departments should be equal if they are equally important to the branch, i.e., both departments should have maximum effectiveness scores of 160. Next, remember that the actual performance roll-up scores are 60 (75, 0, and −15) for the sales department, and 202 (90, 50, 50, −10, and 22) for the service department. To make the two departments contribute equally, the 202 for the service department must be adjusted with a roll-up correction factor. The computation of the correction factor is 370/160 = 2.31, which is used to adjust the 202 (202/2.31) to result in 87.5. The 87.5 from the service department can then be added to 60 from the sales department to get 147.5 (87.5 + 60), the roll-up score for the branch.

Once the problem of equal contribution has been corrected, it is possible to post the rolled-up number on a roll-up chart as described earlier in this chapter and shown in Figure 8.2. Consider the example in Figure 8.3 where the contributions of both departments are considered by the branch manager to be of equal importance. To use a roll-up chart, the branch roll-up score from our last example of 147.5 (87.5 + 60) could be plotted on the chart as the baseline. Afterward, if the branch roll-up score increases in the next month from 147.5 to 170, the point of 170 is added to the chart, and the two points (147.5 and 170) may be connected with a straight line.

Adding New Branch Indicators

Facilitators should be aware of another challenge that may develop when rolling up across target organizations. It is not uncommon for managers of organizational units being rolled up to want an indicator(s) which apply to the higher level organizational unit, and which may or may not have anything to do with work in the lower-level units being rolled up. For instance, in rolling up across departments to a branch, the branch manager may want indicators which are unique to the branch. Such additional indicators can be measures of activities that take place only at the higher organizational level, or of activities that take place in all the lower-level organizations being aggregated. Managers want such indicators that are unique to their level because they feel they measure important parts of their organization's work and that roll-up is incomplete without them. For an example of how to deal with this situation, consider the example of the two departments in the high-tech company described in Figure 8.3.

Suppose the branch manager wishes to add an indicator that applies to the branch and not to the two subordinate departments. To accomplish this, the facilitator leads the branch manager through the usual process of identifying the feasible best, worst, and indifference points (or zones) to develop a feedback chart for the branch indicator. If there is only one branch indicator, the effectiveness points for its feasible best are 100 and for its feasible worst are determined on the negative side relative to -100. This feedback chart will be used to assess performance on the activity measured.

To incorporate this branch feedback chart into the system with the two departments shown in Figure 8.3 the branch manager merely needs to make decisions on the contributions to overall branch performance of the two departments, and the activity assessed by the single branch indicator.

In the earlier discussion of the example in Figure 8.3, suppose the branch manager believes the service department is only half as important in its contribution to the branch as the sales department. Therefore, these departments made contributions of 100 percent and 50 percent. Thus, the maximum effectiveness score and roll-up score of the service department were correspondingly modified by one-half for roll-up. Following the same procedure, before the single branch feedback chart can be rolled up, it must be made relative to the sales department as 100 percent. To accomplish this, the facilitator asks the branch manager the following question:

> You have said that the sales department makes the greatest contribution to branch effectiveness. We, therefore, set its effectiveness score at 100. You also said the service department makes only half as much contribution and, therefore, was set at 50. In this context, what is the contribution of the activity measurement by the single branch indicator compared to 100 for the sales department?

Suppose the branch manager believes the contribution to the branch of the activity measured by the single branch indicator is only one-tenth as important as the contribution of the sales department. The maximum effectiveness score for the feasible best of the branch indicator would be adjusted to .10 of 160, or 16, and the branch indicator roll-up score adjusted with the roll-up correction factor to 10 (160/16).

$$\frac{\text{Roll-up score before adjustment}}{\text{Roll-up score after adjustment}} = \text{Roll-up correction factor}$$

Thus, a roll-up score for actual performance of 85 on the branch indicator is adjusted to 8.5 (85/10) before being added to the corresponding roll-up scores from the sales and service departments.

If the branch manager wants two or more branch level indicators, the development and roll-up process is identical. The feasible best, worst values, indifference points (or zones), and slopes on feedback charts would be developed for all branch indicators. Again, the branch manager would decide the importance of the contribution to branch mission of activities assessed by the branch indicators relative to the contribution of 100 percent for the sales department.

Suppose, as in the earlier example, the contribution of the branch indicators is only one-tenth as important as the sales department at 100 percent. If so, the total maximum roll-up score for all feedback charts of the branch are adjusted down to 10 percent of the maximum roll-up score (160) of the sales department. Then, branch roll-up scores would be adjusted with the correction factor before being added to the roll-up scores of the other two departments.

Roll-Up Across Branches

The logical extension of rolling up across departments to a branch is to roll up across branches to a division and ultimately to the entire company. The process of rolling up across increasingly larger organization units follows the previously described procedures. For example, consider the high-tech company discussed earlier. One of the branches in this company is the one shown in Figure 8.3 which was discussed above. Let's call it Branch A. There is another branch that has three departments. Assume these branches have TQM/MGEEM systems in place. The division manager expresses an interest in having a single number with which to measure the performance of the division. Therefore, roll-up across the two branches is necessary.

Before explaining how to roll up the two branches to the division, it will be useful to revisit the TQM/MGEEM systems already in place in those two branches, and to walk through the adjustments which have been made to roll up to each of the two branches. After that, it should be easy to roll up to the division.

Figure 8.4 includes Branch A with one sales and one service department (described in Figure 8.3), and Branch B with three departments (a sales department and two service departments).

For Branch A, the maximum effectiveness scores are 160 (100 + 50 + 10) for the sales department and 370 (100 + 90 + 80 + 50 + 50) for the service department. Since the manager of Branch A believes the service department is only half as important as the sales department, the service department's maximum effectiveness score is adjusted to 80 (50 percent of 160). This value is shown in Figure 8.4 as the adjusted maximum effectiveness score. The roll-up correction factor for the service department is 4.63 (370/80). The current month's roll-up effectiveness score for actual performance for three feedback charts for the sales department in Branch A is 60 (75, 0, − 15). The sales department's performance of 60 is plotted for the manager of Branch A on a roll-up chart. Similarly, the rolled-up effectiveness score for the actual performance of the service department in Branch A is 202 (90, 50, 50, − 10, 22) and is plotted for the manager of Branch A on a roll-up chart.

If the numbers on the roll-up charts are increasing (showing improvement) or can be adequately explained by the department managers if decreasing, the branch manager would have no interest in seeing the department feedback charts. To roll the two departments up to Branch A, follow this procedure: The roll-up score of the sales department of 60 is added to 43.6 (202/4.63), the adjusted roll-up score of the service department. The sum is 103.6 (60 + 43.6), the branch roll-up score. It

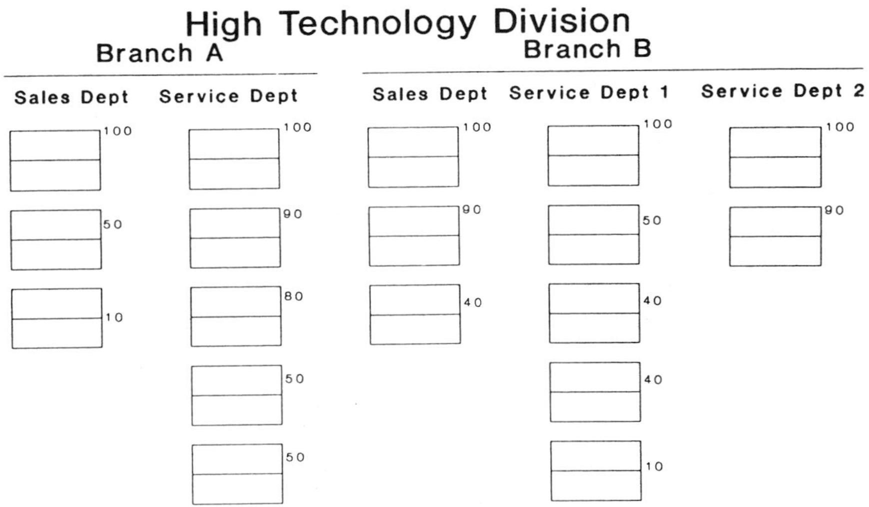

High Technology Division

Branch A / Branch B

	Sales Dept (A)	Service Dept (A)	Sales Dept (B)	Service Dept 1 (B)	Service Dept 2 (B)
Maximum Effectiveness Score	160	370	230	240	190
Adjusted Maximum Effectiveness Score	160	80	76	171	190
Roll-Up Correction Factor	—	4.63	3.03	1.40	—
Roll-Up Effectiveness Score	60	202	200	160	100
Adjusted Roll-Up Score		43.6	66	114	
Branch Roll-Up Score	103.6		280		

FIGURE 8.4 Rolling Up Across Branches

is this number that is monitored by the branch manager with a roll-up chart.

Figure 8.4 shows Branch B with three departments. Their maximum effectiveness scores are 230 (100 + 90 + 40) for the sales department, 240 (100 + 50 + 40 + 40 + 10) for service department 1, and 190 (100 + 90) for service department 2. Suppose for the current measurement period, the roll-up scores for the actual performance of the three departments are, respectively, 200, 160, and 100. (Note that these are actual performance scores, not maximum effectiveness scores.) These numbers are plotted separately on roll-up charts for the respective department managers.

Suppose the manager of Branch B believes the sales department and service department 1 are only 40 and 90 percent, respectively, as important to the branch mission as service department 2. If so, the maximum effectiveness scores of the sales department and service department 1 must be reduced for purposes of roll-up to the branch by these percentages. These adjusted maximum effectiveness scores are 76 (190 × .40) for the sales department and 171 (190 × .90) for service department 1. The corresponding roll-up correction factors are 3.03 (230/76) for the sales department and 1.40 (240/171) for service department 1.

To roll up to Branch B, the roll-up scores for the actual performance of the sales department and service department 1 must be adjusted by the roll-up correction factors to take into account their lesser importance relative to service department 2. These adjustments are 66 (200/3.03) for the sales department and 114 (160/1.40) for service department 2. After adjustment, roll-up for the current period's actual performance is accomplished by adding the rolled up scores of 66 for the sales department to 114 for service department 1 to 100 for service department 2 to a sum of 280.

From the viewpoint of the Branch B manager, the performance of the branch can now be monitored on the roll-up chart. Again, if the numbers on the roll-up chart are increasing (showing improvement), or can be explained if decreasing, the branch manager should have no interest in seeing the department's feedback charts. He/she should appreciate the need for the self-control in subordinate units.

Before explaining how to roll up the two branches to the division, it is important to reemphasize that original feedback charts developed at lower levels are unaffected by adjustments for roll-up. Managers, supervisors, and workers at lower levels may continue to use the feedback charts and other products, such as roll-up charts, as initially developed.

The first step in rolling up the two branches to the division, as summarized in Figure 8.5, involves a discussion between the facilitator and the division manager to secure a judgment about the relative contributions of the two branches to the division mission. This is identical to the procedure used to roll-up across work centers and departments. The branch which the division managers think makes the most important contribution to the division mission is given the rank of 1 and automatically assigned an effectiveness value of 100. The other branch is ranked 2, and the importance of its contribution is determined by the division manager relative to 100. Of course, the branches may be judged to make equal contributions and, if so, would both receive ranks of 1 and effectiveness scores of 100.

If both branches are equally important, then the unequal maximum effectiveness scores for both branches, 240 (160 + 80) for Branch A and 437 (76 + 171 + 190) for Branch B, must be made equal. Consequently, Branch B's maximum effectiveness score must be adjusted to 240 because its importance must be made equal to the importance of Branch A, and therefore its roll-up correction factor is 1.82 (437/240). As a result, the division maximum effectiveness score is 480 (240 + 240).

To roll up the rolled-up scores for the actual performance of the two branches—103.6 (60 + 43.6) for Branch A and 280 (66 + 114 + 100) for Branch B—Branch B's rolled up score must be adjusted to 191.8 (280/1.46) with the roll-up correction factor to make the branch contributions equal. The two branch rolled-up scores may then be summed to 295.4 (103.6 + 191.8), and this may be considered the baseline for a roll-up chart for use by the division manager.

Suppose, on the other hand, the division manager believes that Branch B is only 80 percent as important to the division mission as Branch A. Branch B's maximum effectiveness score of 437 must be adjusted to 192 (240 × .80), and the corresponding roll-up correction factor is 2.28 (437/192). As a result, the division's maximum effectiveness score is 432 (240 + 192).

Before Branch B's rolled up score on actual performance is added to the corresponding rolled up score of Branch A (103.6), it must be adjusted to 122.8 (280/2.28). The two branch roll-up scores for actual performance may then be summed to 226.4 (103.6 + 122.8), and this value may be considered the baseline for a roll-up chart for use by the division manager.

Thus, it is possible for managers at various levels to receive rolled-up data on the actual performance of their subordinate units. Managers are strongly cautioned that misuse of feedback and roll-up charts will defeat the basic objectives of TQM/MGEEM. These charts are not intended as tools for the micro-management of subordinates. To the contrary, they are intended to increase subordinates' self-control and, thereby, restore their

	Branch A	Branch B
Maximum Effectiveness Scores	240	437
Roll-Up Effectiveness Scores	103.6	280
If both branches are equally important:		
Adjusted Maximum Effectiveness Scores	240	240
Roll-Up Correction Factor	—	1.82
Division Maximum Effectiveness Score	480	
Adjusted Roll-Up Effectiveness Scores	103.6	191.8
Division Effectiveness Score	295.4	
If Branch B is 80% as important as Branch A:		
Adjusted Maximum Effectiveness Scores	240	192
Roll-Up Correction Factor	—	2.28
Division Maximum Effectiveness Score	432	
Adjusted Roll-Up Effectiveness Scores	103.6	122.8
Division Effectiveness Score	226.4	

FIGURE 8.5 Rolling Up to a Division

right to take pride in their work, and experience feelings of craftsmanship.

Consequently, managers above the managers of target organizations, wherever they exist within a company, should not expect to routinely monitor feedback charts. They must be content to use roll-up charts as a basis for *how goes its, standups,* or whatever names they use for periodic review sessions with their subordinates. They must leave feedback charts to the use of their subordinate target organization managers as long as performance is satisfactory or explained.

When performance is unsatisfactory, higher-level managers must resist resorting to the fire-fighting tradition of Western management. They must not leap into the breach to solve the crisis themselves.

Instead, utmost care must be taken by higher-level managers to use such problems as opportunities for their subordinate managers to learn and develop their leadership abilities. Here, higher-level managers have opportunities to demonstrate real leadership. They must perform as role models of the true leader's behavior. What does this involve? It involves the role of facilitator, mentor, cheerleader, and guide. It does *not* involve telling subordinates how to solve problems and checking to see that they did what they were told. It involves asking a few key, perhaps solution-suggestive, questions and much listening.

Managers can assess their performance in changing their behavior from micro-manager to that of real leadership in at least two key ways:

First, in encounters with subordinates they can keep mental note of who does the most talking. The worst micro-managing approach is for the manager to do all the talking. "Now, you listen to me. I'll tell you how to solve this crisis. After I tell you, you go do it and I'll come around later to check to see that you did what I told you to do." That's not leadership. Real leadership involves asking questions and listening to help subordinates clarify the situation and map out and evaluate alternative actions. Such questions include: "What's our situation here?" (Note: it's *our* situation, not *your* situation.) "What are 'we' up against?" "Have we got all the key players here to try to get the situation clarified?" "What's your perspective on this thing, Sheree?" "Can you shed any light on this issue, José?" "Fred, you've got some experience here, don't you? Tell us about it." "Now we seem to have two alternatives. Which do you prefer, Kathy?" One of the key jobs of any leader is to develop new leaders in their subordinates.

There is a second way managers can assess their progress in changing their role from micro-manager to that of real leader. This is illustrated by the extent to which the users of feedback charts are target organization personnel and their manager, rather than the higher-level manager.

The worst case is when a higher-level manager calls in subordinates and uses feedback charts to conduct fire-fighting on the spot. "Frank, here's where you went wrong! It's on the 'timeliness of repair' feedback chart. Here's what I want you to do about it."

Of course, the correct approach is to leave the feedback charts where they belong, in the hands of subordinates who built them, and ask questions within the management framework they provide. In a feedback meeting, the charts should remain in the hands of the subordinates. The boss should say such things as, "Frank, what do your feedback charts tell you about this situation?" "Have we got the charts built right?" "Do we need to do some fine-tuning on the charts?" "What are our alternatives for a solution?" Within an environment structured by feedback charts, subordinates talk and the boss counsels, facilitates, cheerleads, and, above all, listens.

Discussions about unsatisfactory performance are at the very heart of the TQM/MGEEM system. Unsatisfactory performance, usually brought out by minus effectiveness scores, must be regarded as opportunities to improve. In these discussions subordinates should be encouraged to study the processes which drive their performance and quality (as measured by the effectiveness scores on their feedback charts). It is here that subordinates can best work to identify barriers to improvement. It is here that managers must mentor their subordinates and take action on their recommendations about how to remove barriers and improve processes. The details of how to use feedback charts for continuous improvement are explained in Chapters 10 and 11.

CHAPTER

9

IMPROVING LEADERSHIP WITH TQM/MGEEM

Chapters 2 through 8 explained how to build a TQM/MGEEM system. This chapter describes opportunities for improved leadership with TQM/MGEEM after it is established. Before exploring this, however, it is important to elaborate on the philosophy of management which promotes an organizational climate conducive to the success of TQM/MGEEM.

TQM/MGEEM Management Philosophy

Managers in the United States and other Western countries share a common set of attitudes about how to operate an organization. There is increasing evidence that rather than helping, many of these attitudes actually reduce organizational effectiveness. The most harmful result of such attitudes is that they prevent managers and their organizations from achieving their full potential. These attitudes keep managers from seeing the paths to genuine success. For this reason, I refer to them as *blinding* attitudes. It is important that these blinding attitudes be identified so that managers may consider rethinking them.

The first blinding attitude can be traced to the thinking of persons whose influential and provocative books appeared over the last several hundred years. Among these is a Scottish economist, Adam Smith, who over 200 years ago wrote that if every individual is allowed to pursue his or her own self-interests, an "invisible hand" will guide the economy so that the welfare of the majority is maximized.

In the mid-1800s, the British philosopher and scientist Herbert Spencer proposed that certain people are better-suited than others to certain environments. It is these people, he said, who will survive. This philosophy has been interpreted to suggest the idea of "survival of the fittest," that only those who are strong and aggressive will prosper.

Philosophies like those of Smith and Spencer encourage rugged individualism, competition, and the expectation that someone must win and someone must lose. Carrying this kind of thinking to an extreme, Western managers see the world of work as a jungle where they must kill or be killed. Subordinates are to be used, burned out if necessary, to enhance one's own career; co-workers are dangerous competitors in the struggle for promotion; superiors are buttered up for their support and then, after promotion, shoved aside. When managers lose a battle in the dog-eat-dog world of corporate and office politics they often bide their time and look for a chance to take revenge.

Beyond the suffering of self, families, colleagues, and subordinates, a harmful result of this competitive attitude is that one's career often takes on a higher priority than leading the organization to accomplish its mission. Rather than doing what is right or is in the best interests of the organization, a highly career-oriented manager may think mainly of self.

There is a confusing dimension to this competitiveness issue. If we conducted a survey of whether people would prefer to live in cooperation or competition, goodwill or hostility, harmony or conflict, is there any doubt about what most of them would say? Do people want cooperation or competition with their spouse? Do people want harmony or conflict among their subordinates? Do people want goodwill and harmony between their kids and their playmates? What are the teachings of every great religious and moral leader across history? Do they teach brotherly love or encourage conflict? Consider the nature of your own moral convictions. Which do you prefer, harmony or conflict? Yet, even though most people want harmony, much of our lives and especially our work lives is based on competition.

Unfortunately, few Western managers see the advantages of cooperation. They believe the world is a zero-sum game. For every winner there has to be a loser. They believe there isn't enough money to go around. For everyone that's rich, someone must be poor. (They weren't paying attention in their finance class during the lecture on the velocity of money.) They believe there are just so many pieces of pie, and too few to provide a piece to everyone, so someone must finish dinner with no dessert. They see the world as six wolves who have only five bones, so one wolf must go without a bone. Like these unfortunate wolves, they think they must continually fight among themselves to survive. Isn't there a better way?

In the story of the wolves, the wolves eventually learned that if they would work together as a pack no one would have to go without a bone. This, of course, led to the development of the wolf pack. Too few Western managers understand the story of the evolution of the wolf's hunting style, or advantages of cooperation. Western managers must learn that there is a time to fight alone, but there also is a time to join forces for even greater victories through cooperation.

There are those who teach managers raised in the competitive tradition to give up their aggressive, self-seeking approach to life. They advise them to consider their religion. They advise them to stop being aggressive and, instead, seek harmony with nature and mankind. To suggest this to a manager who lives in the dog-eat-dog world of fierce competition is like advising a gladiator to put down his sword in the middle of a fight. No sensible manager believes this advice because he/she knows it simply doesn't work. If everyone changed at once, it would be OK, but if one gladiator puts down his sword in the middle of a fight and the other gladiators don't, you know what will happen. The swordless gladiator will be killed. To give such advice to managers only destroys a teacher's credibility.

A better approach is to suggest to managers that they slowly begin a journey from their present attitude of competition, hostility, and conflict to a future attitude of cooperation, goodwill, and harmony. Unfortunately, it may be generations before this change can be fully completed.

The first step is to suggest that managers practice the team approach. According to this familiar approach, it is appropriate to compete among each other to win a position on the team. Once team positions have been determined, however, we must cast aside individual differences and struggle fiercely against the other team. For instance, there is intense rivalry for starting positions on professional sports teams, but once the season starts fights seldom occur between members of the same team. Individual differences are forgotten, and a spirit of teamwork prevails. The focus must be on beating the other team. The same approach should be recommended for application in organizations.

Upon hearing advice that they should adopt the team approach, managers often respond that this is, in fact, how things are done. It is obvious that employees do form teams, since companies are a kind of team, which struggle in fierce competition against other teams.

The real problem is that usually there is little cooperation and often outright conflict among the departments or divisions of the same company. People who work in a certain department often don't see themselves as members of the company team and may have a far stronger sense of loyalty to their department, e.g., the engineers stick together, the accountants stick together, the production people stick together, etc.

Rather than cooperate with other departments for the good of the company, there are menacing, bare-knuckle relations among departments. This is comparable to all the first basemen or pitchers sticking together against the rest of the baseball team. It doesn't make sense. In such rivalries, everyone suffers. When the team loses, the first basemen lose, the second basemen lose, etc.

Strange as it may seem, competition severely reduces effectiveness in Western organizations. Consequently, senior managers must strive to lessen this competition. In particular, senior managers must ensure that company policies do not promote competition within the company. Recognition, reward, promotion, and other personnel systems must respond to actions which evidence intracompany cooperation, and do not promote competition. Personnel systems must not encourage managers to advance their own careers by exploiting their subordinates, or making other departments look bad.

A second blinding attitude about how to manage organizations is based on the half-century-old writings of Frederick Winslow Taylor, the father of scientific management. Taylor and his associates asserted that, through study, the "one best way" to accomplish any job or work can be determined. These "one best ways" are taught to workers, and a cadre of supervisors is established to ensure that workers accomplish jobs exactly as taught (pp. x–xi).[41] Today, Taylor's philosophy pervades the thinking of virtually every manager in the Western world. When an innovative worker says "Hey, boss, I've got a better way to do this job," a Taylor-style supervisor says:

> Look, son, smarter minds than yours and mine developed this approach. Why don't you just fall into step with the rest of us? I'm sure you'll eventually see that our way is best. You don't want anyone to get the idea that you're a troublemaker!

Of course, the problem with Taylor's "one best way" is that the world is constantly changing. Better ways to do things come along every day, but many managers slavishly adhere to the rules. They go by the book, and are unable to show leadership. Leadership is not maintaining the status quo, it is managing in a spirit of continual improvement. Managers who go by the book eventually choke on their own rules as innovative competitors attract away their customers. Going by the rules keeps them doing things the same way year after year as their competitors change and continually improve. By adhering rigidly to the rules, they do great damage to their subordinates, their company, and the country.

Effective managers create organizational climates that welcome change and innovation; they share the planning and improvement of work with their subordinates. In such a climate, suggestions are welcomed with a sense of excitement because they represent opportunities for improvement. The acid test of the existence of this kind of climate is whether workers and managers *welcome* customer complaints as opportunities for improvement. Additionally, how does an organization change and improve in response to a customer suggestion? Remember that a key role of the quality council is to establish a policy on quality. The heart of this policy must be that senior managers will enthusiastically authorize any change that will improve the way business is conducted. To do otherwise would be a demonstration of the council shirking one of its most important responsibilities!

A third blinding management attitude is an overconcern with results, usually short-term results. The reasons why this happens are well understood. One reason stems from the fact that many Western organizations are corporations. As such, they are financed with equity (not debt) and the selling price of their stock is strongly influenced by quarterly earnings statements. Stockholders and Wall Street regard these quarterly earnings statements as measures of the corporation's health. These statements help investors form decisions about where to invest. Consequently, there is pressure on managers to make these quarterly (short-term) statements look good. The emphasis is on the short- rather than the long-term. As is more common in Japan, debt financing places greater emphasis on security of investment and long-term growth. Most Western managers are too focused on the next quarterly earnings statement, pressuring them to think short-run.

A second reason for Western managers' overconcern with results is that often they are so unfamiliar with the work they manage that they must rely on numbers to tell them what's going on.

There are several reasons why managers are so often unfamiliar with the work they manage. (1) Organizations like to diversify into activities that bring in profits in periods when earnings would otherwise be flat or in a slump. Unfortunately, the managers of acquiring companies often do not fully understand the work of the companies thus acquired. (2) There are career, financial, and organizational pressures on managers to move around within the same company and from one company to another. For example, a person with a marketing background gets promoted to plant manager where understanding the work involves knowledge of industrial engineering. Another example is evident in the military where pilots are an elite corps and benefit from fast promotion. Frequently, when their flying careers end to make room for younger pilots, they are made commanders of organizations with activities for which they may have little technical knowledge.

Managers who don't fully understand the work for which they are responsible often must adjust by relying on the bean counting technique of cost accounting and finance to hold the activities to standards. To survive, they learn to think in terms of results. They are forced to adopt a control- and compliance-oriented management style. Unfortunately, the standards they use may not really apply to the organizations in question and frequently restrict the achievement of their full potential. This restriction of potential occurs because personnel must divert time for their core responsibilities to handle the added paperwork required by the standards.

This trend toward reliance on control and compliance has manifested itself across the years in great interest in learning more about managerial accounting and finance. It has made B.B.A. and M.B.A. programs the cash cows of United States universities, and inspired a variety of so-called improvement programs, such as management by objectives (MBO), zero-base budgeting, zero defects, and management by results (MBR).

There also is an unfortunate tendency for managers new to a job to have to quickly produce some form of achievement. Rather than building on what one's predecessor began, new managers often feel the need to start something new that can be measured with accounting to succeed over the short period of time that they are in the job. Starting new programs or changing the orientation and emphasis of existing programs can, of course, have a destabilizing effect on an organization. When this happens, personnel can lose their sense of purpose. When the purpose changes with every new manager, an organization loses its sense of constancy of purpose.

Many problems arise from overconcern with results, including short-term effects detracting from essential long-term planning. Since basic research always is part of long-term planning, funding for this vital activity often gets deleted from planning documents.

Another harmful effect of overconcern with results is that as long as things are going as planned, no one thinks about or improves the work which produces the results. Managers like to say "If it ain't broke, don't fix it." When results do not go as planned, however, the typical Western manager senses a great urgency to find someone to blame for the problem and to "fix" something to put results back on track. Of course, blaming people for problems makes them less willing to take risks and innovate, and fixing something is merely fire-fighting.

Blaming someone and fire-fighting, however, are standard ways of life for almost all Western managers. To overcome this attitude, they should try to realize that work which is understood and properly managed will produce satisfactory results. Their emphasis should be on understanding and improving work, not just on watching results. Enlightened managers consider it essential to make improvements even when things are running smoothly. They appreciate the need to innovate, to continually make things better. Rather than saying "If it ain't broke, don't fix it," they prefer the childhood jingle, "Everyday in every way we are getting better and better." Enlightened managers know that it is important to become intimately familiar with the work they manage and not limit their attention to results. They know that if work is managed properly, results will take care of themselves.

Most Western managers like to think of themselves as being on top of things, as "watching the figures." In such situations, little improvement occurs. The consequences of watching the figures are that stress levels increase, morale goes down, and the organization becomes less effective.

Management by objectives (MBO) and employee performance appraisals are illustrations of too much focus on results and too little focus on methods. In MBO, supervisors and subordinates jointly agree on goals for the subordinates for a next period of performance. Later, subordinates are evaluated against these goals. There is seldom much concern about how to improve the methods or processes by which subordinates accomplish their goals. There is a virtual absence of knowledge in management of the importance of improving processes, such as reducing red tape and other barriers, so subordinates' efforts can be more effective. In MBO, management's interest usually is confined mainly to results, accomplishing the goals, not in improving the means by which goals are to be accomplished. Are employees properly trained to achieve the goals? Do they use the best methods available to achieve the goals? Do they have the proper tools for their work?

In the case of performance appraisals, employees are periodically appraised, again with the focus usually entirely on results. Normally, management shows little or no appreciation for the need to improve the means by which results are accomplished.

A ridiculous example of the use of performance appraisals comes from the teaching field. The teaching effectiveness of professors at many colleges is appraised by questionnaires completed by their students. Questions commonly found on such questionnaires include "Would you take another course from this professor?" "Would you recommend this professor to your friends?" "How does this professor compare with other professors you have known?" "Would you say that this professor is much better, better, about the same, worse, or much worse than the average professor at this university?"

Most university administrators are content to carry this exercise no further than returning summary data on the completed questionnaires to professors as feedback and using questionnaire results to rank professors for merit pay.

Few university administrators understand the necessity of improving the *processes* which produce the results measured by questionnaires. For instance, is training provided on how to be an effective teacher? Are workshops provided on teaching methods? Are opportunities available for dialogue among professors about teaching methods? Are professors asked if there is anything the university administration can do to help them become more effective in the classroom? Are facilities satisfactory? Are lecture halls adequate? Comfortable? Properly air conditioned and lighted?

Consider how a professor must feel to learn from the results of a questionnaire that he or she is ranked by most students as "worse than" or "much worse than" their fellow professors. Suppose the professor wants to improve. Most professors want to improve and do a good job as they seldom are in this profession for the money. Is there any guidance in this kind of feedback about how to get better? There is not! Think how helpless such a professor or any other employee feels when subjected to this kind of cruel performance appraisal.

It's comparable to giving a student a grade of C on an examination without any counseling about how to improve next time. It's as though the grade itself tells the student everything he/she needs to know about how to improve. "Just study harder!" No information is provided about how to reform one's study habits, and there is certainly no recognition of the possibility that a student's grade may be influenced by factors beyond the student's control, such as a poorly written textbook; an ineffective teacher; inadequate homework; or a noisy, crowded classroom.

If a physician merely looks to a thermometer to identify the cause of a patient's fever, it is obvious a different attitude is needed. Results of any kind should be used to kick off a search for problems and ways to improve. Results of all kinds, i.e., a student's grades or a patient's temperature, should be considered as a source of diagnostic information. Results always must be followed up with a search for ways to improve the process which produced the result.

Adopting a different way of thinking about these blinding attitudes is not easy for United States managers. Most Americans grew up competing, trying to beat someone out for shortstop or the lead in a high school play. We competed with peers to enter college or the plumber's union. We cheer for our favorite teams on television. We see competition everywhere, and we compete in many facets of our lives, e.g., we want to drive a better car than the next person; we want a better lawn than the person who lives next door; we want our children to outperform other schoolchildren. We think being an engineer is better than being a bookkeeper or vice versa; we think our department is better than those down the hall; we think that plumbers do more of a day's work than clerks, or vice versa. We were taught that there is a right and wrong way to hold a baseball bat or violin, fix a faucet, or find an error in a ledger. We watch the scoreboard. We say, "If you don't play to win, why keep score?"

For people who think this way, change does not come easy. After some thought, in fact, most managers will insist that their aggressive, competitive attitudes actually have contributed to their success. It's no wonder these attitudes are difficult and, in many cases, impossible to modify. Modifying these blinding attitudes will, however, make leadership with TQM/MGEEM more successful. The remainder of this chapter discusses opportunities for leadership with a TQM/MGEEM system in place.

TQM/MGEEM and Leadership

To discuss how to improve leadership with TQM/MGEEM, consider the illustration of the sales department of the high-tech company discussed earlier and shown in Figure 9.1. The manager and employees of this department have worked through the TQM/MGEEM development process. They have revisited their mission statement, identified customers and suppliers, and developed KRAs, indicators, and feedback charts. In

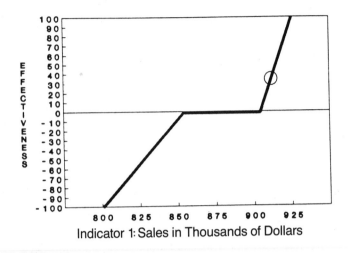

Indicator 1: Sales in Thousands of Dollars

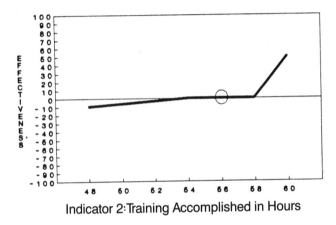

Indicator 2: Training Accomplished in Hours

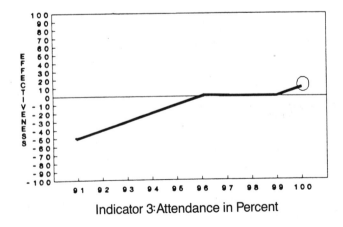

Indicator 3: Attendance in Percent

FIGURE 9.1 Feedback Charts for a Sales Department

the developmental process, the manager was a member of the Blue Team. In that effort, the manager came to better appreciate that the sales department has customers and suppliers. The manager stressed the importance of this knowledge to other members of the department. Consequently, the department established better communication with its customers and suppliers to develop a stronger sense of harmony and cooperation in the interest of continually improving the way business is conducted.

The manager learned that if the department is to improve, management must create an environment conducive to change. The manager discovered that management must authorize the removal of barriers to good work.

Revisiting their mission statement and identifying KRAs helped the manager and workers understand more fully how the efforts of the sales department fit into the company's overall goals. Every leader should understand this relationship and communicate it to his/her subordinates. People must know how their work fits into the overall scheme of things.

TQM/MGEEM as a Management Information System (MIS)

TQM/MGEEM provides much useful information about the operation of an organization. In Figure 9.1's illustration of the sales department, the two KRAs make it clear that the mission is to sell high-tech products and to maintain a well-trained staff. The three indicators provide measures of how well the department is accomplishing its two KRAs. There is one feedback chart for each indicator.

Feedback charts show the relationship between performance on each indicator (on the horizontal axes) and the department's overall effectiveness (on the vertical axes). Slopes on feedback charts show the importance of indicators: A flat slope means an indicator is less important, and a steep slope means an indicator is more important. For example, comparison of slopes on the feedback charts in Figure 9.1 indicates that sales is more important to the department's overall effectiveness than training or attendance. (The slope on the sales chart is steeper than the slopes on the other two charts.)

The charts also show that when the sales department performs at its feasible best on all three indicators, sales of $925,000 has an impact of 100 effectiveness points while accomplishing 60 training hours and 100 percent attendance have impacts of only 50 and 10 effectiveness points, respectively. Thus, feedback charts depict department policy about the importance of indicators. Doing well in sales is more important than doing well in training or attendance. This does not mean that the manager of the sales department can neglect training or attendance. The charts for these two areas show that completing only 48 hours of training has a small negative effect of -10 effectiveness points, but 91 percent attendance has a seriously negative effect of -50 effectiveness points.

As organizations strive to improve, feedback charts provide periodic information to managers on the status of improvements. Results of performance on each indicator are recorded monthly on feedback charts and provided to the manager and all other members of the sales department. Feedback charts also are posted on the department's bulletin boards. Suppose last month's performance on the three indicators of the sales department was $910,000 in sales, 56 hours of training, and 100 percent attendance. Letters representing performance levels for given months are plotted on the slopes of the charts shown in Figure 9.1. In other words, performance through time is noted on feedback curves with letters representing months. For instance, O could represent October, N could represent November, etc. The results posted in Figure 9.1 show that in the current month, say October, the sales department is as effective as currently feasible in attendance (100 percent) and that the training level (56 hours) has no positive or negative impact on effectiveness. The current level of sales ($910,000) is above the indifference point (zero effectiveness) or "don't rock the boat" point, but considerable room for improvement remains. At the end of the next month, performance results will be recorded again on the three feedback charts and provided to the manager and all other members of the sales department. November performance can then be compared with October performance. Thus, with a TQM/MGEEM system in place, managers can monitor performance from month to month to track the results of performance management initiatives and other influences, e.g., seasonal and advertising effects on sales.

Another aspect of a TQM/MGEEM MIS is that a summary of a department's performance can be rolled up each month to the next level of supervision on a roll-up chart. (The technical features of the roll-up chart are discussed in Chapter 8.)

Information from roll-up charts provides a quick overview of performance, e.g., the sales department's effectiveness (the sum of the current period's vertical axis effectiveness scores on each of its three feedback charts) for a given period (one month or an average of several months) is plotted on a roll-up chart. The performance of the sales department for October was 45 effectiveness points (the sum of 35 effectiveness points for sales of $910,000, zero effectiveness points for 56 hours of training, and 10 effectiveness points for 100 percent attendance). The 45 is simply plotted on a roll-up chart as shown in Figure 9.2. Subsequent months' effectiveness scores also are plotted in this manner, e.g., if the next month's (November's) overall effectiveness improved by 10, the new point of 55 would be plotted on the roll-up chart in Figure 9.2. This chart can be useful to the next higher level of management as it keeps him/her apprised of the overall performance of the sales department in a manner that requires no great expenditure of time.

In the early stages of a TQM/MGEEM implementation, the next higher level managers usually will want to review the feedback charts of lower-level units, but with time they should feel comfortable with information only from roll-up charts. Returning to our example, as long as the trend on the roll-up chart is positive (showing improvement), or otherwise adequately explained by the sales department manager, the higher-level manager may continue the business of providing leadership from that level of management. Satisfied with the roll-up chart, there should be no reason for the higher-level manager to want to see the sales department's feedback charts. Remember that the higher-level manager was a member of the Blue Team in the TQM/MGEEM development process, so reviewing the system after its initial development should be infrequent, perhaps never unless the mission changes.

New Management Tools

In addition to displaying performance on indicators through feedback charts, TQM/MGEEM provides several powerful management tools. To discuss these tools, consider again the feedback charts of the sales department shown in Figure 9.1.

The first management tool provided by TQM/MGEEM comes from the fact that the slopes of feedback charts show the importance of indicators and, therefore, suggest priorities for increasing performance. For example, which of the three indicators of the sales department has the greatest potential for improving effectiveness? Should the manager seek to increase sales, training, or attendance? The answer is sales because of its steeper slope. Improving sales from $900,000 to $910,000 will increase effectiveness (on the vertical axis) by 35 points whereas increasing training hours from 56 to 58 has no positive or negative impact on effectiveness, and no gain at all is possible in attendance because it is already 100 percent.

A second and similar management tool provided by TQM/MGEEM is that the slopes of feedback charts are guides to decisions about allocating resources. Almost always resources are allocated to indicators with the steepest slopes and, therefore, where the potential gain in effectiveness is

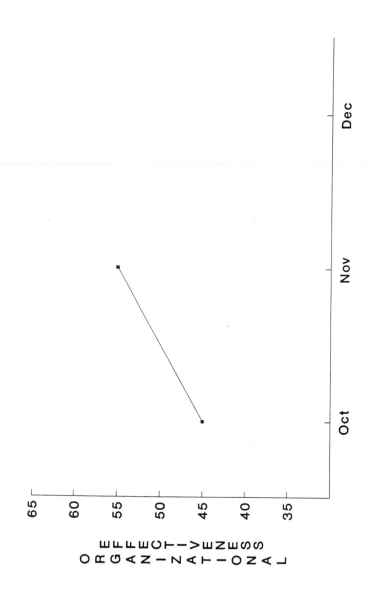

FIGURE 9.2   A Roll-Up Chart of a Sales Department

greatest. However, there are exceptions to this rule. Slopes of feedback charts provide information about potential gain in effectiveness, but do not consider the relative cost of improving performance on indicators. Thus, studying the slopes of several feedback charts may suggest that improvement on one indicator promises greater gain than improvement on a second indicator. A knowledgeable manager, however, may decide to allocate resources to the second indicator, even though it has a flatter slope than the first, because the cost of improvement on the first indicator is too high relative to the gain in effectiveness which will occur. Feedback charts provide no information about how easy or difficult it is to improve on indicators. This information comes entirely from the judgment of experienced personnel and their knowledge of the processes which drive the indicator. Consequently, decisions about resource allocation should never be separated from the judgment of knowledgeable personnel.

Another type of resource allocation decision occurs when managers are required to scale down the activities of an organization. In the public sector, this may result from reduced government appropriations. In the private sector, it usually is reflected in budget cuts. In any case, managers often face tough decisions about where to take the cuts. "Shall I reduce service here or here?" "What shall I stop doing?" "What shall I decrease?" "My customers are still out there, but to which of them shall I reduce support?"

When a TQM/MGEEM system is in place, decisions about scaling down operations are made easier. The key is that the slopes of feedback charts show the relative importance of various components of an organization's mission, its KRAs. Again, when indicators on feedback charts have steep slopes, it means that the KRAs which they measure are important. Less important KRAs have flatter slopes. Remember that operational TQM/MGEEM systems, including the slopes of feedback charts, have been reviewed and approved by at least the next higher level of management. Since the slopes of the charts reflect the importance of KRAs, it stands to reason that the KRAs with the flattest indicator slopes are the mission's least important components and should be the first candidates for resource reduction.

Some resources support several indicators, a few of which may have steeper or flatter slopes. Managers who understand the processes which drive their indicators can make resource reduction decisions which consider such differences. They can reduce resources in noncritical mission areas while maintaining, or even increasing, resources in mission-critical areas. Before using a TQM/MGEEM system as a basis for resource allocation decisions, it is prudent to review it to ensure its relevance to the current situation.

After such a scaling down exercise has been completed it is advisable to reconvene the Blue Team of the target organizations to review the reduced scope of the mission statement. This review should result in management's approval of a reduction in the scope of the mission statement. It is unfair to personnel to reduce their resources while expecting them to maintain the same level of mission accomplishment.

A third management tool provided by TQM/MGEEM stems from the fact that fluctuations on feedback charts can be used to identify problem areas before they become serious. In the illustration of the sales department in Figure 9.1, suppose attendance falls from 100 percent in October to 96 percent in November. To the manager tracking attendance with a feedback chart it will be understood that attendance of less than 96 percent will have a serious negative impact on the department. Below that point, there aren't enough people around to adequately perform the required work. Thus, as long as attendance remains at or above 96 percent the manager may not have any reason for concern. When a downward trend is detected, however, the manager should become aware that there may be a problem with attendance.

Many people believe that most managers know what causes their indicators to fluctuate. Indeed, they *should* know! Understanding the underlying causes of bad and good performance on indicators is a key part of any manager's job. The sad truth is, however, that experience shows that few managers fully understand such causes.

One reason for their incomplete knowledge, as previously mentioned, is that most management training programs involve career broadening. In career broadening, managers are moved through many supervisory positions, presumably to provide a broader knowledge of how the company operates. The truth is, however, that managers usually are moved through various departments so rapidly that most of them never have time to thoroughly learn the work in each area. The problem is further aggravated by the often rapid promotion and mobility of managers.

If that isn't enough, it is a common belief that managers don't really have to understand a job to manage it! According to this view, all it takes to be a manager is to hold a meeting each Monday morning to tell workers what to do during the week and another meeting every Friday afternoon to find out if they did what they were told to do.

"Hold personnel to work standards and quotas! Micro-manage and bird-dog them all day long!" Many managers believe that's all there is to management. They have little conception about helping their subordinates.

The job of management should be to help their people do a better job, but most managers merely examine results. Fifteen years ago they established the *one best way* for workers to do a job, and now have little concern about understanding and improving how workers really get the job done. Such managers seldom listen to the workers. Most managers do more work with their mouths than with their ears. They never go down on the shop floor. They don't know whether the right tools are available. They don't know how often the machines don't function. They don't know how noisy the office gets. They merely view the results.

Another reason why many managers don't understand the factors that affect performance centers on what they do with their results. As mentioned earlier, when results don't go strictly according to plan, managers search frantically for someone to blame. After some poor soul is properly disciplined, fire-fighting begins. The managers try one corrective action after another—usually guesswork. What is needed, of course, is an attitude that takes the emphasis off of results and places it on understanding and continual improvement of the processes that produce the results.

As discussed above, a third management tool provided by TQM/MGEEM is that feedback charts allow managers to track performance to receive early warning signals that problems exist. *When a problem is suggested by an indicator moving in the wrong direction or not moving at all, the process or processes that produce the indicator must be studied to identify the problem.* (The preceding sentence is vitally important. Read it again, think about its meaning, and then read it once more.)

After thorough diagnosis, corrective action should be taken to fix the processes. Further tracking on the feedback chart will show if the processes are fixed. This is a fourth TQM/MGEEM management tool.

If processes are corrected and working properly, monthly tracking on their feedback charts will demonstrate movement on the indicators in the right direction. The key is that monthly tracking on feedback charts allows managers to monitor the effect of *continual improvement* of their processes. In other words, feedback charts detect the inevitable problems that creep into any process, but the emphasis must be on continually improving processes, not just blaming someone and fighting fires. It is important to know as soon as possible if a problem is fixed because often it is necessary to cease a resource-intensive corrective action.

Indicator tracking on feedback charts in TQM/MGEEM provides a fifth tool: evaluating alternative actions for improvement. One action to generate improvement could work better than another. If both actions work well, the less expensive or time-intensive action should be selected. Recognizing which action is best becomes obvious when tracking results on feedback charts. Possessing knowledge of alternative improvement actions' impact is an enormous benefit to managers.

Experienced managers worry that corrective action taken to fix a problem in one area may have an unknown impact somewhere else. Organizations with feedback charts in place are in a position to detect such effects, whether favorable or unfavorable. As a result, the use of feedback charts through TQM/MGEEM provide a sixth advantage: The charts help managers become more sensitive and knowledgeable about their actions' effects.

It may be obvious that feedback charts also can be successfully used to measure the effects of quick fixes and fire-fighting. Although occasionally inevitable, this approach to problem solving is strongly discouraged as a primary way of conducting business. The viewpoint encouraged here is that managers should abhor fire-fighting and seek to reduce it to a minimum. Instead, they should concern themselves with the continuous study and improvement of the processes by which business is conducted in their organization. Results of their efforts for improvement are illustrated by the movement of indicators on feedback charts. Using this periodic information allows managers to continuously learn about the performance of the processes for which they are responsible. When TQM/MGEEM is used, there is far less need for fire-fighting.

Occasionally the suggestion is made that performance on indicators should be presented in standard statistical format, e.g., various charts and graphs, rather than on feedback charts. Undoubtedly standard charts and graphs can play an important role in displaying information. There are, however, many reasons why they cannot replace feedback charts.

Perhaps the most important reason is that when a level of performance is posted on a standard chart or graph, there is no way to determine how bad or good that level is except in terms of past performance. On feedback charts, however, performance on an indicator (on a horizontal axis) is immediately understood in terms of its impact on organizational effectiveness (on a vertical axis). Possessing such knowledge is important to managers.

There is another key advantage of feedback charts over standard charts and graphs. Remember that all indicators are not of equal importance. In developing feedback charts, indicator feasible worsts and bests are weighted against one another, making indicators comparable. Knowing which indicators are more important and when performance on them is bad or good, of course, leads to the many powerful management tools previously explained: suggesting priorities for increasing effectiveness, providing guidance about resource allocation, assistance in scaling down operations, identifying problems, monitoring processes, knowing when processes are improving, knowing when problems are fixed, and evaluating alternative causes of action to take toward improvement. This valuable system is made possible through the use of feedback charts.

Feedback Charts and Control Charts

An insightful remark often made by students of Deming's philosophy is that taking a corrective action based on feedback charts may result in "tampering" with a process (or system). By this, they mean that a given monthly level of performance on a feedback chart may be nothing more than random variation, or chance. As such, they contend that this information is not a sound basis for taking action to change the process which produced it.

This remark is correct and suggests that users of feedback charts may wish to develop upper- and lower-control limits for each of their feedback charts to determine whether they can be considered predictive. (Statisticians will appreciate that the slope on a feedback chart corresponds to the horizontal axis of a control chart. Performance on any given indicator is recorded on the slope of its feedback chart for different time points relative to the "goodness" of the performance level as reflected on the chart's vertical effectiveness axis. It is these sample performance values that can be averaged to establish the nominal value and the standard error of the mean, or percent, for determining upper- and lower-control limits.)

When a process which drives the indicator on a feedback chart is shown by these limits to be out of control, action should be taken to bring it into control. On the other hand, when it is demonstrated by these limits that such a process is in control, the process should be studied for ways to improve it, i.e., to move its nominal value farther into the positive area on its feedback chart.

From the standpoint of statistical theory, feedback charts and control charts are similar to the extent that they meet and violate the same underlying assumption. (The assumption violated by both, of course, is the absence of independence of observations.) The statistical theory of control charts applies fully to feedback charts.

Considerable experience demonstrates that the processes which drive indicators on most feedback charts usually are in poor shape. Typically, their poor condition results from the work of the amateurs who initially designed the processes. These are individuals who do quality planning or front-end analysis in what are often called plans and programs departments. This is why Juran refers to the typical quality planning group as an "alligator hatchery."[22] He correctly suggests that those who originally establish processes usually do an inferior job.

Since processes typically function so poorly, managers who use feedback charts soon realize the depth of the problems they face in trying to improve them. They seldom have the time or interest, at least in the short term, in gathering enough samples to construct control limits. Usually, they are too busy taking the obvious action to improve them.

Despite this problem, strict control chart advocates may object to managers taking action to improve their processes before upper and lower limits have been established on the feedback charts involved. They argue that this may constitute tampering. My answer to this objection is that taking corrective action this early may be appropriate or inappropriate, depending on the situation.

The decades of experience of the Japanese Union of Scientists and Engineers (JUSE) suggests that 90 percent of all process problems can be identified for solution with simple statistical tools, not including the control chart. Furthermore, at a more practical level, many managers who are experienced in process improvement observe that the root causes of many process problems are so obvious that no form of statistical analysis is needed! They claim that what is required is leadership willing to listen to worker comments on what needs to be changed and enough courage to test and implement those suggested changes. For instance, workers may say "Get the delivery truck down here earlier," "Move the spare parts inventory closer to the work site," "Provide us with our own copier," "Get us the right tools for the job," "Provide the right kind of training," "Get us better lighting," "Clean up the toilets around here," or "Reduce the fire hazards." Obvious changes like these don't require control limits. Anyone can see that these changes are necessary. Such suggestions will be made by workers who aren't afraid to speak up about barriers, and appropriate changes will be authorized by managers who have been trained to listen and understand that improving processes is their responsibility.

The fact is that enormous gains can be made by these kinds of changes. (Chapters 10 and 11 provide details on how to use feedback charts and simple statistical techniques, such as the flow chart and cause-and-effect diagram, for this purpose.) After these types of improvements have been made, however, and in a variety of special situations, control charts can play a role for which no other statistical method is a substitute. However, I believe it is naive to think that every feedback chart must have control limits before beneficial action can be taken.

CHAPTER
10

CONTINUOUS IMPROVEMENT
WITH TQM/MGEEM

In addition to making possible improved leadership (as explained in Chapter 9) TQM/MGEEM is a process for creating continuous improvement. This takes place through the use of feedback meetings. To use feedback meetings effectively requires knowledge in the following areas:

1. Understanding the purposes of feedback meetings.
2. Conducting feedback meetings.
3. Involving customers and suppliers in feedback meetings.

The Purpose of Feedback Meetings

Feedback meetings have two basic purposes. The first purpose is to provide feedback to personnel on the results of their work. A considerable amount of research shows that feedback has many positive effects. Favorable feedback makes people feel good—it is motivational. Unfavorable feedback, when presented in a positive, constructive manner, represents a challenge and gives people something for which to strive. In many ways, such challenges can be used to train, build, and strengthen.

Additionally, people learn from feedback. They learn what does and doesn't work, and what to continue and stop doing. Whether feedback is positive or negative, people appreciate it because they like to know how they're doing.

The second purpose of feedback meetings is to give target organization managers feedback from their subordinates about what must be done to improve the way business is conducted. It is unfortunate that many Western managers resist using information from their subordinates as a basis for improvement. They are accustomed to telling subordinates what to do, not to listening to their ideas. In the best tradition of Western management, they believe improvement transpires because of revolutionary innovation. Such innovations are big jolts initiated by someone besides workers, usually the staff or a group of technical specialists, and are commonly capital-intensive. Normally, workers are only involved in these kinds of innovations in a passive way, when they are taught to use them. Examples of big jolts include new machinery, computers, and robots.

Instead of focusing entirely on big jolts to create improvement, managers must be taught to appreciate that hand-in-hand with dramatic, but infrequent, big jolt improvements there should be a companywide attitude of continual improvement in everything. This type of improvement is at least as important as that brought about by big jolts, and many observers believe it is more important. This kind of improvement occurs on a small, step-by-step basis. Usually, it is not capital-intensive, but involves everyone's direct participation in building on existing technology.

To achieve this type of improvement, all employees should be taught that everything about their work should be the object of study and improvement. Everything about their individual jobs and the entire company must be improved continuously in a deliberate, patient, never-ending manner. The outputs of every organization must improve in terms of higher quality and lower cost. These kinds of improvements often are imperceptible through time so that customers hardly notice them. When such an attitude is present, however, the products and services which internal and external customers receive simply continue to improve.

In feedback sessions, it is essential that managers demonstrate that the ghost of Frederick Winslow Taylor with his "one best way" does not haunt their organization. Managers must convince subordinates that they are sincere about improving the way business is conducted.

Remember, despite managers' statements to this effect, not all workers will initially participate by offering their ideas about improvement. They won't believe managers are serious. They have seen improvement programs come and go, and believe TQM/MGEEM is just one more way for managers to try to look good to the big boss.

Usually workers are justified in not trusting managers because many Western managers view workers as a resource to be exploited to enhance their own careers. Therefore, it is critical that managers *demonstrate* their commitment to improvement. The only way to demonstrate this commitment is to accept an employee's idea for an improvement and carry it out. Managers must actually make a change or remove a barrier which improves things. All the big talk and promises in the world won't convince workers of a manager's sincerity. Only actions will convince them!

It is ironic that the only way to convince most workers of management's sincerity is for management to take action to improve things. In other words, managers must do the job for which they are paid! Usually such improvements should have been made years ago.

Unfortunately, most Western managers don't realize that it is their job to make improvements. They think their job is to ensure compliance with rules and procedures by setting deadlines and exhorting workers to do a day's work. Many managers believe improvement is best achieved through fear by creating a reign of terror. In the meantime, they sit back and wait for big jolts to improve things. For many such managers, the big jolt comes in the form of offshore competition which puts their company out of business and them out of a job.

Many managers raise the question of whether workers really care if improvements are made in the way work is conducted. They reason that, unless workers are on incentives or piece rates, they get paid the same whether work methods are improved or not. Therefore, why should they care? Aren't most workers in their jobs just for the pay?

In one sense, this reasoning is sound. Like everyone else, workers must pay bills, put kids through college, and save for something special. My experience, however, suggests that they also are deeply concerned about improving the way work is conducted. Why is this? Because workers know better than anyone else that barriers stand in the way of their doing a good job. They realize that doing a satisfactory job makes them feel good about their work and themselves. They know that when their job performance is hampered by barriers it denies them the opportunity to do work of which they can be proud.

Who wants to do bad work? Who wants to be a poor performer? Who wants to work with bad tools? Who wants to work with replacement parts that don't fit? The answer is no one. Everyone wants to be proud of their work, and considered as a great employee. Everyone values the joy of being involved in important, meaningful work! For direct evidence of this, see the study by Weaver and Matthews.[47]

Besides being ironic, it is almost funny that the only way management can convince workers of their sincerity is for management to remove barriers. What is funny about this is that the barriers that prevent workers from doing a good job were put there in the first place by the managers themselves! In most companies, managers obsessed with control and compliance build mountains of red tape, paperwork, rules, regulations, and redundancy that stand in the way of genuine organizational effectiveness. Regardless of how hard workers try, these barriers almost always overpower their efforts and prevent them from realizing their full potential. Therefore, it is simply justice that the managers who created these barriers accept the responsibility for removing them.

How to Conduct a Feedback Meeting

Soon after a target organization's monthly performance results have been posted on feedback charts, the charts should be given to the manager for study and then provided to all personnel at feedback meetings. (In a large target organization it may be necessary to have several feedback meetings so everyone can be included.) As explained in Chapter 3, there are many target organizations in every company. This means that many feedback meetings should take place each month throughout a company using TQM/MGEEM. All of the personnel in each target organization, including the manager, supervisors, secretaries, part-timers, etc., should be present at its meetings. Before each meeting, everyone, especially new employees, should understand how feedback charts are built, what they mean, and how they are used.

Little formal structure or planned agenda is needed for a feedback meeting. Perhaps the position of chairperson should rotate among personnel on a lottery basis. When the first feedback meeting is held, the chairperson should start things off by distributing the current month's feedback charts with performance results noted on the slopes (with different letters representing the current month's and past several months' performance). Usually meetings begin with the chairperson posing a nominal question like, "How can we do better on our charts?" or a specific question about how to improve on a particular chart.

When workers feel secure, rest assured that they will have plenty to say in response to such questions. A general measure of how well TQM/MGEEM is working is the extent to which personnel are willing to speak their minds in feedback meetings.

After meetings have continued for several months and management feels secure with TQM/MGEEM, an even bolder question can be used to start the meetings. This question is, "What can management do to help us do a better job?"

The first few feedback meetings frequently turn into forums for airing grievances, abuses, and insults which personnel have suffered for years in silence at the occasionally unwitting hands of present and past management. Processing these feelings is healthy, and the chairperson, who for the first few meetings may be a trained facilitator, should focus on team building and urge everyone to bury the hatchet on old business. (In the many organizations where it is suspected that abuses of personnel have taken place, it may be helpful to precede the first feedback meeting by conducting a team building exercise, usually available through training departments.) Eventually the air will clear of expressions of grievances and a never-ending journey can begin to improve things.

An easel with chart paper should be available so the chairperson can write things down for all to see. Participants then begin to give answers to a nominal question such as, "How can we do better on our feedback charts?" or "What can management do to help us do a better job?" When team members are free to express their ideas as they come to mind, the discussion method is called *unstructured brainstorming*. In this approach, there is less pressure on participants to contribute ideas because anyone who wishes may refrain from participation, but there is a tendency in this method for aggressive and high status members to dominate. An alternative which prevents this by ensuring that everyone receives repeated opportunities to participate is called *structured brainstorming*. In this method, each participant is called on, in-turn, and given a chance to contribute. Of course, a reluctant, shy, or fearful person can say "Pass" and not participate, but each person is given repeated opportunities to speak. Continual nonparticipation throughout a structured brainstorming session occurs only in organizations filled with fear.

In a number of companies using TQM/MGEEM, the NGT (explained in earlier chapters) has been successfully used in feedback meetings as the vehicle for soliciting suggestions from feedback team members about areas in need of improvement. Some justify this use of the NGT on the grounds that some workers may be reluctant or fearful about speaking up in an open forum about supervisors or co-workers who they think are part of a performance problem. The NGT can be used in a manner that allows such workers to make anonymous inputs. For instance, suppose in a certain organization there is an uneven workload. Unknown to the manager, several workers sit in a back office and read the newspaper and visit with each other for the first hour of each work day. This is likely to concern other harder-working personnel who regard this as an injustice. They want to see everyone carry their fair share of the work, and the work load problem corrected. They may, however, be reluctant to introduce the problem in a feedback meeting in front of the malingerers because they might be their valued friends. Lack of training, motivation, pride in themselves, or, what is far more likely, past abuses by the system occasionally produce workers who will take advantage of their co-workers by not doing their fair share of the work. Of course, management wants to know about such problems to take corrective action. Thus, in feedback meetings there may be need for an alternative to *verbal* feedback.

During silent generation on the nominal question, answers are written on 3×5-inch cards, one answer per card. The instructions should be that no names or other information which could be used to identify workers submitting recommendations can be written on the cards. The completed cards are collected and shuffled in front of all participants. A short break is then taken while the chairperson and an assistant write the recommendations on sheets of chart paper, perhaps three or four suggestions per sheet. The cards are then disposed of so that no one can look at them to try to identify sponsors of suggestions from their handwriting. The feedback team is then reconvened to discuss the recommendations, one at a time.

To further ensure anonymity in a feedback meeting, participants may be called on in round-robin fashion to comment on a given recommendation even though all but one of them did not make it. In this approach, potentially unpleasant information can be presented and discussed in a manner that protects the identity of its sponsor.

The perspective in a feedback meeting where unpleasant information about personnel is presented should not be accusatory. No effort should be made to identify and reproach guilty persons. A better point of view is that we are all trying to improve the way we do business. Making changes for improvements is a way of life for us. In our earlier example, the work load problem is fixed and nothing is ever said to the malingering workers who afterward will carry their fair share of the work.

In feedback meetings, managers should listen intently and try to learn how to improve things, not play the role of judge. Reigns of terror should be ended. In feedback meetings, managers should help subordinates understand how important their work is in relation to the company's greater aims and how the mission of the target organization contributes to the company's larger mission. Managers should help their subordinates focus on improving relations with suppliers and customers. In this new role, some companies change titles from manager or supervisor to *coordinator*. Managers must create trust, reduce fear, and become role models of listening and learning. Managers must study Deming's philosophy of leadership.[7]

In conversations with subordinates, managers should do more work with their ears and less work with their mouths. This is an important initial step in the transformation of management style from that of creating a reign of terror to true leadership.

One way to do this is to use the *talk-listen* ratio. In conversations with subordinates, managers should be aware of how much time they talk in relation to how much time subordinates talk. Who talks the most? In the beginning, it is almost always the manager who talks the most. "I'll tell you what to do and you do it!" This is hardly what Deming means by leadership. This kind of statement must change to "What can I do to help you?" Managers must lessen the amount of time they talk and increase the amount of time their subordinates talk. Initially, this change will shock and surprise subordinates, but they will adjust quickly to the joy of being treated as an adult. Beyond this, however, managers must demonstrate their commitment to continuous improvement with action. They must "Walk like they talk!"

Naturally, changing the way business is conducted represents a considerable change for most United States managers trained in the finest traditions of Western management, including the belief that there is one best way to do things. Remember, however, the old management style is the path to economic ruin. A preferable view is that everything must get better and better. Nothing stays the same. Things either improve or degrade. (A few managers may need professional counseling to help them make this critical adjustment. This is money well spent by the company.)

In feedback meetings, discussion should focus on how to upgrade things. "How can we improve performance on our feedback charts?" Doing better on feedback charts, of course, means a higher level of mission accomplishment because feedback charts track performance on indicators which measure KRAs, the mission's key components.

As previously explained, experience shows that nearly all performance and quality problems result from barriers (e.g., unnecessary paperwork, needless layers of management, and an obsession with control and conformity) rather than from personnel being unwilling to work hard.

Therefore, it is almost always a waste of time to expect lasting gains in performance and quality by exhorting and micro-managing subordinates.

Unfortunately, there are many occasions when exhortation and micro-management have resulted in higher performance levels for a time period. These techniques work when managers have created such deplorable working conditions, devoid of joy and full of fear, that the only employees willing to tolerate such conditions are those who cannot find work elsewhere. Such employees are painfully grinding out the hours, putting in time until the 5 o'clock whistle blows and longing for Friday to come. When you pass them in the hall, they are the ones who say, "TGIF!" ("Thank goodness it's Friday!") They are forced to endure managerial abuses to put their kids through college or to pay off an unexpected debt, but they take no joy in their work. These poor souls have been reduced to working strictly for the money. How sad, but how common!

Almost everyone is willing to put their best efforts into their work, and to work hard. Almost everyone wants to accomplish something, and take pride in their work. Almost everyone wants their spouse and kids to be proud of what they do at work. Often, when employees don't work hard it is because they don't understand what they are supposed to be doing. They have not been trained. That is management's fault.

Other employees who don't work hard lack the aptitude for their job and should be transferred to a job in which they can be trained to excel. It's management's job to match people's abilities with job requirements, but by far, the largest share of employees who don't take pride in their work are responding to a work environment created by management which *itself* limits any real accomplishment.

Employees would gladly put more into their work if they could see any possibility of meaningful results. They review the past years and remember contributing many maximum efforts only to be frustrated time and again by barriers, e.g., equipment that didn't work properly, poor quality supplies, inadequate support, and supervisors who took credit for the results of the employees' labor.

Consequently, rather than exhorting subordinates to work harder, managers must understand that for the most part serious gains in performance and quality result from their own efforts to improve the manner in which work is conducted. A manager's most important responsibility is to improve work processes. Managers who fail to recognize and act on this responsibility are simply blind to the immense damage their inaction is doing to their subordinates, their company, and the United States.

How to Involve Customers and Suppliers in Feedback Meetings

In this text, emphasis is on creating harmonious, cooperative relationships between target organizations and their customers and suppliers. This involves real people talking about real problems. When customers, suppliers, and target organization personnel meet in feedback meetings they quickly develop a capacity to learn and to solve problems right where the action is. When empowered by enlightened senior management, faster, more realistic decisions are made in these *flexible networks* of customers, suppliers, and target organization personnel. There is no need for them to wait for wisdom from above before they solve a customer problem.

The purpose of working with customers in feedback meetings is to better understand their expectations. It is through understanding that target organizations can continually improve the way they do business to better satisfy customer expectations. The purpose of working with suppliers, on the other hand, is to enable suppliers to better understand and satisfy the expectations of their customer — the target organization. In feedback meetings, suppliers quickly learn to appreciate the need to continually improve the quality of their outputs. With ever-increasing quality inputs from their suppliers, target organizations are a leg up on improving their value-adding activities so that they, in turn, can produce outputs that lead to increasingly greater satisfaction for their customers.

In the early stages of TQM/MGEEM implementation (as explained in Chapter 4), target organizations are led by a facilitator through exercises to define, identify, and prioritize both customers and suppliers. These exercises result in identifying the *critical few* and *important many* customers and suppliers. The critical few suppliers are those who provide the inputs that are critical to the efforts of the target organization to accomplish its mission. Conversely, customers who are critical are those who receive the bulk of the goods or services produced by the target organization, usually defined in terms such as sales or mission-criticality.

For as many as six months, feedback participation should be limited to members of a target organization so training can be conducted about the philosophy of continuous improvement and how feedback from customers will be used. The first time outsiders are invited to a feedback meeting, it might be best to invite only customers. It also might be best to first invite people who work for only one customer organization (perhaps one manager and several key workers).

During this feedback meeting, target organizational personnel should be taught more about how to deal with feedback from customers as a basis for improvement.

The essence of this training is that customer feedback must not be taken personally, but considered as an opportunity for improvement. As this training takes hold several more customers can be added to the next feedback meeting. Eventually, people from one supplier organization can be invited to attend and, later, more suppliers can be invited as target organization personnel learn to deal with suppliers in the interest of improvement. Of course, the teachings of the quality philosophers should form the basis of this training. Perhaps the most important result of this training is that everyone surrender the attitude that there is one best way to do things and adopt a new attitude of seeking continual improvement. The key measure of this training's successfulness for continual improvement is whether target organization personnel view customer feedback as criticism or opportunities for improvement.

After the critical few have been dealt with, representatives from the important many customers and suppliers should be invited to feedback meetings. They are invited so target organization personnel can learn how to better understand and cooperate with them. As the expectations of the important many customers are better understood, it is hoped that they will move up to the status of the critical few. This results in expanded sales, market share, and mission for the target organization.

The reason to invite the important many suppliers to feedback meetings is that they, too, need to learn about continual improvement. Enlightened suppliers who are external to the company can be expected to be highly motivated to participate in feedback meetings. They want to move up to join the ranks of the vital few suppliers. They want to increase their sales to the target organization.

Similarly, suppliers who are internal to the company can be expected to be highly motivated to participate in feedback meetings. They should be beginning their own TQM/MGEEM implementations. They, too, should be learning the importance of close contact with their customers to better understand their expectations. Playing the role of processor in one TQM/MGEEM feedback meeting, supplier in another, and customer in another establishes a network structure which helps everyone understand the interconnectedness of their work. This understanding breaks down barriers between departments and is the basis for making harmony and cooperation a reality.

Learning about the expectations of their customers comes fast in a target organization when customers are brought into feedback meetings. There the customers are, sitting at the table looking at the feedback charts of their supplier, the target organization. Talking to a real live customer is much better than looking at a stack of completed questionnaires. A questionnaire can tell you that your service was rated as "average," but it won't talk to you about how to become "excellent." Customers can be asked how the target organization did last month in meeting their needs. "Tell us the worst so we can give you our best!"

Target organization personnel using feedback meetings with customers present don't have to rely so much on printouts of trends, demographics, and market segments. They can look their customers right in the eyes and find out if they get what they need. This is the safest and surest route to understanding what customers want.

There is less need to use questionnaires or telephone calls to get information about customer expectations and evaluations of the target organization's performance. There is less need for the target organization's manager to go to lunch with the managers of internal or external customer organizations to learn if their expectations are being met. The feedback-at-lunch approach seldom works well anyway because it doesn't usually involve workers from both organizations, only managers. It is important that workers, too, be taught the importance of harmony and cooperation. This learning occurs in feedback meetings.

When customers are asked in feedback meetings to "tell us the worst so we can give you our best," they are likely to do just that — they will tell the worst. Honest answers must, therefore, be expected and planned for by target organization personnel. They must be prepared to hear some rough statements. "This is all wrong!" "That is all wrong!" "You people have never done this right!" "Why can't you get it here on time like you promised?"

In preparation to hear this, target organization personnel should be taught the attitude that, as an organization, we are continuously getting better. To get better we must appreciate that a customer complaint is an *opportunity* for improvement, not a criticism. Everyone must see customer complaints as a rich source of information about how to improve, not as criticism or a basis of argument. Here's what they should say:

We are going to be the best department in the company. We are going to be the best in the industry! Feedback meetings with customers are our way of gathering information about how we can improve. Rather than being insulted when a customer tells us "the worst," we see such comments as information about how to improve, as opportunities to get better. So, when we hear a customer complaint, we don't argue. We don't see customers as rivals or competitors. We must take care of them. We say "OK, we understand. We'll take care of it. We'll fix your problem." In the next month's feedback meeting we say to them, "We tried to fix that problem for you. How did we do? What else do you need? What else can we do for you? How else can we satisfy your requirements?"

Again, customers may discuss more serious problems, and, again, they are fixed. This process repeats itself month after month, with the target organization only getting better. The target organization becomes relentless about improving quality. They never quit! Finally, customers have nothing to say except "Gosh! You guys *are* the best in the company!" Customers begin to brag about the target organization. Now everyone knows they are the best!

Occasionally in feedback meetings customers are reluctant to express their true attitudes about a target organization. Some customers hesitate to discuss the poor service they have been receiving from the target organization. Facilitators who suspect this may wish to try to make it easier for them to do so. For instance, the first customers invited to a feedback meeting could be those known for their largely positive attitudes toward the target organization. These customers may have better relations with the target organization and feel more secure about expressing their true attitudes, favorable and unfavorable. In subsequent meetings, customers whose attitudes are a bit less friendly may be invited, e.g., former customers who were identified through marketing research as those who became so dissatisfied with the service that they quit conducting business with the target organization. They may even have to be offered incentives to attend a feedback meeting.

This process of moving from friendly to unfriendly customers also has the advantage of giving target organization personnel a measured exposure to possibly severe customer feedback so they have time to learn to see customer feedback as opportunity for improvement.

Aside from receiving verbal customer feedback, there is another way which guarantees anonymity and, consequently, may reduce customer reluctance to express their true attitudes. In this method, customers and everyone else in a feedback meeting are asked to record their comments about ways to improve on 3 × 5-inch index cards, one comment per card. After everyone has completed their cards, the cards are shuffled in plain view. The facilitator then writes the comments on chart paper, one at a time, for general discussion. Since anyone can begin discussion of a suggestion, it usually is impossible to associate a comment with the customer who voiced it. This degree of anonymity usually makes even the most reluctant customer comfortable enough to contribute.

Feedback meetings are a valuable forum in which customers can be called on to express their needs and expectations. For instance, an organization might think that to their customers' price means everything and, consequently, work hard to keep prices down. Eventually they may lose customers to competitors who provide what customers really want, perhaps better service. Possibly their customers would even be willing to tolerate higher prices if they could obtain excellent service. Target organizations can easily lose customers if they lack knowledge of what customers really want. Such losses occur every day, but such knowledge can be gained effortlessly in feedback meetings.

Target organization personnel must be taught that the expectations of their customers are complex. Often what customers really want is quite different from what target organization personnel have traditionally believed. Common sense suggests, for instance, that customers seldom want only one feature in a product or service, but usually want a variety of features which vary in importance. For example, reliable performance through the life of a product may be of prime importance, but price and on-time delivery may run a close second; the product's color may not matter at all. Often the most important feature is service and more service. Target organization personnel must be taught that it usually takes time and patience to really understand customer expectations.

Target organization personnel also often fail to fully appreciate another commonsense notion about customers. Customers have choices when they purchase services or products. Consequently, personnel must be trained to be aware of what competitors have to offer and how the competitors' products and services compare against their own in their customer's eyes. Often the little things count the most to customers, e.g., the attitudes of target organization personnel who interface with them. Examples of interface personnel are service representatives, receptionists, and secretaries. Do they smile? Are they cheerful? Do they have integrity? Are they honest? Or, do they give the impression that "This would be a great place to work if it weren't for the customers"?

It also is important that managers not rely merely on the regulations, standards, procedures, and requirements that are supposed to focus the organization on satisfying customer expectations. For most organizations, this kind of guidance was written years ago by some well-meaning managers who were trying to ensure that customers get what they want. The customers who existed when these documents were written have undoubtedly changed, or at least their needs and expectations have changed. Markets change, expand, shrink, and disappear in response to a multitude of factors, including demographics, technology, and competition.

Therefore, it is essential that organizations remain in continual contact with their customers and their expectations. Otherwise, a change will occur and an ignorant and, therefore, unresponsive company will be put out of business. Monthly feedback meetings provide a forum for continual contact with customers. Feedback meetings provide the vehicle for continuous adjustment through information to an uncertain, changing environment.

There are countless other advantages in hearing directly from customers in feedback meetings. Of course, face-to-face contact with customers makes it easier to learn what they really want. Service? Immediate attention? Speed? Integrity? Life-cycle reliability? Concern? Respect? Recognition? A feeling of importance? Securing this information in feedback meetings is at the heart of TQM/MGEEM and forms the basis for continual improvement essential to success.

Additionally, face-to-face contact makes it easier to translate information about customer expectations and problems into changes in how target organizations do business. This is because customers sitting in feedback meetings can be asked what changes should be made and later can be asked to appraise the effects of these changes.

An interesting and valuable realization often occurs for target organization personnel when customers participate in their feedback meetings. In the course of exploring customer expectations, target organization personnel come to realize that some parts of their TQM/MGEEM system are incorrect and need revision. For instance, they may realize that, despite the fact that customers were members of their Blue Team, their Blue Team was wrong in some ways about what customers want.

Maybe the Gold Team created indicators in the belief that strict adherence to engineering requirements produces quality, but conversations with customers in feedback meetings changes their minds. They learn that product adherence to requirements means nothing unless customers want to buy the products that result. A product can be great from a specifications point of view but, for any number of reasons, it won't sell. The specifications may be correct, but when compared to the products of competitors, the product may be technologically obsolete, lack key features, or cost too much. Getting it right the first time is meaningless unless customers want what is produced. Experience may have taught customers that the company's after-sale service capability for a given product is inadequate or not timely.

In response to realizations that their Blue and Gold Teams might have made some errors, target organization personnel must revise their TQM/MGEEM system, e.g., with different slopes on feedback charts, different indicators, or new or revised KRAs. In many cases, more accurate knowledge of customer expectations will cause a target organization to modify or rewrite its mission statement. Any changes in a TQM/MGEEM system which make a target organization more sensitive to customer expectations should be encouraged. After all, quality should be defined by the customer and everything about a company, including TQM/MGEEM, must continually improve.

Remember that making changes that lead to increased customer satisfaction and to the resolution of customer complaints virtually always requires management action. It is well documented that workers can influence only a small part, perhaps less than 10 percent, of the factors in an organization that relate to customer satisfaction. Influencing the other 90 plus percent requires management action. Therefore, the ultimate success of efforts to satisfy changing and ever-rising customer expectations rests almost entirely with management.

When you consider your own personal contact as a customer with businesses, it is easy to understand that it is almost always management who must change something to increase your satisfaction. When you have to wait too long to check into a hotel, pick up a rental car, get a waiter at a restaurant, receive spare parts, check out at a grocery store, or see a doctor, was it the fault of the workers involved or the management? Who designed the system? Who decided how many people will be available to serve customers? Who decided on the number of hotel clerks, rental agents, waiters, parts clerks, checkers, etc., to be on duty on each shift? Who is trying to reduce labor costs to make more profit? Who bought the checkout counters at the grocery store that force you to unload your own groceries onto a conveyor belt? Who made the decision to save labor costs by forcing you to serve yourself? Who reduced the hours of the supply shop from full to half-days? Who made the decision that you must put up a $50 deposit? Who made the decision that the requisition you are trying to fill out must be signed by your supervisor and branch manager? Who made the decision that a cashier won't give out change for a soft drink machine 10 feet away? Who installed the telephone answering equipment in which a machine puts you on hold for 15 minutes? Who built the bureaucracy and terrible compliance systems which keep workers from doing a good job? It wasn't the workers!

Experience probably has taught you how little good it does to complain to a reservations clerk or waiter. They sheepishly say, "I'm so sorry, but it's our policy that. . . ." or "Hey, man, I'm sorry, but I only work here." Their statements really mean "If it were up to me, I'd do what you ask but the boss won't let me."

Bosses raised in the tradition of accounting and finance mistakenly focus on reducing costs when what is really important is satisfying customers. These bosses must be taught to listen to customers. The valuable process of listening to customers transpires in feedback meetings.

When managers learn in feedback meetings what their customers really want, most move quickly to provide it. Others, however, respond with an interesting remark such as, "Gee, I'd like to provide the service you need, but I'm simply not resourced or budgeted to do that. I'm sorry!" Or, managers may say, "I'm so sorry, but it's against company regulations or policy."

What should a facilitator do when these types of remarks are made to a customer in a feedback meeting? (Remember, facilitators are trying to get managers to accept their responsibilities to change things so that customers can be satisfied. Here are managers who apparently understand the need to satisfy customers but can't because of a lack of resources or because of company policy and regulations.) What is the answer? The answer lies with higher management. If providing customer satisfaction is in the target organization's mission statement, as it should be, then adequate resources for that purpose and policy and regulations in the form of guidance should be provided by higher management.

In these examples, higher management is holding lower levels managers to budgets and regulations rather than asking "What can we do from our level to help you and your people do a better job for your customers?" Here the level of service to customers is mistakenly driven by budgets and regulations instead of customer feedback. Consequently, customers simply don't get what they need! A budget developed months ago doesn't provide sufficient resources or staffing. This makes the comptroller happy but eventually drives away customers. And how can organizations improve their processes when they are frozen in place by company policies and regulations? These are examples of how an accounting- and regulation-driven approach to management can utterly ruin a company. Eventually everyone, including the comptroller, will be on the street looking for another job. It happens every day in the United States.

In my experience, customers are deeply impressed when they attend feedback meetings in which their supplier (the target organization) is working on ways to do a better job for them. They appreciate having a direct voice in how their supplier can improve its products and services. Wouldn't you be impressed if one of your suppliers (such as the service advisor where you have your car repaired, your dentist, physician, barber, travel agent, mortgage company, insurance agent, grocer, or minister) invited you to a meeting to seek your advice on how to better serve your needs? Wouldn't you be impressed if after you made a few suggestions, they actually took action on them! Through time, customers come to depend on an improving level of quality from target organizations and, consequently are able to vastly improve their own quality and effectiveness because of it. This is the point of TQM/MGEEM.

Imagine the impact of holding monthly feedback meetings in *every* department within a company. In addition to all the motivational and leadership-enhancing benefits, the cross-feeding and networking among various departments deepens everyone's appreciation of the benefits to quality of harmony and cooperation. Personnel from different departments are processors in some feedback meetings, suppliers in others, and customers in still others. Walking in the moccasins of every player in the quality effort—suppliers, processors, and customers—is a profound and enlightening experience. As feedback teams become empowered by enlightened senior managers, faster and more realistic problem solving takes place in these flexible networks where the focus is on satisfying customer expectations. There is less need to wait for guidance from the hierarchy. The impact on a company's effectiveness can be enormous.

(Chapter 11 presents more information on how feedback teams do their work, particularly how they increase effectiveness by identifying, understanding, and improving processes.)

CHAPTER

11

PROCESSES AND THEIR IMPROVEMENT

A central purpose of feedback meetings is to discover how to improve the way work is conducted. Feedback charts play an important role in making these discoveries. Feedback teams use the charts to consider what can be done to improve performance. Knowing how to use feedback charts to improve organizational performance requires an appreciation that all work is a process; that processes can be understood, usually with simple statistical tools; and that processes must be improved continuously.

It is important that members of feedback teams understand that the levels of performance shown on their feedback charts result from various causes. They must understand the commonsense notion that performance doesn't just happen. It is caused by something. Something makes performance low, moderate or high. For example, if sales were high last month, something happened to make sales high. Perhaps it was an effective advertising program, or improved training, or better service. Similarly, if attendance was low last month, something happened to make it low. Maybe it was poor morale, or hunting season, or unseasonable weather. It is imperative that managers follow and teach the practice of trying to understand the factors, events, and circumstances that drive the levels of performance on their feedback charts. The purpose of developing an understanding of the factors which affect performance is, of course, to take one action after another to continuously influence these factors to produce increasingly higher performance. A variety of excellent tools for use with feedback charts will be detailed later in this chapter. These tools help feedback teams understand the factors that affect their performance.

A key to improving organizational performance is understanding that all work is a process. A process is a group of factors which work together to produce some result. To be more specific, a process uses resources (from internal and/or external suppliers) to do some work (value-adding activities) which results in goods or services, usually for internal and/or external customers.

Processes are everywhere. For instance, brushing your teeth is a process. You use resources: a toothbrush, a tube of toothpaste, water, and a mirror. You do some work: squeeze the tube, brush your teeth, and rinse your mouth. You get a result: clean teeth and a bright smile. To improve results, you must identify, study, and improve the process that produced the result. This is a common sense idea, but it is important.

In the last example how could you get cleaner teeth and a brighter smile? The answer is to study the process and seek to improve it. Improving a process involves examining its various parts, such as the resources. How can the resources used to brush your teeth be improved? A better toothbrush? Better toothpaste? Purer water? Maybe rinse with mouthwash? Clearer mirror? Next, improvement could involve looking for better methods: brush up and down instead of sideways, and start using dental floss.

To learn more about process improvement, think about these simple processes. How you could improve flossing your teeth, changing a typewriter ribbon, arranging for corporate travel, hiring a new employee, washing a car, keeping the fleas off your dog, caring for hospital patients, educating students, writing a letter, repairing a jet engine, playing a game of pool, washing a dog, and fishing.

Feedback teams should understand that if we want to survive and prosper, we must not be concerned solely with results. In the flossing example, it is important that you inspect and admire your clean mouth in a mirror and perhaps keep count of how many times a week you floss. The main focus, however, should be on doing a better job of flossing. If you continually improve the way you do the job, the result will take care of itself. For instance, what's the best dental floss for you to use? When should flossing be done? What's the best way to actually do the flossing? Continual improvement of processes is what's important.

Consider the example of keeping fleas off of your dog. Although it's important to occasionally check the dog for fleas, the main work is to improve the process. In the past, the process used was to catch each flea and kill it. Later, use of DDT improved the process. When DDT was banned, many other materials were developed to improve the process. Today, knowledge is spreading that a teaspoon of brewer's yeast powder sprinkled each day on a dog's wet food will permanently repel fleas. This is an example of process improvement through innovation and awareness.

The education of feedback teams about processes should begin with simple exercises to identify processes and to consider how to improve them. For instance, after defining the term *process* and giving several examples, a facilitator should ask team members to write down three processes present in their personal lives or at home. There are literally countless examples, e.g., getting dressed, shaving, putting on makeup, ironing a shirt or blouse, cooking breakfast, waking up the kids, getting the kids ready for school, and driving to work.

The facilitator should then ask each team member to choose one process from his/her list and write down how the process is currently done. Next, team members are invited to think of three ways their process could be improved. In other words, how could their current way of getting dressed be improved? One answer could be laying out your clothes and shining your shoes before going to bed. Another solution could be ironing your shirt or blouse the evening before. With such simple, everyday examples team members can begin to think in terms of processes and their improvement. Then, the team could be asked to identify processes in their work and discuss ways to improve them.

Now consider a simple process which will be used to discuss how processes fit into TQM/MGEEM. Consider the process of making a sandwich. The resources in this process are people (a cook, a dishwasher), machinery (a stove, refrigerator, cabinet, knife, plate, spoon), raw materials (bread, meat, lettuce, tomato, mustard), methods (a recipe), and environment (a kitchen). The work is slicing meat, lettuce, tomatoes, spreading mustard on the bread, etc., which results in the output — sandwiches. In TQM/MGEEM, providing sandwiches to customers could be one of the KRAs, one of the principal intended accomplishments of a sandwich shop. If the shop's employees want to know how well they are doing on this KRA, they could generate some indicators. Effectiveness indicators would tell them, for instance, if the sandwiches look appetizing, taste good, and are nutritious. Efficiency indicators would tell them how many pounds of mustard were required for X number of sandwiches. Feedback charts would show the levels of performance on these indicators (on the horizontal axes), and the slopes would translate these levels into effectiveness scores (on the vertical axes). If a slope is steep, the indicator is important. If a slope is flat, the indicator is less important. For instance, the fact that the sandwiches look appetizing may not be as important to customers as their taste. If so, the slope on the feedback chart on appetizing would be flatter, and the slope on the chart on taste would be steeper. On the other hand, suppose customers are deeply concerned about their health. They don't care much about sandwiches looking appetizing or tasting great as long as they have high nutritional value. In this case, the slopes on the appetizing and taste feedback charts would be flatter and the slope on the nutrition chart would be steep.

Members of feedback teams should be taught that performance on each of their feedback charts is the result of a process or several processes. To improve performance, they must identify the processes involved and consider action to improve them. This activity should occur in feedback meetings. To improve performance, feedback teams must not be obsessed with results, only worrying when a problem arises, such as a customer complaint. Instead, they must identify, study, and continually improve the processes which produce the result. It is also essential that managers strive to create an environment in which feedback teams can take joy in their work and in which employees, customers, and suppliers feel free to make suggestions about how to improve processes.

Consider, again, the sandwich shop example. Suppose the feedback chart on sandwiches looking appetizing has a steep slope. That means it is important that the sandwiches appear appetizing. Now suppose that customers report in a feedback meeting that the sandwiches don't look appetizing. What should be done? First, the manager and employees of the sandwich shop should not become offended and argue with the customers about whether the sandwiches look appetizing. They should try to see customer comments as information which they can use to study and improve the sandwiches, to stay in business, to outsell their competitors, and to prosper.

More specifically, what approach should the sandwich shop use to improve their process so that their sandwiches appear more appetizing? Perhaps they can get some specific ideas from their customers in feedback meetings. For instance, their customers might suggest that the way they wrap the sandwiches gives them a crushed appearance. Maybe they will suggest that the lettuce looks wilted, or the buns don't *look right* somehow. Where does the shop purchase its buns? Does it buy them from the bakery that charges the lowest prices? Does the shop have a close, cooperative relationship with a bakery? Does the baker understand the shop's needs? Can the shop's manager and employees network with the baker and his employees in feedback meetings to solve the bun problem?

As another example, consider the sales department discussed in Chapter 10. The personnel in this department must understand that sales result from one process, training from another process, and attendance from yet another process. To most people, it makes sense to think of a large process as being made up of several smaller processes which, in turn, may be made up of several even smaller processes. Ultimately, the key to success for the sales department is to work in feedback meetings to understand and improve the processes that influence their performance. What causes sales to increase? Exactly what is involved? What factors cause training and attendance to fluctuate? The manager and employees of the sales department should know. It is the manager's responsibility to authorize action after action to improve processes so that performance continues to increase.

Workers are an endless source of ideas about how to improve processes, and work smarter. After all, many of them have been working with various processes for years. Although they may not think of their work as part of a process, or call it a process, they know what makes their operations tick. They certainly have some good ideas about what's wrong with them. They know what needs to be changed so that their processes will work better.

Think about your own job. You know what needs to be changed to allow your performance to increase. Remember a few of your past jobs, e.g., that job you had in high school. Think about the processes that were involved. (It's a good training exercise to try to actually name each of the processes that were involved.) Didn't you understand what was wrong with these processes and what needed to be changed to improve things? You knew that most of those needed changes were beyond your control as a worker. The boss should have done something, and if your boss had been willing to listen to your suggestions and make changes, improvement surely would have followed. If the changes had been made, you would have been able to do a better job and take greater joy in your work.

Years of experience show that so much is wrong with the processes by which most United States organizations do business that huge gains usually can be achieved by making the obvious changes in them. For instance, in the first step of the TQM/MGEEM process, enormous improvements result when personnel simply better understand what their processes are supposed to achieve, that is, understand their mission.

Notice that developing or reviewing a mission statement is itself a process. As repeatedly stated in this text, many people in United States businesses who are working hard are actually working on the wrong things. They don't understand their mission. Understanding the mission is a process that needs improvement in virtually every organization in the United States.

Other dramatic improvements often are made in TQM/MGEEM when personnel become aware of the other players in their processes. They must recognize that they have both internal and external customers to whom they are responsible for quality products and services. Developing an awareness of customers is another process. Personnel also need to recognize that they have both internal and external suppliers, and that their own quality can be no better than the quality of the support they receive from these suppliers. Developing an awareness of suppliers is yet another process.

As networking transpires with customers and suppliers across a series of feedback meetings, attitudes continue to change, and improvements and processes begin to advance in a slow, deliberate, never-ending manner. Perhaps the most significant improvements occur when managers begin to remove the many senseless barriers that prevent workers from doing their best. Recognizing and removing the barriers is another process.

Before organizations can take full advantage of opportunities for the improvement of their processes, managers usually must experience an attitude change. They must relinquish the attitude that workers are the main cause of the organization's quality and performance problems. They must realize that most workers try to do their best, and that it is management's responsibility to make improvements in the processes by which work is conducted. They must accept the fact that workers want to do a good job and that when they don't, it's almost always because of a flawed process which only management can fix.

Managers must learn to accept what is said in feedback meetings as an important basis for improving processes. Managers must accept the fact that there is no one best way. Rather, they must appreciate that change and improvement is a better way of life. They must create a work environment in which improvement can take place in a slow, step-by-step, never-ending manner. They must learn that everything should be in a constant state of improvement. Nothing is static. Things either improve or degrade.

Using Statistics in Feedback Meetings

Many suggestions made in feedback meetings concern work-related problems which are obvious to workers but somehow have never been exposed to management. For example, "These instructions aren't clear." "More training is needed with this equipment." "These tools are out-of-date." "Our spare parts are seldom delivered on time, and often the order is wrong." "The people we have to depend on are not well trained."

Conversely, many suggestions made in feedback meetings pertain to problems that represent personal irritants to workers. Examples of these kinds of suggestions include, "All of us want to ban smoking in our office." "It's too cold or noisy in here." "The restrooms around here are not cleaned often enough." Suggestions related to personal irritants should be considered by management to be at least as important as those that appear to be more directly job-related. Managers must regard employee statements about personal irritants not as criticism, but as opportunities for improvement. Can you do a good day's work when your nose gets stuffed up by the smoke from someone's pipe, when the office is too cold, when the restroom is dirty, or when some other irritant is on your mind?

After the obvious barriers to performance have been encountered, problems of a more obscure, technical, and complicated nature may be addressed. For these problems, it is better to base recommendations to management for improvements on evidence rather than on judgment. Rather than going to a manager with a recommendation for an improvement based on a feedback team's opinion, it is preferable that team recommendations be based on facts. It is better to express recommendations as "The facts show that..." rather than as "It's our opinion that...."

To illustrate this, consider an effort in a certain department to improve an approval process required to purchase new equipment. Everyone who had to deal with this process agreed that it took far too much time. Moreover, it was well-known that one of the four managers who reviewed these requests was the source of the delays. Rather than forwarding a recommendation for a change in this process based on judgment and opinion, however, it was far more convincing and less dangerous politically to gather and present the facts. Study showed that acquiring approval on the most recent 14 requests for new equipment averaged 24 days (with a small standard deviation). The data further showed that over half of the 24 days were taken by one of the four managers whose signatures were required. Here data were used to pinpoint the problem. Data add an undeniable sense of objectivity. Results based on data are easier for everyone to take. The bottleneck manager was not made to feel embarrassed over this incident because he/she was doing his/her best. It was the *process* that needed fixing. In this case, the manager in question merely needed to be made aware of the problem to fix it by hiring an assistant. The important point is that data should always be the basis of recommendations for improvements to a process. Process recommendations should not be based on judgment.

Another even more important reason for basing recommendations on data rather than judgment is that the real problem with a process may not be what a feedback team thinks it is. Opinion may be that one thing is the problem when in reality the problem is something entirely different. Data are far more reliable than opinion in discovering a problem. Many senior managers who understand the importance of data have signs on their walls saying, "In God we trust, all others bring data!" This sign sends a clear message to feedback team members that they should base their recommendations for changes on data, not opinion.

There is an interesting way to think about why it is necessary to gather data on process problems. Rather than using the *genius approach,* in which feedback team members express their opinions and judgment about what is wrong with a process, it is better to let the process tell us about its problems. Strange as it seems, processes can speak! They can tell us what is wrong with them. Just as a patient can tell a physician, "Doc, I have a stomachache," or "Doc, something in my elbow hurts," the voice of all processes is statistics.

An example of this voice is the simple statistic used in the previous example which demonstrated that over half the average of 24 days of approval review time on new equipment was taken up by one of the four managers. An average is an example of the type of simple statistics which are the voice of processes.

Because it is important to use statistics to let processes speak, all members of feedback teams should acquire a basic knowledge of statistics. Experience shows that this knowledge should not be taught simultaneously to everyone in the company. I have been teaching statistics since 1963 and I know that to really understand statistics, you must use it. If you teach everyone in the company statistics, it may be many months before some have the opportunity to use it. Over those months, many will forget much of what they were taught. Therefore, it is important that training in statistics be made available on an as-needed basis. When a feedback team needs statistics, provide the training.

There are a number of simple statistical tools available for use in the analysis of processes. These tools can help feedback teams achieve a far better understanding of how their process works. Additionally, these tools can be valuable in discovering what is wrong with processes.

Every public or college library has many books on statistics; it is not my purpose here to provide a complete guide to their use. My purpose is simply to identify the most useful of these statistical tools and provide several illustrations of how they can be used in the process improvement dimension of TQM/MGEEM. For details on the statistical tool most useful to process improvement, see *Guide to Quality Control*[19] and *The Memory Jogger: A Pocket Guide of Tools for Continuous Improvement.*[1]

Of the many statistical tools available, it is fortunate that those that are the easiest to understand and use are the same ones that are the most valuable for understanding processes. The tools most often used to understand processes are called The Seven Tools, but there is some disagreement as to which tools make up the list. Probably the most widely accepted list includes the cause-and-effect diagram, Pareto chart, check sheet, histogram, scatter diagram, control chart, and various graphs. Other tools often listed among the seven include stratification and the flow chart.

If a statistician is hired from a local college, it is important that this person appreciates and has experience in the use of statistics to improve processes. Most statisticians can lecture at length on various statistical subjects, but few understand how to use statistics to improve processes. It also is important to locate a statistician with good teaching skills. It is one thing to know statistics; it is another thing to be able to teach it. The best way to determine if a statistician can teach is to talk to his/her customers—the students.

Generally experienced statisticians agree that the statistics used to understand processes should be thought of as a kit of multipurpose tools. Each tool can be used for several different purposes in the various stages of working with a process. Depending on a statistician's background and experience, some prefer certain tools over others (e.g., many statisticians prefer to use the flow chart and the check sheet for problem identification, but the histogram, control chart, and Pareto chart for the problem analysis.) Another experienced view is that the simplest tools from the aforementioned list of The Seven Tools can be used to successfully diagnose 90 percent of all process problems. According to this view, one additional tool, the control chart—a more complex tool than the others—can be used to diagnose 5 percent of the remaining problems. Thus, these seven tools collectively can be used to diagnose 95 percent of all process problems.

A collection of Seven New Tools has been proposed to work out the remaining 5 percent of the problems. Unfortunately, each of these new tools, described in Mizuno's *Management for Quality Improvement: The Seven New QC Tools,* are more complex than the most complex of the other seven, the control chart.[26] These new tools are the relations diagram, affinity diagram, systematic diagram, matrix diagram, matrix data analysis method, process decision program chart, and arrow diagram. A somewhat different set of seven management and planning tools is provided in *The Memory Jogger Plus +* by Brassard.[2]

It is widely agreed that the most useful tool to begin the analysis of any process is the flow chart. It provides a thorough description of all phases of a process, from its start to its finish. It also provides valuable information about what parts of a process need improvement. A flow chart uses symbols, e.g., rectangles, arrows, and diamonds, to show the work in a process as a sequence of steps.

As defined earlier, every process begins with inputs (resources), moves on to value-adding activities (the work itself), and ends with output (goods and services). For example, a flow chart of the various steps in a contract review process could be worked out by a feedback team. On a sheet of paper or chalkboard they could begin with a *rectangle* showing that contracts originate in the purchasing department. An *arrow* from the *rectangle* to a *diamond shape* shows that the next step is that contracts move from purchasing to inspection where decisions are made about their conformity to legal requirements. If contracts conform, another *arrow* shows that they move on to a second *diamond shape* for a second inspection decision, this time concerning conformity to federal guidelines.

Conversely, if contracts do not conform on the first inspection, a different *arrow* out of the diamond illustrates that they are returned through a *loop* to the purchasing department for correction. A feedback team studying this process would use these types of symbols to lay out all the steps involved. The level of detail depends on how the team defines the scope of the problem. Larger processes have more steps than smaller processes. Flow charts serve as the basis for recommending improvements to processes, such as studying what must be done to eliminate loops, identify areas where training is needed, search for ways to increase throughput, find ways to cut costs, reduce errors, reduce handling damage, and, in general, simplify a process.

An effective way for feedback teams to use flow charts is to first develop an *as required chart* to show a process as it is directed in company regulations. An *as is flow chart* is then developed to display the process as it actually exists. Feedback teams usually find that a process that actually exists is quite different from the process called for in regulations.

Next, a *should be flow chart* is developed to illustrate the process in what the feedback team believes is its ideal state. Comparisons among these three charts provide a wealth of ideas for process improvement.

After developing flow charts, the next step is to use other statistical tools, such as Pareto charts, cause-and-effect diagrams, histograms, and check sheets, to document the importance of problems identified in the flow charts. For instance, what percentage of all looping (when products are kicked back to earlier steps in the process for rework) occurs from different points in a process? Where in the process does the most looping occur? Why does the looping occur? What percent of the looping is associated with various reasons? Does the main reason for looping, say at a key inspection point, suggest that additional training is needed? Or, does looping suggest that workers at this station have inadequate tools or out-of-date methods?

A tool described by Ishikawa for the understanding of processes is the cause-and-effect diagram (also called the fishbone diagram because of its shape).[19] With an easel and chart paper a chairperson or facilitator of a feedback meeting can use this tool to help a feedback team better understand their processes. The general form of a cause-and-effect diagram is shown in Figure 11.1.

In a cause-and-effect diagram, an "effect" or problem is written in the box on the right side of the diagram. As possible causes for the effect are identified by a feedback team, a facilitator writes them on the lines on the left side of the diagram.

Suppose the director of a certain training department wants to increase his/her trainers' insight into the factors that affect their teaching performance. Using a cause-and-effect diagram on a large chalkboard, the director writes the words "trainer's teaching performance" in the effect box on the right. He/she then calls on each trainer, in turn, to identify and explain one factor that influences this effect. As answers are brainstormed, the director tries to group similar answers and writes them on the lines on the diagram's left side. A cause-and-effect diagram can be useful in identifying and increasing insight into the possible causes of various problems or measures.

To users of TQM/MGEEM, it is helpful to know that the effect box on the right side of a cause-and-effect diagram can be a feedback chart. This suggests a new statistical tool uniquely suited to help understanding of the processes which cause fluctuations in indicators. The new tool is a combination of a cause-and-effect diagram and a feedback chart, as shown in Figure 11.2.

The new tool is called a cause-and-effect feedback diagram. To use this tool the name of an indicator is written under the effect box, and the box

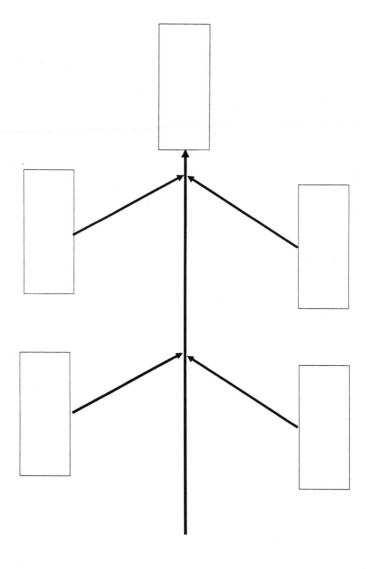

FIGURE 11.1   General Form of a Cause-and-Effect Diagram

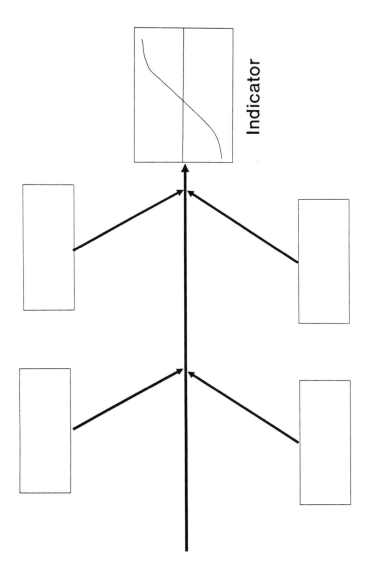

FIGURE 11.2 General Form of a Cause-and-Effect Feedback Diagram

itself is the familiar rectangle for a feedback chart. Feedback teams may use this tool to brainstorm causes which might influence the indicator.

To start the brainstorming, a chairperson or facilitator asks, "Let's try to think of factors which affect this indicator. What makes our performance on this indicator go up or down?" As team members supply answers, the chairperson lists them in the order given on a chalkboard or chart paper. After all of a team's suggestions are listed, they are grouped on the lines on the diagram's left side.

As an example, assume a target organization has a cause-and-effect feedback diagram for an indicator on the timeliness in which a given product gets to customers. The exact indicator could be "percent of times products were delivered on time." The equation for computing it could be

$$\frac{\text{number of on-time deliveries}}{\text{total number of deliveries}} \times 100$$

to make the measure a percentage.

The effect box on the right is a feedback chart with the feasible best, feasible worst, and indifference points for timeliness on the horizontal axis, organizational effectiveness on the vertical axis, and a slope showing the impact of effectiveness of alternative feasible levels of timeliness, as shown in Figure 11.3.

Remember that the purpose of the cause-and-effect feedback diagram is to help feedback teams develop insight into the possible causes of fluctuation in their indicators (in this case timeliness). With several months of timeliness values posted on the slope of the feedback chart, which is the effect box, the chairperson may wish to begin a feedback meeting on improving timeliness by asking team members to brainstorm factors which could cause fluctuation in the timeliness with which they get their products to customers.

Answers from the team, e.g., late receipt of orders, orders filled out incorrectly, insufficient supply of spare parts, personnel out on sick leave, delivery truck unavailable, and deliveries made to wrong locations, are written in the order given on a chalkboard or chart paper. When no one can think of another cause, they are grouped by the team into broad categories: personnel, mechanical devices, tools, methods, and environment. There may be more or fewer categories, and a feedback team may prefer different categories or different names for categories. The emphasis should not be so much on the rules for developing the diagram, but on achieving a deeper understanding among feedback team members of the causes which drive the indicator.

A second emphasis, of course, is to not be as concerned about results

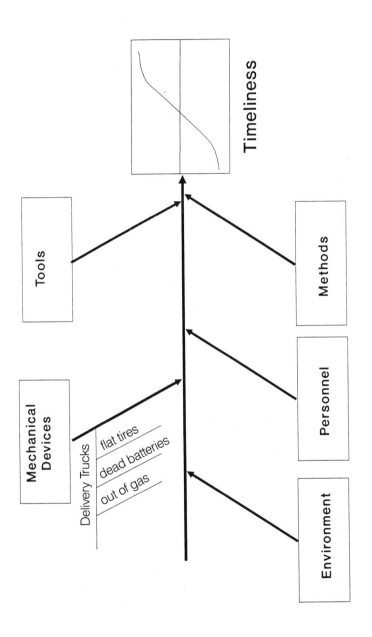

FIGURE 11.3 Example of the Cause-and-Effect Feedback Diagram

as with understanding and improving the process which produces those results.

The chairperson works with the team to group their suggested causes under broad categories. For instance, it may become evident in the discussion that several suggested causes have to do with mechanical devices. So "Mechanical Devices" is written in one of the boxes on the chart's left side, as shown in Figure 11.3. Other suggested causes are similarly grouped.

After the broad categories have been identified, suggested causes are written on the limbs, branches, and leaves under the broad categories. For instance, consider the broad category of mechanical devices shown in Figure 11.3. Suggested causes which have to do with mechanical devices, such as delivery trucks, would be placed on *limbs* leading off of the mechanical devices' *trunk*.

Suggested causes on limbs can be further broken down and placed on the branches leading off of limbs. Suggested causes which could be a further breakdown of delivery trucks are flat tires, dead batteries, and running out of gas; these causes are placed on the branches. Suggested causes on branches could be further broken down and written on *leaves*. Suggested causes associated with other broad categories are similarly graphed on limbs, branches, and leaves as appropriate.

Some facilitators prefer to use cause-and-effect feedback diagrams in a slightly different way. They have the five broad categories (personnel, mechanical devices, tools, methods, and environment) already written in the boxes on the diagram's left side before the feedback meeting starts. The first thing the feedback team does is brainstorm answers to a nominal question such as, "What factors play a role in whether we are early, on time, or late in the delivery of our product to customers?"

As answers are offered by the team, the facilitator uses his/her experience to write the causes on the appropriate limbs, branches, and leaves of the diagram. For instance, if a team member says "delivery trucks," the facilitator knows this suggestion goes on a limb off of the mechanical devices trunk. If someone says "flat tires," the facilitator knows this suggestion goes on a branch off the delivery truck limb. (Since much erasing and rewriting usually occurs in the use of cause-and-effect feedback diagrams, it is helpful to use a white or chalkboard.)

Facilitators who use this method claim that it develops greater team understanding of causes than the other approach in which team members simply brainstorm possible causes and, while they are on a break, the facilitator groups the causes under broad categories. Facilitators claim that when team members participate in grouping they see possible causes that otherwise wouldn't come out.

For instance, suppose during the brainstorming someone suggests delivery trucks as a possible cause. The facilitator suggests that delivery trucks goes under mechanical devices, the team agrees, and delivery trucks is written on a limb off of the mechanical devices' trunk. This makes team members consider how delivery trucks figure into whether they are timely. As a result, someone thinks of flat tires and suggests flat tires as a possible cause. The facilitator obtains agreement that tires runs off of the delivery truck limb and that flats are listed on a leaf on the tires' branch.

This focuses team members to think about what else can go wrong with the tires besides flats to possibly affect timeliness. So, involving team members in the grouping process may produce a more complete set of possible causes and contribute to a deeper understanding of the processes involved.

A feedback team can never be 100 percent certain that it knows everything about the causes of a given indicator. However, there are several rules-of-thumb, including the *bushy rule* for evaluating cause-and-effect feedback diagrams. This rule says that a team's knowledge of the causes of an indicator is generally meager unless the left side of the diagram is bushy, like an old, used hairbrush.

Having suggested causes on many branches and leaves going in every direction means a team's knowledge is fairly complete. A rather barren area on the left of a diagram means that a team has little understanding of the causes which drive the indicator in question.

Another approach used in evaluating a team's depth of understanding of an indicator's cause is to submit the list of causes they developed to a subject matter expert for his/her opinion. This person could be experienced in the same function area in a different department or different division, or a trade association representative with experience in this field.

After a feedback team has developed a reasonable understanding of the causes which produce fluctuation in a given indicator, they should progress to the next step, determining what specific actions can be taken to improve the process. Although the basic idea is to continuously improve and innovate a process, the first step in this undertaking is to fix whatever is wrong with it. This approach is acceptable as long as the feedback team does not fall into the fire-fighting tradition of Western management. They shouldn't stop fixing processes after they correct what they regard as the key problem's area. They must maintain this repair activity so that, as attitudes change, continuous fixing becomes continuous improvement and innovation.

The next step in determining what specific actions can be taken to fix a process is to use more statistical tools after the flow chart and cause-and-effect feedback diagram have been used. For instance, after completing a cause-and-effect feedback diagram, a team could keep a log, or tally, for a defined period to count the number of times a particular cause occurred.

In the timeliness example shown in Figure 11.3, a team could learn many times a month that problems occur in the five broad categories of personnel, mechanical devices, tools, methods, and environment, or in important parts within each category. For example, each time a product is late the cause could be identified and traced back to one of the five categories or parts of a category.

Managers must be careful that identifying causes does not create a witch-hunting atmosphere. Remember, it is a process we want to fix. We must resist the impulse to "find and punish the guilty party."

In our example suppose the largest number of delays are in the mechanical devices category in general, and in the inavailability of delivery trucks in particular. It would be a mistake to embarrass the person who schedules delivery trucks even if the person's work appears to be the focus of the problem. The key is to network with that person and his/her staff to get their opinions about how to fix the truck scheduling problem. As a show of good faith, accept a reasonable suggestion and make the necessary changes. Track the effects of these changes with the indicator on the appropriate feedback chart.

After improving the delivery truck scheduling problem, does the feedback team stop thinking about the issues associated with delivery schedules and delivery trucks? No. All improvement efforts must be endlessly repeated. These repetitions are best thought of as a cycle. For instance, the most well-known version of these repetitions is called the Deming Cycle.[7] When the team meets every month to review its feedback charts, the chairperson raises the issue of further considering how to improve on this timeliness indicator. The ensuing discussion should again focus on causes as the team is reminded of the causes they identified on their cause-and-effect feedback diagram for timeliness. Delivery trucks are part of this diagram. Remember that everyone is now in the spirit of continuous improvement.

I have sat in on many feedback meetings. Team members willingly rack their brains to think of better ways to do things. It is human nature for them to want to improve. It's not unusual for team members to use their free time to read about factors that affect their indicators, i.e., delivery schedules in the example. Using that case, team members might go out on Saturdays and examine new delivery trucks as the new year's models appear. They can be expected to become enthusiastic about inviting customers to feedback meetings to get their views on how indicators can be improved.

You may wonder whether customers will be interested in coming to these meetings to participate in trying to improve timeliness. You bet they will. The timeliness of their suppliers often means money in their pockets! Customers may suggest something like just-in-time deliveries, which would allow them to reduce their inventories.

Suppliers also are invited to feedback sessions. In our example, the supplier of the delivery trucks and the supplier of the computer software that runs the delivery system are invited. Are they motivated to improve timeliness? Absolutely! They know that if their customer does better, they do better. They want to innovate so they can sell more trucks and so they can keep the software contract. This networking with customers causes suppliers to mobilize their best efforts in the customer's behalf.

There are many occasions when barriers to organizational effectiveness are beyond the control of a given department and its feedback team. As Juran points out, a process in need of improvement may extend across two or more functional areas.[22] For instance, suppose a feedback chart in one department shows that the process of bringing new employees on board is operating too slowly. Part of this process is in the department that has the feedback chart, but the process extends across several other departments, including accounting, personnel, and training. If a process is too slow or otherwise ineffective, there usually is little that one of the involved departments can do to fix and improve it if the problems lie in another or several other departments. Managers of other departments where such problems lie often are reluctant to consider change.

Remember, typical Western managers believe they have the one best way to operate a process, usually through excessive control and compliance. Because they were designed wrong in the first place or have never been improved, many cross-functional processes in United States businesses are notoriously inefficient and ineffective. They have been the subject of outcry for years by internal and external customers who are required to use them, and by the unfortunate employees who have had to operate them. Since so many cross-functional processes seem to be set in concrete, how can they ever be fixed and improved? What does TQM/MGEEM do about these problems?

Solving Cross-Functional Process Problems

There are at least two ways to fix and improve processes which extend across two or more organizational units. The approach used depends on whether TQM/MGEEM has been implemented throughout the entire company or at the lower hierarchical levels.

If TQM/MGEEM has been implemented throughout an entire company, processes are improved by the first organizational unit within the hierarchy that contains and is responsible for the process that needs attention. The process is cross-functional at lower levels, but not to the higher level that contains it.

To demonstrate this idea, consider an example of a process that brings new employees on board. To various lower-level departments, this process is cross-functional, but not to the higher level unit that contains the departments into which the process extends. What higher-level organizational unit contains and is responsible for this process? It's not accounting, personnel, training, or any other lower-level department. It's an organizational unit above the department level. It may be at the level of corporate or division headquarters.

Let's say this process is owned at the corporate level. Corporate owns the process and the departments into which the process extends. If TQM/MGEEM has been implemented throughout the company, there will be a TQM/MGEEM system in place at the corporate level. Members of corporate's Gold Team will be the CEO's subordinates, the directors of accounting, personnel, training, etc. (Since those department managers have their own TQM/MGEEM systems, they sit on two teams, the Blue Team in their own departments and the Gold Team at the corporate level.) Corporate's TQM/MGEEM system will have KRAs and indicators. The feedback team at corporate has learned that each of their indicators is driven by a process. One of the indicators at corporate almost always includes having an adequate staff of trained personnel on board. This is the indicator that is driven by the cross-functional process of concern in this example.

The corporate feedback team also has learned that it is their responsibility to improve this process. To accomplish this, they have the necessary players. The managers of the departments that contain the slow process are on the corporate team, as is the CEO. Thus, the corporate feedback team fixes this process. When TQM/MGEEM is implemented throughout an entire company, higher-level feedback teams work process problems that are beyond the control of the feedback teams at lower levels.

When TQM/MGEEM has been implemented only at the lower hierarchical levels, e.g., only at the department level, a different approach to solving cross-functional process problems is required. In such situations, there are no feedback teams in place at the higher organizational levels to work process problems beneath them in the hierarchy. Therefore, it is necessary to *create* a feedback team for every important cross-functional process. Because these teams deal with cross-functional processes, in TQM/MGEEM they are called cross-functional feedback teams.

Although the main concern of both feedback teams and cross-functional feedback teams is improving processes, the composition of their memberships is different. Rather than being composed entirely of members from one target organization, as is true of feedback teams, cross-functional feedback teams include a member from each target organization into which the process of interest extends. This provides horizontal linkage. Cross-functional feedback teams also have vertical linkage through a member who is a senior manager at the first hierarchical level which contains the process. Often a senior manager who sits on the quality council (discussed in Chapter 3) is requested to serve on a cross-functional feedback team. Either of these two senior managers can authorize changes in the process. Thus, either of these managers can be said to own the process since it is under his/her control.

Cross-functional feedback teams also have a member who is a subject matter expert whose regular job is a key position in the process itself. This member is thoroughly familiar with company regulations on the process.

Finally, there is a member who is designated as the action officer. This person is given sufficient time away from other duties (perhaps 10 percent) to work the team's administrative tasks, such as calling meetings, acting as recorder, preparing memoranda, and employing the statistical tools necessary to diagnose problems in the process.

As explained in Chapter 3, organizations that are serious about improving performance usually have a quality council composed of the CEO and other senior managers. In addition to encouraging and supporting other TQM/MGEEM activities, members of the quality council often serve as the vertical connection in corporate management for all cross-functional feedback teams.

One of the council's responsibilities is to decide which cross-functional processes require a feedback team. Processes recommended for cross-functional feedback teams are identified in at least three ways: (1) The most common way is for regular feedback teams in target organizations to petition the council through channels that certain cross-functional processes restrict improvement on their feedback charts and, consequently, are in need of improvement. (2) The council can call for nominations from personnel in the organization as a whole, say through an announcement in the company house-organ or through a memorandum. (3) The council itself can identify cross-functional processes for improvement.

This last method is common in the early stages of a TQM/MGEEM effort because it usually is well-known in most organizations that certain cross-functional processes are out-of-date and so poor that they urgently need improvement. After improvement is well along on the worst cross-functional processes, however, it is best to identify others through petition by feedback teams. This method is vastly superior to detecting them strictly through judgment because the teams have actual measures through their feedback charts of which cross-functional processes most restrict their performance.

The first cross-functional process identified by a quality council for improvement should possess certain key characteristics. The most important characteristic arises from the fact that the companywide quality improvement effort needs a winner, a showcase, a success story that will provide the critical early evidence to skeptical employees that management is serious about improvement. Therefore, the first cross-functional process selected for improvement should have high visibility and should be feasible. Obviously, it is not in the best interest of the TQM/MGEEM campaign to start with a process that is too broad in scope or politically difficult. For example, it is not wise to select a cross-functional process for improvement, regardless of how bad it is, that was originally designed and currently managed by a politically powerful person who is opposed to change. These processes must come up for improvement, but it is best to wait until TQM/MGEEM has developed some momentum. For an excellent treatment of the criteria for selecting cross-functional projects, see Juran (Chapter 3).[22]

Both feedback teams and cross-functional feedback teams use the statistical tools, such as flow charts and cause-and-effect diagrams, described in Ishikawa,[19] Brassard,[1, 2] and Mizuno,[26] but cross-functional feedback teams do not always have the benefit of their own feedback charts to monitor the effects of corrective actions taken. Of course, having these charts is a significant benefit to regular feedback teams. Nevertheless, the widespread availability of feedback charts throughout a company is also of benefit to cross-functional feedback teams because the charts make possible the indirect measurement of their efforts.

Improvements in cross-functional processes should show up in feedback charts that are directly or indirectly affected by the process being worked. For instance, improvement in the cross-functional process of contract review should show up in the feedback charts of the various departments involved in creating, reviewing, and executing contracts. It is reasonable for a cross-functional feedback team to develop a feedback chart of its own to monitor its process. The flow chart and cause-and-effect feedback diagram would also work well here as diagnostic tools.

Considering the evolution of the use of teams in the history of organizational development, it has been suggested that feedback teams are the ultimate form of quality circles. They increase morale through emphasis on teamwork (as was characteristic of the early use of quality circles by the Japanese). Typical of the use of quality circles in the United States, the main emphasis of feedback teams is on improving the manner in which business is conducted. In sharp contrast to quality circles as originally conceived, however, feedback teams have the benefit of feedback charts whose slopes guide their improvement efforts into the areas that are most mission-critical. Furthermore, feedback charts are the measurement devices which monitor the effects of corrective actions taken. These powerful features have led to the observation that feedback teams are enhanced quality circles.

CHAPTER 12

A LOOK TO THE FUTURE

Successful companies continuously improve in response to advancements in technology, expanding competition, and spiraling customer expectations. This book has explained how TQM/MGEEM can guide any company in a never-ending journey of improvement.

Much has been said in this book about how to start and continue a TQM/MGEEM journey and where this journey leads. Broadly speaking, this experience leads to dramatic improvements in organization effectiveness. As has been explained, this occurs when TQM/MGEEM changes an organization's culture by successfully implementing the teachings of the quality philosophers, improving leadership, and increasingly empowering workers. Experience shows, however, that enlightened senior managers facilitate the natural tendency of TQM/MGEEM to create other kinds of changes in their organizations which lead to even higher levels of effectiveness.

Pressures to make these other types of changes in an organization develop for a particular reason. When TQM/MGEEM is first implemented, it gives members of feedback teams sharply increased responsibilities, e.g., networking with customers and suppliers, and recommending barriers for removal by management. As teams' responsibility increases, so does their sense of ownership and commitment. With these changes teams seem to want even more responsibility. Thus, it is the workers' desire for increased responsibility that creates pressures for other changes in an organization. To better understand this process, consider the following:

Imagine you are a member of a feedback team that has been given increased responsibilities by TQM/MGEEM. You were a member of a Gold Team which developed indicators and feedback charts. You now meet with your feedback team to work with customers and suppliers. Your team identifies barriers for removal by management and at every turn management encourages your team to accept even more responsibility. If you are a typical worker, you enjoy this additional responsibility to have more than the usual input about your work. You like to feel more in control. You delight in not having a supervisor constantly looking over your shoulder telling you what to do. Furthermore, you discover that as your sense of responsibility increases, so does your sense of commitment because having greater responsibility increases your sense of ownership. You're not merely helping some supervisor with his/her job — it's your job!

Now, suppose business picks up, and your feedback team must add a new member. Would you be enthusiastic about some supervisor or the personnel department selecting someone for this job? You know that selecting the wrong person can have negative effects on the team and its performance. So, you and the other team members would prefer to get the team involved in selecting all new members.

What about training? Would you be happy to see the training department train new team members on the important parts of the job? Who knows the most about what new team members must know about your customers and suppliers? Who knows the most about what new team members must know about feedback charts? Who knows the most about what new team members must know about why some of the slopes on your charts are steep and some are flat? Of course, the answer for all of these questions is that the team itself knows more about these things than anyone else. So, to ensure that new team members get the right kind of training, you and the other team members would prefer to do the training yourselves.

Thus, any feedback team that has the expanded responsibilities brought about by TQM/MGEEM and the resulting sense of commitment will want even more responsibility. They will want to get involved in virtually every decision that affects their team and its work. Senior managers who see the benefits of increased worker commitment will allow teams to gradually assume more of the functions formerly regarded as the responsibility of supervisors and various staff departments.

As TQM/MGEEM increases the responsibilities and commitment of feedback teams, recall that it also is generating a change in the role of supervisors that further encourages the empowering of workers. As TQM/MGEEM is implemented, the supervisor's role evolves away from its traditional functions toward those proposed for leadership by Deming, i.e., facilitator and people builder.[7] Rather than cracking the whip running things, supervisors become coordinators whose main function is to help feedback teams do a better job. Instead of solving their problems, supervisors teach teams how to solve their own problems. This form of supervisory behavior leads to even greater empowering of workers. Senior management reinforces and accelerates this transition in the supervisory role by selecting, training, and rewarding supervisors for these new skills.

As previously explained, feedback teams tend to want more responsibility. With the support of an enlightened senior management, they gradually assume more of both the traditional and new supervisory functions resulting in eventual displacement of supervisors. Supervisors disappear. Without supervisors, team members interface through their rolled-up feedback charts with the next level of management. Futhermore, as team skills increase, they eventually assume functions formerly the responsibility of staff departments, e.g., selection, training, budgeting, quality control, and compensation.

When functions formerly performed by supervisors and staff departments are assumed by feedback teams, mounting pressures create even more changes. One such change is that the number of levels in the organizational hierarchy can be reduced, at least to the extent that supervisors become obsolete. Staff departments that have lost functions or significant parts of functions can be consolidated or will disappear, resulting in a flatter, more decentralized organizational structure.

Furthermore, the organizational structure tends to become more horizontal as empowered feedback teams network with customers and suppliers. With less hierarchy, there is reduced need for teams to wait for authority from above and a greater tendency for them to respond horizontally: in one direction to customer needs and problems, and in the opposite direction to create harmony and cooperation with suppliers. This results in much shorter response time and is exactly what is needed in highly competitive times.

TQM/MGEEM brings about significant changes in an organization's culture and produces highly positive impacts on organizational effectiveness. Exactly how does this happen? Remember that feedback teams are involved through monthly feedback meetings in flexible networks with customers and suppliers. The main reason for this networking is, of course, to stay in touch with customer expectations and to cooperate with suppliers to secure their best support. TQM/MGEEM gets feedback teams close to their customers and gives teams increased responsibilities for satisfying customer requirements. Feedback teams in this position are customer-driven. At least once a month, they network with customers in feedback meetings. They visit customer facilities. They know better than anyone else what customers want. They bring this information about customer expectations into the company. Feedback teams are the authority on customer expectations into the company. Feedback teams are the authority on customers and on what customers want.

Having customer-driven feedback teams with responsibilities for satisfying customer expectations produces an interesting cultural change. Suppose that as a result of working with its customers, a feedback team requests from a staff department a certain kind of support which is not authorized by company policy. The staffers refuse the request saying, "Your request is not authorized. It's outside of company policy. We can't allow it." The feedback team responds, "We need this support to meet customer expectations, to beat competition, and to stay in business!" This dispute goes around and around until it finally is brought to the attention of the owner of this small company.

Who do you think will win this argument, the staffers or the team? Will the team receive the support it needs? Think about the problem from the owner's viewpoint. Does the owner want to keep profits rolling in or continue to work within policy and lose business? Will the owner authorize changes in company policy so that current customers are satisfied and new customers can be drawn away from competitors?

Let's be more candid about what the owner wants. Does the owner want to keep up the payments on that vacation home at the lake? Does the owner want to keep buying a new luxury car every year? Does the owner like the prospects of possibly laying off workers? Rest assured, the owner will agree with the feedback team and authorize the needed support.

It is in this manner that authority comes to feedback teams. Through their close contact with customers, they become known throughout the company as those who speak for customers, i.e., the customers' voice. When you think about it, this is the purest and best type of authority. It comes from the customers' purchasing power. Consequently, when team members speak, managers and staffers listen.

This represents a significant cultural change. No longer do workers merely listen and do what they are told. No longer are they disinterested in their work and operating below their potential. TQM/MGEEM expands their responsibilities. Now they have commitment; now they are experts on the customers.

Similarly, this cultural change affects managers and staff departments. To truly be effective in this situation, managers and staffers can't afford to do all the talking. They must listen to feedback teams who speak with the customers' authority. When managers and staffers do speak, they learn to ask feedback teams the question that is in keeping with their new role, "What can we do to help you do a better job of satisfying customer expectations?" No longer should managers lay down the law and crack the whip. The law is determined by the customers' expectations and feedback teams know more about this law than anyone else. The managers' new job is to coordinate and support feedback teams.

No longer should staffers sit back and interpret company policy on what can and cannot be done to satisfy customer expectations. Customer expectations are constantly spiraling. There is now little company policy for the staffers to interpret except to continually adjust and improve the company to satisfy customers. The staffers' new job is to help feedback teams meet customer expectations.

Almost everyone believes that authority in business comes from ownership. If someone owns a business, they or their representatives are thought to have the authority to tell the people they hire what to do. An owner can say to a newly hired worker, "This is my business. I own it. I own the building. I own the tools. I pay your salary. Therefore, I tell you what to do." If a worker doesn't do what the owner says, he or she can be fired. This is the traditional explanation for the source of business authority, but it is only partially correct.

Having enough money or ownership to start a business is important, of course, but it is certainly not the most important factor in making a business successful. If this were true, everyone who could afford to start a business would automatically make it a success. Unless an owner has a monopoly or is lucky, what it really takes to be successful in business is knowledge of what customers want and the skill to manage a company to provide it.

Typically, owners of successful businesses have had to struggle to survive. This struggling goes a long way toward teaching them what customers want and how to manage their business to provide it. The authority of owners to tell workers what to do arises not so much from ownership, but from owners knowing what customers want and what it takes to provide it. Knowledge of customer expectations is the real source of authority in business.

Through the years, many things have happened to upset the arrangement whereby owners know their customers and how to manage to provide for their needs. As explained in this book, many of these changes relate to the attitudes of Western managers. What is needed to overcome the crisis which faces Western business and industry is the development of owners who are truly knowledgeable of customer expectations. To accomplish this, the traditional wedding cake bureaucracy must be turned upside-down with fewer layers, and feedback teams serving as *owners* in direct contact with customers. Management's role in this setting is critical. Management must support, facilitate, and coordinate the efforts of feedback teams to meet and exceed customer expectations.

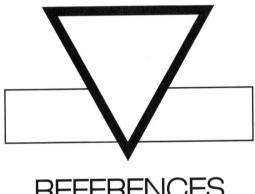

REFERENCES

1. Brassard, Michael (Editor). *The Memory Jogger: A Pocket Guide of Tools for Continuous Improvement.* Methuen, MA: GOAL/QPC, 1988.

2. _____. *The Memory Jogger Plus +.* Methuen, MA: GOAL/QPC, 1989.

3. Crosby, Philip B. *The Eternally Successful Organization.* New York: McGraw-Hill, 1988.

4. _____. *Quality Is Free: The Art of Making Quality Certain.* New York: McGraw-Hill, 1979.

5. Delbecq, A. L., Van de Ven, A. H., and Gustafson, D. H. *Group Techniques for Program Planning: A Guide to the Nominal Group and Delphi Processes.* Middleton, WI: Green Briar Press, 1986.

6. Deming, W. Edwards. "On Some Statistical Aids Toward Economic Production," *Interfaces,* Vol. 5, No. 4 (August 1975), pp. 1-15.

7. _____. *Out of the Crisis.* Cambridge, MA: MIT, 1986.

8. Faltermayer, Edmund. "Is 'Made in America' Fading Away? *Fortune,* Vol. 122, No. 7 (September 7, 1990), pp. 62-65, 68, 72-73.

9. Fahey, Liam (Editor). *The Strategic Planning Management Reader.* Englewood Cliffs, NJ: Prentice-Hall, 1989.

10. French, Wendell L., and Cecil H. Bell, Jr. *Organizational Development. Behavioral Science Interventions for Organizational Improvement.* 4th Edition. Englewood Cliffs, NJ: Prentice-Hall, 1990.

11. Garvin, David A. *Managing Quality. The Strategic and Competitive Edge.* New York: Free Press, 1988.

12. Gitlow, Howard S., and Shelly J. Gitlow. *The Deming Guide to Quality and Competitive Position.* Englewood Cliffs, NJ: Prentice-Hall, 1987.

13. Gitlow, Howard S., and Paul T. Hertz. "Product Defects and Productivity," *Harvard Business Review,* Vol. 61, No. 5 (September-October 1983), pp. 131-141.

14. Glenn, Norval D., and Charles N. Weaver, "Enjoyment of Work by Full-time Workers in the U.S., 1955 and 1980," *Public Opinion Quarterly,* Vol. 46 (Winter 1982-1983), pp. 459-470.

15. Hagan, John T. "The Management of Quality: Preparing for a Competitive Future," *Quality Progress.* December 1984, p. 21.

16. Harrington, H. J. *Excellence the IBM Way.* Milwaukee, WI: ASQC Quality Press, 1988.

17. Heinritz, Stuart F., and Paul V. Farrell. *Purchasing: Principles and Applications.* 4th Edition. Englewood Cliffs, NJ: Prentice-Hall, 1965.

18. Imai, Masaaki. *Kaizen: The Key to Japan's Competitive Success.* New York: Random House, 1986.

19. Ishikawa, Kaoru. *Guide to Quality Control.* Tokyo: Asian Productivity Organization, 1987.

20. Ishikawa, Kaoru, and David J. Lu. *What Is Total Quality Control? The Japanese Way.* Englewood Cliffs, NJ: Prentice-Hall, 1985.

21. "Japanese Assets in 1987 Reportedly Surpassed U.S. for First Time," *Wall Street Journal,* August 22, 1989, p. A10.

22. Juran, J. M. *Juran on Leadership for Quality: An Executive Handbook.* New York: Free Press, 1989.

23. Lee, Sang M., and Gary Schwendiman. (Editors). *Japanese Management: Cultural and Environmental Considerations.* New York: Praeger, 1982.

24. Lewis, Howard T. *Procurement: Principles and Cases.* Chicago, IL: Irwin, 1948.

25. Morita, Akio, Edwin M. Reingold, and Mitsuko Shimomura. *Made in Japan: Akio Morita and Sony.* New York: E. P. Dutton, 1986.

26. Mizuno, Shigeru (Editor). *Management for Quality Improvement: The Seven New QC Tools.* Cambridge, MA: Productivity Press, 1988.

27. Naylor, James C., Robert D. Pritchard, and Daniel R. Ilgen. *A Theory of Behavior in Organizations.* New York: Academic Press, 1980.

28. Ouchi, William G. *Theory Z.* New York: Avon, 1982.

29. Pascale, Richard Tanner, and Anthony G. Athos. *The Art of Japanese Management: Applications for American Executives.* New York: Warner, 1982.

30. Peters, Tom. *Thriving on Chaos: Handbook for a Management Revolution.* New York: Alfred A. Knopf, 1987.

31. Peters, Thomas J., and Nancy Austin. *A Passion for Excellence: The Leadership Difference.* New York: Random House, 1985.

32. Peters, Thomas J., and Robert H. Waterman, Jr. *In Search of Excellence: Lessons from America's Best-Run Companies.* New York: Harper and Row, 1982.

33. Pierce, John A., II. "The Company Mission as a Strategic Tool." *Sloan Management Review,* Vol. 23, No. 3 (Spring 1982), pp. 15-24.

34. Pierce, John A., II, and Fred Davis. "Corporate Mission Statements: The Bottom Line," *Academy of Management Executive,* Vol. 1, No. 2 (May 1987), pp. 109-116.

35. Price, Frank. *Right Every Time. Using the Deming Approach.* Milwaukee, WI: ASQC Quality Press, 1990.

36. Pritchard, Robert D., Steven D. Jones, Philip L. Roth, Karla K. Stuebing, and Steven E. Ekeberg. *Organizational Productivity Measurement: The Development and Evaluation of an Integrated Approach* (AFHRL-TR-86-64, AD A183 565). Brooks AFB TX: Manpower and Personnel Division, Air Force Human Resources Laboratory.

37. Scherkenbach, William W. *The Deming Route to Quality and Productivity. Road Maps and Roadblocks.* Milwaukee, WI: ASQC Quality Press, 1988.

38. Shapiro, Harris Jack, and Teresa Cosenza. *Reviving Industry in America: Japanese Influences on Manufacturing and the Service Sector.* New York: Ballinger, 1987.

39. Shewhart, Walter A. *Statistical Methods from the Viewpoint of Quality Control.* New York: Dover, 1986.

40. "The Global Giants," *Wall Street Journal,* September 21, 1990, R27-R30.

41. Taylor, Frederick Winslow. *Scientific Management.* New York: Harper and Row, 1947.

42. Tuttle, Thomas C. *Productivity Measurement Methods: Classification, Critique, and Implications for the Air Force.* (AFHRL-TP-86-3, AD A105 627). Brooks AFB TX: Manpower and Personnel Division, Air Force Human Resources Laboratory.

43. Tuttle, Thomas C., and Charles N. Weaver. *Methodology for Generating Efficiency and Effectiveness Measures (MGEEM): A Guide for Air Force Measurement Facilitators.* (AFHRL-TP-86-36, AD A174 547). Brooks AFB TX: Manpower and Personnel Division, Air Force Human Resources Laboratory.

44. Walton, Mary. *The Deming Management Method.* New York: Putnam, 1986.

45. Weaver, Charles N. "What Workers Want from Their Jobs: Evidence from the National Surveys," *Personnel,* Vol. 52, No. 3 (May-June 1976), pp. 48-54.

46. Weaver, Charles N., and Larry T. Looper. *Methodology for Generating Efficiency and Effectiveness Measures (MGEEM): A Guide for the Development and Aggregation of Mission Effectiveness Charts.* (AFHRL-TP-89-7, AD A208 353). Brooks AFB TX: Manpower and Personnel Division, Air Force Human Resources Laboratory.

47. Weaver, Charles N., and Michael D. Matthews. "What White Males Want from Their Jobs: Ten Years Later," *Personnel,* Vol. 64, No. 9 (September 1987), pp. 62-65.

INDEX

 **Printed on Recycled Paper**